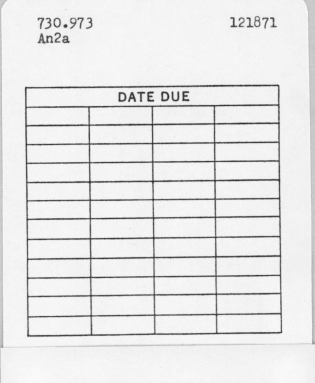

AMERICAN SCULPTURE IN PROCESS: 1930/1970

AMERICAN SCULPTURE IN PROCESS: 1930/1970

Wayne Andersen

NEW YORK GRAPHIC SOCIETY
BOSTON, MASSACHUSETTS

Library of Congress Cataloging in Publication Data

Andersen, Wayne V
American sculpture in process, 1930–1970.

    Includes bibliographical references and index.
    1. Sculpture, American. 2. Sculpture, Modern—
20th century—United States. I. Title.
08212.A43   730'.973   74-21498
ISBN 0-316-03681-1

Designed by Margaret Dodd

First printing

New York Graphic Society books are published by
Little, Brown and Company.

Published simultaneously in Canada by Little, Brown
and Company (Canada) Limited.

Printed in the United States of America

For Mark

CONTENTS

FOREWORD

The speed of jetcraft nowadays is snail-paced compared to the rate at which this book follows a point-blank trajectory through forty years of American sculpture. No fraction of my readership will more poignantly recognize the shortcuts I have taken than the sculptors about whom I have written. The abbreviation of an artist's production over many years to a few paragraphs and reproductions should, in fact, strike every reader as intrepidly, if not presumptuously adventurous, involving as it does the pretense of making the appearance of a self-evident whole out of a selection of parts. But it is in the nature of expository writing that facts, events, and examples, considered objectively and without creative or imaginative alterations— once sorted out and arranged—become fixed in place or taken over by a structuring schema which comes to stand for the whole.

It is easy enough, therefore, to explain the limitations I have accepted in this coverage of American sculpture over four decades. Had the quantitative contingencies of publishing it allowed even a doubling of the factual material and reproductions, this book would have been significantly different only in size. More difficult to explain—and obviously more subjective—is the choice of schema that I allowed to take possession of the factual material.

"American sculpture in process" assumes a linear action of continuous movement through each of a succession of activities, events, or even developmental stages—the action being both progressive and cumulative, often intrinsically dialectical and cybernetic. As an endless interlocking chain of causation and concomitance, the action constitutes the process of modern American sculpture. In adopting this schema, I have accepted that the passage of time is linear in human awareness and that, being a time-bound action, process can be reconstructed through a chronological arrangement of facts, events, and artifacts, and recognized as a reasonable approximation of historical truth.

This schema has, in one way or another, dominated art history surveys; in favoring it as a working hypothesis, I also have accepted its faults. The most outstanding of these is that the older sculptors whose work I deal with have not been carried beyond the point in the process where their individual developments, even while remaining influential, ceased being critical to the forward progress. For example, I stopped discussing David Smith, Herbert Ferber and Seymour Lipton, among others, at the opening of the fifties, even though their developments continued unabated. The reader should not interpret this—in these cases or in any others—as a personal judgment about their later work, which I may like as much or more than the earlier. Attention to the entire course of a sculptor's production depends on a monograph format.

Omitted from these pages are many sculptors whose work I know: some whose principal activity has been in Europe or whose work adhered to European figurative tendencies while avoiding contact with native developments; others who worked in parts of this country where strong regional schools did not develop. I have applied the same criteria to sculptors whose work in a particular style got underway too late to be an innovative factor in the larger process or was at best elaborative rather than generative to the process. Future scholars of contemporary American sculpture will rectify what errors of omission I have committed.

In constructing this book I kept in mind a text of general value to the layman and of special value to the teacher of modern art. Having avoided complex theoretical or critical discussion, I feel that any teacher can overlay my text with interpretive analysis. I have tried to be simply factual, descriptive and informative; anything beyond that would have required a very different and more personal approach.

I am grateful to all those sculptors—many of them my friends—who, over the years, have answered my inquiries and supplied me with photographs. Some of the bibliographical research and interviewing of sculptors and dealers was done by occasional research assistants and secretaries, all of whom were paid for their work. I remain indebted to two people, however, whose efforts and results far exceeded their salaries: Miriam Rosen, who conducted extensive interviews on my behalf and assembled large portions of the text for my final writing; and Marjory Supovitz, who double-checked the facts, and over the final weeks of labor brought the text to a higher level of clarity and balance than I had the patience to do by myself. My thanks as well to Sue Ruotolo for inordinate skill and persistence in getting several essential photographs from the most reluctant of sources and for assistance in every phase of this task's completion. To Muriel Harman of the New York Graphic Society, my gratitude for making the publication of this book as pleasant and effortless as possible.

WAYNE ANDERSEN

THE THIRTIES

By the second decade of the twentieth century the age of the machine had become a reality. For Henry Adams, recalling in 1918 the Paris World's Fair of 1900, the machine was charged with the birth-giving miraculousness that his Christian ancestors had sensed about the Virgin herself. As Christianity had dominated the art of the Western world, supplying its subject matter while administering the flow of its production, so too would the machine age draw art into its theo-technology and determine its matter and techniques; art would reflect mechanization while embracing in its process the doctrines of a mechanized society.

The center of the new fertility cult would be America, where the load of both the classical and Catholic traditions in art was lighter and easier to throw off. As early as 1915 the French artist Francis Picabia could crystallize the full potential of industrial science for art by a single visit to New York City: "Almost immediately upon coming to America it flashed on me that the genius of the modern world is in machinery and that through machinery art ought to find a most vivid expression." [1]

Others, however, did not receive the onrush of technology in the same spirit as Picabia. Lewis Mumford would strike out against the "mechanical ideology" which he felt was limiting the provinces of the senses and confining sense operations to the blind world of matter and motion.[2] The Puritan downgrading of the senses was being recognized by such writers as William Carlos Williams as a central problem in American culture. To the extent that the "mechanical ideology" was becoming theological—an extension of both the Puritan and Protestant ethic—it invited detractors like Mumford who saw it as threatening to the wholeness of the personality, dwarfing the human and severing the senses from the mechanical body. In such an atmosphere Alfred Stieglitz, though championed as a missionary if not a messiah of "machine art" because of his promotion of photography and such Futurist-machinist painters as Picabia and Severini, was looked upon by many in his time as a secular savior of instinctual life in America for showing in his 291 Gallery such American painters as O'Keeffe, Marin, and Dove. For these painters sensual liberation was basic to social progress and the fullness of creative life.[3]

The dialectic between a mechanical ideology and a creativity which was tied to the life of the senses was already established by the 1920's as a polarity of artistic value. So consistently has this binary construction been superimposed on the production of art since the nineteenth-century issue of the classicists versus the romanticists that one might assume its significance to be independent of the issues which have collected along its lines of force. Like the poles of a magnet that consistently align the positive and negative, the formula casting classicist-machine art in opposition to the art of the romanticized senses is a handy defining device which keeps issues clear and serves to delimit the field of artistic activity.

This polarity became a major issue in the 1930's, especially for those sculptors whose materials and processes of production could be more easily aligned along the lines of machine production than could those of painters. In the 1940's it contributed to what became known as "the fusion of Constructivism and Surrealism," a fusion that was as much an ambivalence as a method of reconciling the dichotomy in both painting and sculpture of the 1940's: the conflict between the rationality of geometrical abstraction and the vitalism and passion of Surrealism.[4]

"Mechanism" manifested itself in the representation of machine parts as well as in their use as materials; the creation of non-functioning machines and the fabrication of a work of art as a useful machine, and with Archipenko's 1924 *Archipentura*—the use of a machine to produce art. Alfred Stieglitz championed the cause of the camera as an art-producing machine, and his comrade at the 291 Gallery, Paul Haviland, characterized the new human ideal as machinomorphic: "Man made the machine in his own image," he wrote. "The phonograph is the image of his voice; the camera the image of his eye. . . . He has made the machine superior to himself. That is why he admires her." [5]

In Europe the years that preceded the First World War witnessed an unprecedented amount of experimentation and innovation in art based on the machine. After the initial achievement of the Cubists in Paris in setting traditionally static imagery—portrait, still life, landscape—into virtual motion, Italian Futurism, Russian Rayonnism and English Vorticism carried it further and gave it social implications. There followed the well-known mechanization of imagery by the artists Marcel Duchamp and Francis Picabia, the machine-like figures of Fernand Léger and Raymond Duchamp-Villon, the relief constructions of Alexander Archipenko, the metaphysical engineering symbolism of Giorgio de Chirico, and the anti-art reaction of the Dadaists, who were fascinated by the human body as a machine. The post-war period saw another burst of activity, marked by the emergence of Constructivism in Russia, De Stijl in Holland, the Bauhaus in Germany, and Surrealism in France. Each movement had contributed something, directly or indirectly, to machinomorphic art. The American breakthrough came in the thirties, largely as a response to the wealth of stimulation from Europe; it was characterized by the variety of choices among aspects of the several European styles perhaps because, from afar, the European movements appeared fragmentary and only partially relevant to the American sensibility.

Limited exposure to European movements had existed in this country since the early twentieth century. Even before the shock of the 1913 Armory Show, which carried the works of the Paris avant-garde to New York, Chicago, and Boston, Alfred Stieglitz was promoting the interests of contemporary art at his 291 Gallery, and later at his Intimate Gallery. Throughout the twenties the East Forty-Seventh Street Gallery featured one-man shows of Archipenko, Duchamp-Villon, Kandinsky, Klee, Léger, Malevich, Miró, and Schwitters. In 1920 Katherine Dreier and Marcel Duchamp founded the *Société Anonyme*, which sponsored the International Exhibition of Modern Art at the Brooklyn Museum in 1926–27. The following year Albert Eugene Gallatin instituted the Museum of Living Art at the Washington Square campus of New York University, where, for the next fifteen years, students and Greenwich Village artists were able to see the works of Arp, Brancusi, Braque, Cézanne, Delaunay, Duchamp, Gabo, Giacometti, Gris, Kandinsky, Klee, De la Fresnaye, Léger, Lipchitz, Matisse, Miró, Mondrian, Picasso, Schwitters, van Doesburg, and Vantongerloo. Late in 1929 the Museum of Modern Art opened in New York, committed to the dissemination of advanced European art.

A distinctive feature of American sculpture in the thirties lay in its overlapping styles, its studied incoherence. The broad spectrum of European modes orchestrated very nearly all that had happened to sculpture since the 1880's: naturalism, archaism, expressionism, and also academic classicism, which still retained a strong hold on public sentiment. In addition, each of the general styles had bred "modernistic" offspring; for the naive public and most critics as well, these were difficult to distinguish from the authentically modern. Most coherent in the midst of the American melee was the carve-direct school which was primarily concerned with simplification and analysis of form and with the inherent properties of materials.

The carve-direct movement began in France in the early 1900's as a reaction to traditional studio techniques and production that depended upon commissions to meet the expenses of production. American carve-direct artists like José de Creeft, Chaim Gross, Robert Laurent, and William Zorach, with their emphasis on materials and form, conditioned American sculptors to Constructivism. To a lesser degree their counterparts, the American expressionist sculptors, whose emphasis was more on emotional content, somewhat primed the ensuing acceptance of Surrealism, which would merge in the forties with Constructivism to form the most general and superficial appearance of the new sculpture. In the thirties the Constructivist-Surrealist dichotomy, in its broadest application, was already implicit in the work of Alexander Calder, Isamu Noguchi, David Smith, Theodore Roszak, and Ibram Lassaw, and to a lesser extent in that of José de Rivera, but it failed to make an impact as a coherent new direction, perhaps because it hewed too closely to both European and American avant-garde painting.

By 1930, those American sculptors who were to be the pacesetters of the thirties were in their early formative stages. Their individual developments during this decade had in common the move toward an abstract imagery that fused the geometric with the organic into a hybrid form that would establish the formal dialectic of most sculpture in this country over the following decades. They were also, but each in his own way, dedicated to the perpetuation of the credo of materials which had been advanced by the European carve-direct and Constructivist sculptors alike and widely propagated on an institutional and industrial level by the Bauhaus. Calder was soon to assimilate the near polarity of Constructivism and a light, Miróesque Surrealism into his personal idioms of mobile and stabile; Smith—and later Lassaw—was to develop the machinist welding technique of the Spanish artists Picasso, Gonzalez, and Gargallo; Roszak and De Rivera were to adopt the machine aesthetic of the Bauhaus, which by 1930 was geographically widespread.

Alexander Calder was the first American sculptor to gain international recognition. Born in 1898, he had been dividing his time between Paris and America since 1926. Calder was perhaps the most directly allied with both the Constructivist and Surrealist factions of the European art world. As a result, his development in the thirties and early forties often anticipated the paths that his contemporaries working in the States were to follow. Among the visitors attracted to Calder's miniature circus performances of the late twenties in Paris were Joan Miró, Jean Arp, Frederick Kiesler, Piet Mondrian, Fernand Léger, and Theo van Doesburg. In 1931 he joined *Abstraction-Création*, a group devoted to abstract art, which included Arp, van Doesburg, Jean Hélion, and the Belgian sculptor and painter Georges Vantongerloo; Calder traveled to Spain with Miró in 1932, and exhibited with Miró, Arp, and the Constructivist Antoine Pevsner at the Galerie Pierre in 1933.

When Calder arrived in Paris in 1926, he had a degree in mechanical engineering from the Stephens Institute of Technology and work experience as a seaman and logger. He was something of a showman, a Frenchman's idea of what an

Figure 1. Alexander Calder with his circus, New York, 1936.

American was like: unsophisticated in the Parisian sense, nonchalant, rustic. As if to counter his timidity in the context of Parisian café life, Calder displayed himself in a racy tweed suit of orange background with yellow stripes, and a straw hat ornamented with a fraternity ribbon. Among the café crowd he soon became known as "the cantaloupe with the straw hat."

Calder's mother was a painter; his father and grandfather were well-known academic sculptors. Calder had taken drawing lessons and studied painting with George Luks and John Sloan at the Art Students League between 1923 and 1925. What he would later recall most vividly about his experiences was a fellow student who could draw a nude with two pencils at once, one black, the other red, "by starting at the feet and running right up"; that those in his group learned to draw rapidly, racing with their pencils; and that he had learned how to draw with a single line.[6] This talent got Calder his first job as a commercial illustrator for the *National Police Gazette*. Assigned to cover the Ringling Brothers Circus of 1925, Calder recalls spending practically every day and night of the circus's stay sketching there. His drawings were mannered and weak, generally accompanied by ingenuous captions but in the context of the cartoon humor of the twenties, and in contrast to the content of contemporary paintings, they were no less engaging than Disney's Mickey Mouse. Shortly thereafter he had garnished circus toys made by a Philadelphia manufacturer, and had begun making his own toys in wire and wood, several of which were exhibited at the Salon des Humoristes in Paris and later sold to a toy manufacturer in Wisconsin. The toys soon became complete miniature circuses, and by the spring of 1927 his circus performances in Paris attracted the attention of several famous circus critics including Legrand-Chabrier, and such circus producers as Paul Fratellini. Miró, who had himself brought circus motifs into his paintings in the twenties, began attending in 1928; by 1930 Calder's audiences included many avant-garde artists, writers, and critics. During his visits to the United States he gave performances in New York. Isamu Noguchi, whom he had known in Paris, once acted as his assistant.

Another member of the Paris group, the artist-critic Michel Seuphor, describes Calder's circus in his *The Sculpture of This Century:*[7]

I went twice with Mondrian, in 1930 I believe . . . We sat munching peanuts, perched on the steep wooden tiers, while Calder, below, in the only corner of his studio left free, brought out his show. Not only did he make them turn, dance, jump from one trapeze to another, he had made them himself with his ingenious fingers. It was the period of the great vogue of circuses. We would gather in a gang at the Cirque Médrano to commune in the circular show, whose minor aspects and accessories particularly interested us. For this reason Calder's circus captivated us by its attention to detail, by the minute observation of the conventions. (Figure 1).

Calder's production during these years included wood sculpture: the earliest was the *Flattest Cat* (1926) and the tradition continued with such pieces as *Horse* (1928). He also made all-wire figures in 1927–29 like the first *Josephine Baker* (Figure 2), at the suggestion of California painter Clay Spohn, as well as some crank-operated mechanical fishbowls dating from 1929. Calder exhibited the wire figures in his first one-man show, held at the Weyhe Gallery in New York in 1928, and the following year he showed both wire and wood sculpture at the Fifty-Sixth Street Gallery.

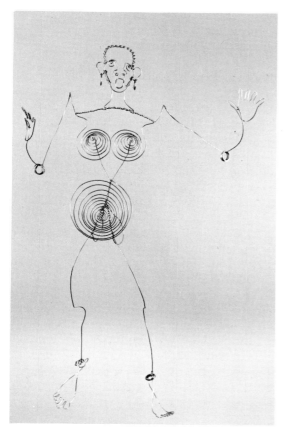

Figure 2. Alexander Calder. *Josephine Baker.* 1927–29. Iron wire, 22¾″ x 39″ x 9¾″. (The Museum of Modern Art, New York.)

Figure 3. Alexander Calder. *Lion and Tamer Behind Bars.* 1932. Ink drawing,
21⅛″ x 29⅞″. (Perls Gallery, New York.)

Calder's two-dimensional, frontal wire figures reverse the traditional relationship of sculptural mass and displaced space; they are, as James Johnson Sweeney
describes them, somewhat like drawings with the paper cut away.[8] The continuous
line which develops the imagery surely depends on the single-line exercises Calder
remembers doing in art school in New York, and parallels his later circus drawings,
like the *Lion and Tamer Behind Bars* of 1932 (Figure 3), and the *Man on Slack
Wire* (1932), where depth is compressed into surface pattern through continuous
outlines. The visual wit of Calder's figures, moreover, invites comparison with a
number of drawings from the early 1920's by Paul Klee, such as Klee's circus-
oriented *Lions–Beware of Them!* and his *Josephine Baker*-like *On the Lawn* (1923).
Nevertheless, Calder's early works had little to do with the formal concerns of his
comrades in Paris, however much they approach the work of Miró and Klee—whose
work was being exhibited in Paris and New York from 1925 on. Rather they
reflected his personal interest in the circus and in toys and mechanical devices.

It was only in 1930 that Calder began to respond to the contemporary
movements around him. He pinpoints his visit to the Paris studio of Mondrian in
1930 as the impetus for his entry into abstract art. "This one visit," he recalls, "gave
me a shock that started things. Though I had heard the word 'modern' before, I did
not consciously know or feel the term 'abstract.' So now, at thirty-two, I wanted to
paint and work in the abstract." [9] "I was particularly impressed by some rectangles
of color he [Mondrian] had tacked on his wall in a pattern after his nature. I told
him I would like to make them oscillate—he objected. I went home and tried to
paint abstractly, but in two weeks I was back again among plastic materials." [10] After
his paintings (Figure 4), which shared the two-dimensional concerns of Mondrian
expanded in the direction of Hélion and Sophie Tauber-Arp, Calder made—and
exhibited in 1931 at the Galerie Percier—a group of abstract geometric wire
constructions, some of which, he later recalls, vibrated slightly in the breeze.

Calder had begun experimenting the year before with works involving movable
objects in a fixed frame—works like *Construction* of 1932 (Figure 5)—and in the
winter of 1931 he conceived his first mechanized constructions. There were many
precedents, however, for the use of motion in developing the form of a sculpture.
Umberto Boccioni's *Technical Manifesto of Futurist Sculpture* of 1912 declared

6

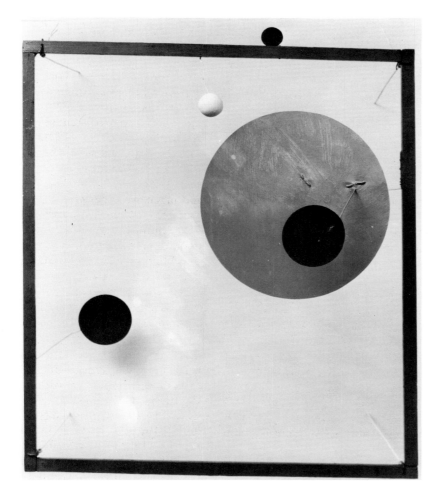

Figure 4 *(top)*. Alexander Calder.
Composition. 1930. Oil on canvas,
18″ x 27″. (Photo: Pedro E. Guerrero.)

Figure 5 *(bottom)*. Alexander Calder.
Construction. 1932. Painted wood, metal.
30½″ high. (Philadelphia Museum of Art,
Philadelphia, Pennsylvania.)

7

that the Futurists broke down the concept of repose and put forward that of movement: "the in-and-out of a piston in a cylinder, the opening and closing of two cog wheels . . . the turbine of a propeller, are all plastic . . . elements of which a Futurist work in sculpture must take account." By 1915 the Italian Futurist sculptors Giacomo Balla and Fortunato Depero were making sculpture set in motion by mechanical means. Brancusi placed his *Fish* (1922) and *Leda* (1924) on revolving bases, and Archipenko invented his *Archipentura* machine to demonstrate paintings set in motion. Among the Constructivists, Naum Gabo in 1920 made a kinetic construction, a vertical length of spring steel vibrated by means of a motor, which described a virtual space; László Moholy-Nagy worked on his kinetic *Light Space Modulator* from 1922 to 1930 (in 1930 he published *The New Vision*, which included a section on kinetic sculpture as the final stage in the evolution of sculptural form); Vantongerloo was experimenting with problems of movement within a sphere, and the Russian Vladimir Tatlin designed an entire building set into motion, the *Monument to the Third International*, which reached the mockup stage as a wire and wood construction in 1919–20.

A more subjective, fanciful approach to mechanization had been adopted by the Dada and Surrealist factions around the same time. Calder cites the example of Klee's *Twittering Machine* (1920) and recalls that he himself had once intended to make a bird that would open its beak, spread its wings and squeak by means of a crank, but had abandoned the project when he learned of Klee's drawing. Implied movement and humorous or satirical machine forms are also combined in Duchamp's *King and Queen Surrounded by Swift Nudes* (1912) and *The Bride Stripped Bare by Her Bachelors, Even* (1915–23), and in Picabia's *Child Carburetor* (1919). Duchamp, moreover, experimented with optical effects produced by mechanical motion in the *Rotary Glass Plates* of 1920 and *Rotary Demisphere* of 1925.

Calder's motorized constructions are significantly different from these earlier works, however, in that the focus of his attention is not the motor or the mechanical device itself, not even the motion, but rather the changing relationships of moving parts in time and space (Figures 6 and 7). He wrote in the magazine *Abstraction-Création* in 1932:[11]

How can art be realized?
     . . .
every element able to stir, move,
oscillate, come and go in its
relation to other elements of
its universe;

     . . .
. . . abstractions which resemble
nothing in life except their
manner of reacting.

Calder exhibited fifteen motorized constructions and some fifteen others moved by hand cranks at the Galerie Vignon in April 1932. Duchamp at this time christened Calder's works "mobiles"—a term he had used in 1917 to describe the "weight with nine moulds" in his *Bride Stripped Bare*. Shortly afterwards, Arp suggested the name "stabile" for the non-moving constructions exhibited the year before at the Galerie Percier. "The mobile," Calder explains, "has actual movement

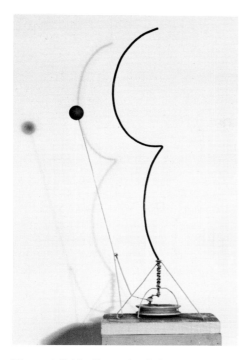

Figure 6 *(left)*. Alexander Calder. *Motorized Mobile*. 1932. Wood, metal, wire, 36″ high. (The Berkshire Museum, Pittsfield, Massachusetts.)

Figure 7 *(right)*. Alexander Calder. *A Universe*. 1934. Motorized mobile. Iron pipe, wire, wood, 40½″ high. (The Museum of Modern Art, New York.)

in itself, while the stabile is back at the old painting idea of implied movement. You have to walk around a stabile, or through it—a mobile dances in front of you." [12]

Although he would continue working with motorized constructions until 1935, Calder had made his first wind mobiles (which were anticipated in Paul Klee's wind propelled sculpture and to a certain extent in Calder's own 1931 abstract wire works) back in 1932, shortly after the show at the Galerie Vignon. One of the earliest of these was *Calderberry Bush*, a standing mobile of sensitively balanced geometric components (see Figure 8). Calder now depended upon random movements generated by air currents instead of the predictable patterns of his mechanized pieces. The mobiles do not involve the unified movement of a single volume in space; rather they create multiple movements and describe multiple virtual volumes of interrelated parts. In this respect, the wind mobiles remain an outgrowth of Calder's initial response to the art of Mondrian: eliminating the background support of a painting, Calder made the geometrical shapes "oscillate" as if they were suspended from the top of a picture frame or series of frames (see Figure 5). In the same fashion, but without the possibility of movement, Tatlin's 1916 corner reliefs were extended from an implied frame, which was the wall intersection. Similarly, random objects, including coins, washers, buttons, and bolts were suspended in such collages of Kurt Schwitters as *Merz 13A* (1919) or *Schwimmt Merz* (1921). Duchamp, in effect, had "suspended" the various parts of the *Bride* on the transparent glass picture-plane. Calder himself emphasized the floating quality of the mobile shape as follows: "the use of a very long thread, or a long arm in cantilever as a means of support seems to best approximate this freedom 9

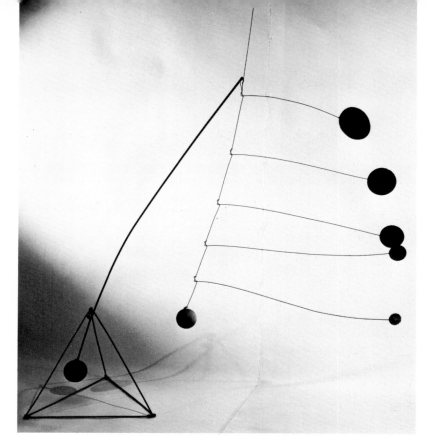

Figure 8 *(top left)*. Alexander Calder. *Calderberry Bush.* 1932. Mobile. Steel wire, rod, sheet aluminum, wood, 84″ high. (Private Collection, New York. Photo: Herbert Matter.)

Figure 9 *(bottom left)*. Alexander Calder. *Agnes' Circle.* 1935. Mobile. Steel wire, rod, sheet aluminum, 36″ high. (Vassar College Art Gallery, Poughkeepsie, New York. Photo: Paulus Leeser.)

Figure 10 *(bottom right)*. Alexander Calder. *Swizzle Sticks.* 1936. Mobile. Plywood panel, wire, wood, lead, 48″ x 33″. (Collection, Mr. and Mrs. James Thrall Soby, New Canaan, Connecticut.)

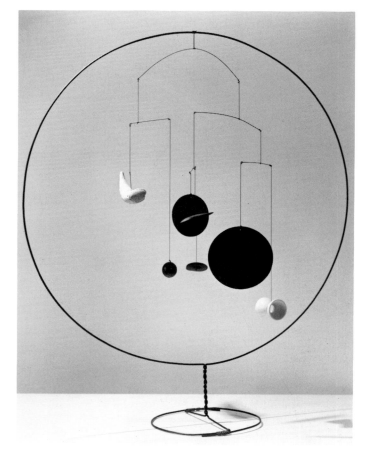

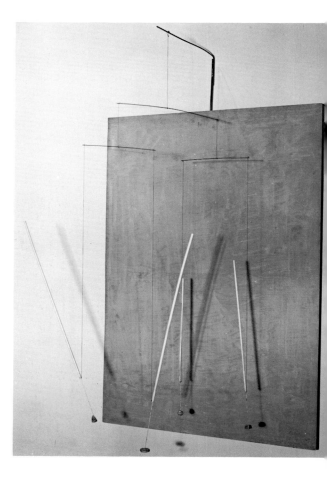

from the earth."[13] The surrounding framing shape is maintained in the rectangular motorized *White Frame* (1934) or *Agnes' Circle* of 1935 (Figure 9) while in *Swizzle Sticks* of 1936 (Figure 10) the rod "figures" are liberated from, but suspended in front of, a two-dimensional background. In this way, too, Calder's works are related more to Cubist painting than to any mode of earlier sculpture (in the same way as Gabo's *Heads*). What remains sculptural, in the traditional sense, is Calder's transference of the weight and motion of the mobile, such as *Calderberry Bush*, to a single point of suspension which also serves as an axis, or median line, as in classical contrapposto.

The element of pure chance introduced by the elimination of the motor also departs from others' earlier experiments with motion. Previously, Duchamp had used the term "canned chance" to describe the combination of accident and careful planning that was already seen in the Dada works of Arp. Arp's 1916–17 collage *Squares Arranged According to the Laws of Chance* exhibited an idea which still occupied Arp in 1929–30—that of reliefs made of scraps of torn paper or wood randomly dropped on the background and consciously rearranged, as in his *Navels* of 1930 (Figure 11).

Calder's panel mobiles represent the three-dimensional realization of the paintings of Miró's circle, the *Abstraction-Création* group, which by 1930 were largely reduced to strictly flat, hard-edge and linear shapes set against a two-dimensional plane and interconnected by lines. By pasting cut-out wooden biomorphic shapes to a two-dimensional surface, Arp had already responded to the three-dimensional potential of this form. The complete omission of the background presented itself as the next step, and Calder took it in works like *White Frame* and *Agnes' Circle*. Thus the transition from Miró's paintings to Calder's mobiles was as sequential as the transition from Analytical Cubism to three-dimensional assemblages.

About 1934, while retaining something of the geometric organization of Constructivism, Calder had adopted many of the playful forms of the Surrealists Arp and Miró.[14] Availing himself of the free, or *a-géométrique* forms of Arp, he developed contrasts among the planar shapes and linear accents in the manner of

Figure 11. Jean Arp. *Navels*. 1930. Varnished wood, 10⅜″ x 11⅛″. (The Museum of Modern Art, New York. Photo: Soichi Sunami.)

Figure 12 *(top)*. Joan Miró. *Dutch Interior, I*. 1928. Oil on canvas, 36⅛″ x 28¾″. (The Museum of Modern Art, New York.)

Figure 13 *(bottom)*. Alexander Calder. *Steel Fish*. 1934. Mobile. Iron, sheet steel, steel rod, sheet aluminum, 120″ high. (Photo: Pedro E. Guerrero.)

Miró. Within Miró's *Catalan Landscape* (1923–24) and his *Dutch Interior, I* 1928 (Figure 12), are contained the essentials of Calder's formal vocabulary, expanded to a monumental scale in works like Calder's standing mobile *Steel Fish* of 1934 (Figure 13).

Some recent criticism of Calder's work has credited him with little more than having set the shapes of Arp and Miró in motion; yet it was Calder's special achievement to have recognized the fully three-dimensional implications of others' configurations. Calder's constructions, however much they depend on Miró's compositions or the biomorphic shapes of Arp's reliefs, invoke a much stricter geometry and are another step removed from involvement with defining the spatial quality of a physical object. The creation of a measurable space, rather than an illusionistic one, may be determined as an outgrowth of Cubism and the real space of the Cubist collage and the Cubist relief, as further evolved by Boccioni in his *Development of a Bottle in Space* of 1912 and by Gabo in his constructed *Heads* of 1915–16.

However valuable Calder's early motorized works have been for the advancement of kinetic sculpture (the foremost spokesman for kineticism, George Rickey, has denied any value at all), he remained a sculptor in the traditional sense; that is, one who defines the interrelationship of parts through gravitational equilibrium and a unified three-dimensional form. At the same time, and more successfully than most of the kineticists, Calder moved away from the primacy of the object that displaces or defines space as if space were a measurable, or circumscribable substance. Calder, as well as David Smith, took his lead from painting and thus avoided the concern for the outward expansion of form against a restraining surface that, as a tradition, all sculptors in this century have had to acknowledge in one way or another.

In his introduction to the catalog of the Percier show in 1931, Calder's close friend Léger placed him in a league with composer Erik Satie, Mondrian, Duchamp, Brancusi and Arp, but pointed out at the same time that Calder remained "one hundred percent American" in his display of mechanical ingenuity and wit. The playful Surrealism of Miró and Arp undoubtedly appealed to Calder's inherent sense of the comic, just as his mechanical instincts had earlier led him to Constructivism. With the monumental stabiles of the late thirties, beginning with *Whale* of 1937 (Figure 14), Calder was able to develop Arp and Miró's biomorphic shapes into a formal alliance with Constructivism, especially the work of Gabo (Figure 15), and establish himself as the first American sculptor to mold a singular style out of the fusion of the dominant European styles.

At the same time that Calder was involved with the Paris avant-garde, his friend Isamu Noguchi was serving an apprenticeship there with Constantin Brancusi, the leading figure among European carve-direct sculptors. Noguchi's previous training in America had been thoroughly academic. A short assistantship in Stamford, Connecticut, to Gutzon Borglum—the sculptor of the Mount Rushmore heads, who was in 1922 beginning his massive figural *Wars of America* for the Newark, New Jersey, city park—left Noguchi with little more than a knowledge of plaster casting. He then enrolled at Columbia University in a pre-medical program, but at his mother's suggestion began to study sculpture again—this time at the Leonardo da Vinci Art School. Under the academic tutelage of the school's director, Onorio Ruotolo, Noguchi became proficient. At the age of twenty-one he was showing regularly and was elected to the conservative National Sculpture Society. By 1926 Noguchi was motivated to abandon his conventional style; he applied for and received a Guggenheim Fellowship to spend one year studying stone and wood carving in Paris and two years working in China, Japan, and India. Born in Los

)4, the son of a Scotch-American mother and a Japanese father (a
d scholar of Japanese art), Noguchi had spent twelve of his first
n Japan. In his Guggenheim application he expressed his new desire
't to West'' through abstract sculpture.

ival in Paris, Noguchi entered into apprenticeship with Brancusi,
: he had first seen in 1926 at the Brummer Gallery in New York.[15]
Noguchi improved his skill with tools and further developed his
al materials, but he was also easily distracted from Brancusi's
nal media. In his own studio in Paris, he undertook experiments
orks in a variety of materials. He made also a study for a neon
ure, and in 1928 he made several brass sheet constructions in curvilinear
orm that suggested potential movement through being loosely assembled and held
together by tension and gravity. In addition Noguchi constructed an abstract work
of two turned brass rods suspended in space. Though built along lines of the
Constructivist's formal program, most of these works echoed the form of Brancusi's
sculpture. For all his experimentation, Noguchi's sympathies remained with
carve-direct precepts. He later recalled being disturbed with the idea of transforming two-dimensional materials like sheet metal into three-dimensional constructions,
and feeling that purely geometric objects represented too great a departure from
reality.[16]

Having lost his fellowship through his prolonged stay in Paris, Noguchi
returned to the United States in 1929. An exhibition of his Parisian abstract works
at the Eugene Schoen Gallery in New York gained him some recognition among the
art public but no sales, and for the next half decade he was forced to support

Figure 14 *(left)*. Alexander Calder. *Whale.* 1937. Stabile. Sheet steel, 78″ high. (The Museum of Modern Art, New York.)

Figure 15 *(right)*. Naum Gabo. *Head.* 1916. Large version, corten steel, 72″ high. (Tate Gallery, London. Photo: E. Irving Blomstrann.)

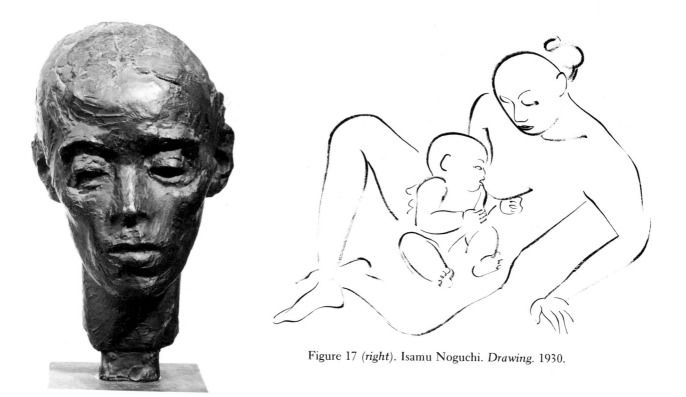

Figure 17 (*right*). Isamu Noguchi. *Drawing.* 1930.

Figure 16 (*left*). Isamu Noguchi. *Head of Martha Graham.* 1929. Bronze, 12″ high. (Honolulu Academy of Arts, Honolulu, Hawaii.)

himself through portrait commissions in both bronze and terra cotta. He achieved a modicum of fame with his portrait work in the early and mid-thirties; those that were included in the 1934 exhibition of his work at the Marie Harriman Gallery were praised by influential New York art critics Edward Alden Jewell and Henry McBride. Included in his fashionable successes of this period were busts of Martha Graham (Figure 16), George Gershwin, José Orozco, and Buckminster Fuller.

As if seeking his own roots at the same time as he was examining the roots of his sculpture, Noguchi returned to the Orient in 1930. He first studied brush drawing in Peking (Figure 17), and then, deciding that drawing was not sufficiently relevant to the practice of sculpture, took up pottery making in a factory near Kyoto under the direction of Uno Jinmatsu, a notorious forger of Korean antiques. Noguchi became particularly interested in primitive Haniwa and Dogu mortuary figures; he executed a number of terra cottas in their manner in 1931, such as *Erai Yatcha Hoi!* and *The Queen* (Figure 18). Although it contributed both a simplifying and enlivening effect to his style, Noguchi's Eastern period sculpture still showed the influence of Brancusi, whose own works, like *Boy* (1907), reveal certain orientalizing traits. Noguchi's fusion of primitive Haniwa stylization with the contemporary abstraction of Brancusi becomes more apparent in *Miss Expanding Universe* (Figure 19), which was executed immediately after his return to the United States in 1932.

During the period of the Depression and afterward, Noguchi became deeply involved in left-wing politics and art as social commentary, as were most artists in New York at that time. As a result, his activities were expanded to include industrial and environmental design and city planning. In 1933 he planned a *Musical Weather Vane* wired for light emission, and made drawings and a model for three public projects, *Monument to Ben Franklin, Play Mountain,* and *Monument to a* 15

Figure 18 *(left)*. Isamu Noguchi. *The Queen*. 1931. Terra cotta, 45″ high. (Whitney Museum of American Art, New York.)

Figure 19 *(right)*. Isamu Noguchi. *Miss Expanding Universe*. 1932. Aluminum, 40⅞″ high. (The Toledo Museum of Art, Toledo, Ohio.)

Plow (Figure 20)—all of which were in the 1934 show at the Marie Harriman Gallery along with his portraits. The Franklin monument commemorated the inventor-statesman's discovery of electricity with the erection of a great vertical kite and key construction on the banks of the Schuylkill River in Philadelphia. *Play Mountain*, a communal playground for Manhattan, included skating facilities, a gymnasium, a pool with water slides—to be constructed in steel, glass, brick, and reinforced concrete. In order to expand the area of the available space, he planned to make the playground in the shape of a gradually slanting, tiered pyramid which would be usable inside as well as outside. *Monument to a Plow*, envisioned on a prairie site, consisted of a stainless steel plow atop a giant pyramidal mound of earth twelve-thousand feet wide, with furrowed earth on one side, and wheat planted on the other.[17] Inspired by Indian mound architecture, *Play Mountain* and *Monument to a Plow* explore the possibility of "carving" the environment, and constitute an innovation in the direct transformation of landscape into sculpture. The concept, however, remains linked to the aspirations of his first teacher, Borglum, who in 1917 was at work in Atlanta on a commission to carve a whole mountain into an image of General Lee.

Noguchi's social preoccupations were manifested more heavily in his sculpture in 1933, as it took a sharp turn toward social commentary. Working from a photograph of a lynched and burned black man, published by the International Labor Defense, he created a three-foot high nickel-bronze statue titled *Death* (1933–34). The superficial form of this piece retained Brancusi's synthesis of representation and abstraction, highly exaggerated, but the subject brought Noguchi back into an alliance with the American social realists of the carve-direct school. In 1934 Noguchi designed an emblematic sculpture depicting the virtues of labor for the auditorium of the Carl Mackley Housing Project in Philadelphia, and

16

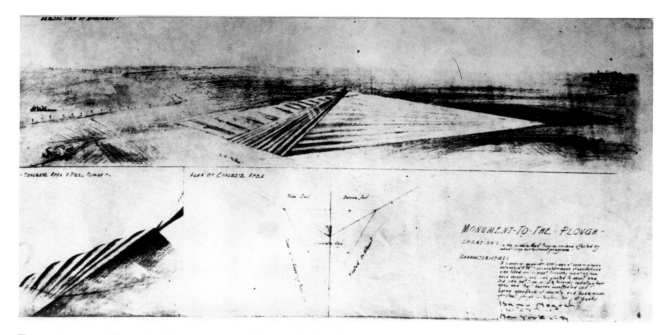

Figure 20. Isamu Noguchi. *Monument to a Plow*. 1933. Pencil drawing.

in 1935 he executed a seventy-two foot relief mural in polychrome cement for the Mercado Rodriguez in Mexico City, illustrating the history of Mexico, complete with the conventions of deprived workers and oppressive capitalists.

Noguchi had been excluded from participation in WPA projects because of his Japanese background; therefore he was forced to support himself through private commissions and design competitions. These included the Associated Press contest design, which Noguchi won in 1938 with a stylized relief in stainless steel depicting examples of modern press facilities. In 1938 he was selected to design a fountain for the Ford Motors' pavilion at the New York World's Fair. That same year he also won the Dole Pineapple competition with a wooden sculpture titled *Hawaiian Spear Fisherman*.

While in Hawaii carrying out the Dole commission, Noguchi met Honolulu's park architect and through him became interested in designing playground equipment. This kind of work permitted him to combine aesthetic and social concerns in utilitarian rather than solely in political or ideological ways, as had the earlier experiment with *Play Mountain*. "For me," he would explain later, "playgrounds are a way of creating the world." [18] He made models for the Honolulu parks, but these were never executed; later, New York authorities rejected the same plans on the grounds that the kind of equipment Noguchi had in mind would be dangerous to life and limb. In response, Noguchi designed in 1941 a *Contoured Playground* (Figure 21) which had no separate equipment, but rather, slides, climbs, mounds and jumps molded out of the earth. But these novel plans failed to reach fulfillment as a result of the onset of the Second World War.

Ultimately, the basis for the major thrust in Noguchi's work of the forties will come from his study of Haniwa and Dogu figures and the environmental sculptural ideas that he initiated in the thirties. From prehistoric Japanese stylization, he came to really understand how representation could be fused with abstraction. It was Buckminster Fuller, however, who finally released him to fully explore this problem. "Bucky was for me," Noguchi has said, "the truth of structure which circumvented questions of art. He taught me, but left me free to seek my own way." [19] In addition, seminal in *Play Mountain* and *Monument to a Plow*—and more developed in his *Contoured Playground*—is the concept of abstract sculpture employed in utilitarian   17

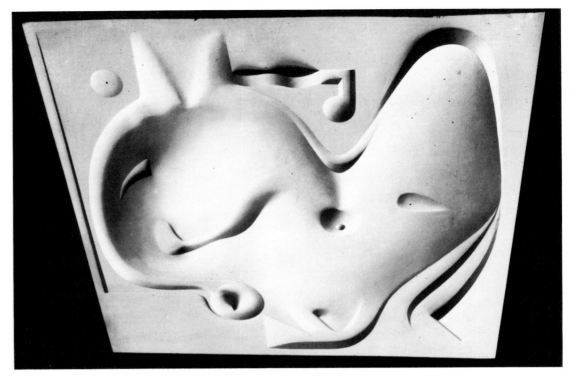

Figure 21. Isamu Noguchi. *Contoured Playground*. 1941. Plaster model. Proposed size about 100 feet square.

contexts, relating the social to the formal value of art. Noguchi's growing concern with free-form abstraction here and in his works of the late thirties, combined with his fervent social attitudes, led him into the mainstream of Surrealist sculpture in the forties.

David Smith, Theodore Roszak, and José de Rivera occupy a position midway between the European-oriented Calder and Noguchi and the native-trained artists who would emerge in the forties. All had visited Europe before the war but did not train there. Moreover, David Smith and Theodore Roszak began their careers as painters. Smith (1906–1965), after brief periods of academic study at Ohio University and at George Washington University in Baltimore, plus some work experience as a riveter in a Studebaker plant in South Bend, Indiana, enrolled part-time at the Art Students League in 1926. At this point, he would later recall, "I always thought of art as oil painting." [20] The following year he became a full-time student at the League, where his principal teachers were John Sloan and Jan Matulka, a Czech immigrant who had studied with Hans Hofmann.

Sloan, since 1907, had been a vigorous proponent of American Scene painting. Though fairly conventional in technique, Sloan was a lusty realist who approached painting straight from his eye, with no intermediating aesthetic to soften the perception. He favored back-alley scenes which offered all of the detritus of slum life—decrepit buildings, old board fences, telephone poles, trash cans, clotheslines with hand-washed laundry frozen stiff, feisty children, and alley cats. By 1927, when Smith entered his classroom, Sloan was feeling the groundswell of abstract painting, but it would be two years before he let himself be caught up in the movement. Smith has not credited Sloan with any influence on his early work. Rather, he singles out Matulka for having provided him, as Sam Hunter describes it, an antidote to the preoccupation of American painters with the current social commentary.[21]

18

It is unlikely, however, that over the six-year period of Smith's study at the Art Students League (part-time in 1926, full-time from 1927 to 1932), he would have escaped indoctrination into American Scene or social commentary painting—in fact he had a marked propensity toward it. The simple act of declaring himself rid of its infectiousness as a result of the Matulka "antidote" does not automatically remove its imprint on his subsequent work. Smith's published remarks on his early training are post-thirties—a time when most sculptors and painters alike were busy dissociating themselves from involvement with the American Scene or social commentary.

Smith had rejected American Scene painting while still at the Art Students League. In 1928 he studied privately with Matulka, who was no longer at the League; and through him was introduced to the art of Mondrian, Kandinsky, and Picasso. Matulka also was showing his students the latest trends as transmitted through European art periodicals. By 1932 Smith's paintings showed an assimilation of these trends and could be identified—along with works by Jean Xceron, Stuart Davis, and John Graham—as American-Style abstraction. In rejecting the way of Sloan and his circle, Smith had also rejected nativeness; if he was to adopt Matulka's attitudes he would have to suppress his American sensibility in favor of an imported "Frenchness," for Matulka's paintings were strictly late-Cubist style studio tableaux, arrangements of art-props painted in a mannered style and pulled together by the kind of decorative clichés that could easily be taught to and digested by art school students; lacking was the strength of directness that marks the character of primary innovation.

A few years later, about 1939, in an outrage against the Second World War, Smith would throw himself into a highly personal genre of social commentary that would not subside until the late forties. The impact of Surrealism on American art at that time is the critics' favorite, and not unreasonable, explanation for Smith's turn of mind, but his shift toward a more explicitly humanistic imagery may have been caused by a massive resurfacing of the social commentary tendencies that he had repressed in the thirties.

At Matulka's suggestion, Smith began using foreign materials to enhance the texture of his paintings. This evolution into relief included the use of lengths of turned wood, metal, and found objects; and, as he later explained, "gradually the canvas was the base and the painting was a sculpture."[22] Smith was also consulting pictures of Russian Constructivist works in German art magazines and Picasso's drawings for sculpture in *Cahiers d'Art*, which made him aware that art could be made out of iron. "My first liberation toward iron," he recalled in 1960, "which I was acquainted with manually, was from Picasso's sculpture of 1928–29. At the time I did not know that Gonzalez had done the welding for him. Nor did I know when I saw the Gargallo exhibition at Brummer's that Gonzalez had taught him welding."[23]

During this time Smith had been experimenting with free-standing wooden constructions, and then incorporating found objects into them—bits of coral and seaweed, which he had collected on a trip to the Virgin Islands in 1931 (Figure 22). Smith's first sculpture, *Head*, was constructed of wood in 1932 (Figure 23). He also briefly tried soldered pieces in aluminum, brass, tin, iron, and wire, but while vacationing at Bolton Landing in upper New York State in 1932, he switched definitively to the welding techniques he had first learned at the Studebaker plant. In the following year, with his studio set up at the Terminal Iron Works in Brooklyn,[24] he made three of a series of welded heads: *Head with Cogs for Eyes* (Figure 24), *Saw Head*, and *Agricola Head*. These were open, additive, humorous constructions made out of cut and shaped boiler plate in the manner of Picasso and Gonzalez and somewhat suggestive of the early transparent sculpture of Lipchitz. As

19

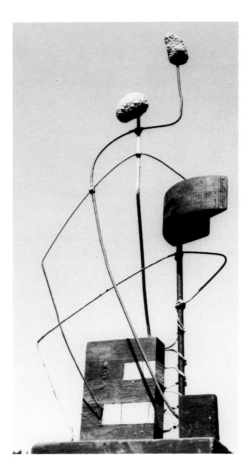

Figure 22 *(top left)*. David Smith. *Construction.*
1932. Polychromed wood, wire, nails, bronze,
coral, 32¾″ x 8⅝″ x 7¼″. (Estate of David
Smith. Photo: Hugo Mulas.)

Figure 23 *(top right)*. David Smith. *Head.* 1932.
Polychromed wood, 26⅛″ x 6⅜″ x 8⅜″.
(Estate of David Smith, Photo: Hugo Mulas.)

Figure 24 *(bottom right)*. David Smith. *Head with Cogs
for Eyes.* 1933. Steel, 14¾″ x 6⅝″.
(Collection, Mr. and Mrs. Carl Fisher, New York.)

20

was earlier true for Picasso, Smith's first metal sculptures are a direct outgrowth of his constructions, and they use the Cubist vocabulary of displacing characteristic features, replacing solid with void and vice-versa, and giving the work a double meaning in the form through the imaginative use of random objects. Picasso's painted iron *Head of A Woman* of 1931 (Figure 25) is comparable; and similar devices are found in Gonzalez' work of that period, such as *Inclined Head* of 1929 (Figure 26), *The Rabbit* (1927–30), and also *Mask* (1927–28). Smith's heads, however, are much more geometrically structured, less pictorial, and evidence his growing interest in Constructivism.

Gonzalez, a fringe member of the Paris avant-garde, was the pioneer welder among the Europeans. Except for a critical period of collaboration with Picasso in the late twenties and early thirties he generally worked by himself. Gonzalez' background prefigures that of Smith in two significant respects: he was trained as a metalworker (in a Renault factory during the First World War) and his formal art education was confined to painting (at the Barcelona School of Fine Arts). Gonzalez apparently did not reach maturity as a sculptor until 1926—his fiftieth year, and even within the next few years his work followed the varying directions of Cubism, the transparencies of Lipchitz, the mannerism of Gargallo, and to some extent, the abstraction of Brancusi. In his collaboration with Picasso, however, his own style of open-form, direct-metal sculpture was crystallized.

John Graham was another member of *Cercle et Carre*, the Paris-based artist circle to which Gonzalez belonged. A painter and collector, Graham was the first American to purchase Gonzalez' work, beginning with three pieces in 1930—the year that Graham met Smith. According to Smith, "His annual trips to Paris kept us all apprised of abstract events, along with *Cahiers d'Art* and *Transition*." [25] In 1934 Graham gave Smith the *Mask* (1927–28) by Gonzalez; the following year they

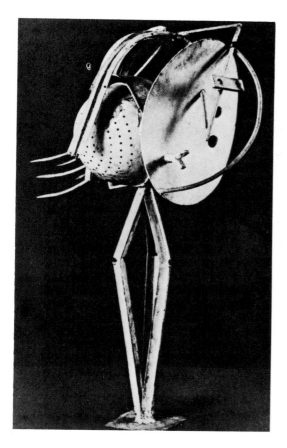

Figure 25 *(left)*. Pablo Picasso. *Head of A Woman*. 1931. Iron, 40″ high.

Figure 26 *(right)*. Julio Gonzalez. *Inclined Head*. 1930. Iron, 6¾″ high. (Collection, M. & Mme. Richet, Paris.)

visited Gonzalez' studio in Paris, but the Spanish artist had moved and Smith never met him. Later Henry Goetz, another American artist in Paris, sent Smith photographs and descriptions of Gonzalez' work.

Smith also was inclined to minimize the importance of the welding technique. In an article on Gonzalez he asserted that "art lies in the concept, not the technique." [26] Citing examples of iron welding and iron working in many periods of culture and in both art and daily life, including the early twentieth-century works of the Cubists and Constructivists, he maintained that the question of who initiated the welding technique of metal sculpture was irrelevant. For Gonzalez, he said, "Craft and smithery became submerged in the concept of the sculpture. The esthetic end was not dependent upon its mode of travel." [27] Smith believed, moreover, that his particular medium, metal, in its broadest implications had little art historical precedence. "What associations it possesses," he has affirmed, "are those of this century: power, structure, movement, progress, suspension, destruction, brutality." [28]

Smith considered the theoretical influence of Kandinsky, Mondrian, and the Cubists the counterpart to the technical influence of Gonzalez and Picasso, recalling that he was exposed to Mondrian, Cubism, Constructivism, and Surrealism all at once, without even knowing the difference between them. Indeed, Smith's first piece of welded sculpture, *Chain Head* of 1933 (Figure 27), brings the collage into sculpture on more than the formal grounds of the Constructivists, drawing on the

Figure 27 *(left)*. David Smith. *Chain Head.* 1933. Iron, 18½" high. (Estate of David Smith.)

Figure 28 *(right)*. Pablo Picasso. *Anatomical Drawings.* 1933. Pencil.

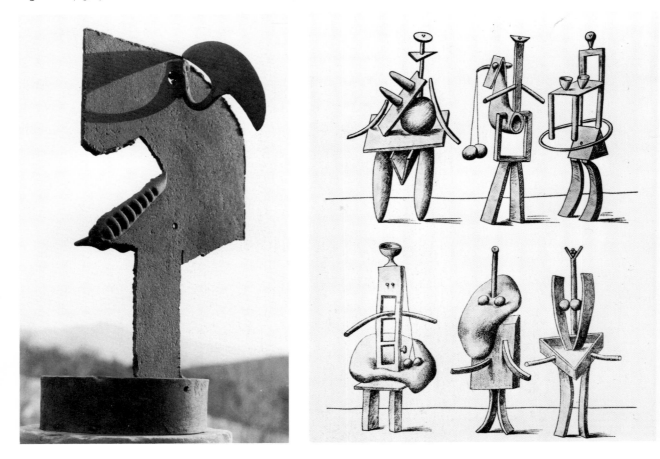

Figure 29. Alberto Giacometti.
Woman with Her Throat Cut. 1932.
Bronze, 8″ x 34½″ x 25″. (The
Museum of Modern Art, New York.)

associative wit of the Cubists and the Dadaists' practice of elevating found objects.
The influence of Picasso's paintings from around 1930, e.g. his *Seated Bather*
(1929), is evident in Smith's imagery and in the way that the image is cut out of the
plate. At the same time the flatness and angular geometry of his sculpture reflects
the more general planar tendency in all European post-Cubist abstract art, including
Constructivism. Smith's insistence on line, plane, and curved surfaces states his debt
to Cubism, which was of a kind similar to that of such American painters as Stuart
Davis, whom Smith met in 1930 and whose descriptive scenes of American life are
strongly reflected in the paintings by Smith of that time.

During his extended visit to Europe in 1935 Smith finally decided to commit
himself to sculpture. He began making wax molds for bronze castings in Greece, but
abandoned the project because of the poor quality of the castings. Around this time,
however, he must have seen a reproduction of the anatomical drawings that Picasso
had made in 1933 (Figure 28), as well as of Giacometti's *Woman with Her Throat
Cut* of 1932 (Figure 29), for from 1935 to 1938, he executed a group of small metal
constructions which fuse the influences of Gonzalez, Picasso and Giacometti in
their most Surrealist bent. Smith's *Head as Still Life* of 1936 (Figure 30) recalls
Picasso's anatomical abstractions, which stress the shape of bones and joints covered

Figure 30. David Smith. *Head as
Still Life.* 1936. Cast iron, bronze,
steel, 15⁵⁄₁₆″ x 8⅜″.
(Photo: A. Fuller.)

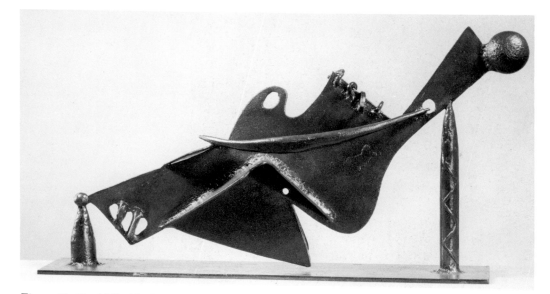

Figure 31. David Smith. *Reclining Construction*. 1936. Iron, 14″ x 27″ x 6″. (Collection, Mr. & Mrs. M. Lebworth, Greenwich, Connecticut. Photo: O. E. Nelson.)

with lean flesh and taut skin, and often contain viscera,[29] while the *Suspended Figure* (1935) and *Reclining Construction* of 1936 (Figure 31) both relate directly to Giacometti's *Woman with Her Throat Cut*. Unlike Picasso and Giacometti, however, Smith reveals his Constructivist tendency toward geometric form—a tendency that already anticipates his works of the early fifties. As a painter, Picasso positions the elements of his construction within the conceptual framework of a

Figure 32. David Smith. *Amusement Park*. 1938. Steel, 22⅝″ x 21⅞″ x 6″. (Collection, Mr. & Mrs. Walter Da▨ New Orleans, Louisiana.)

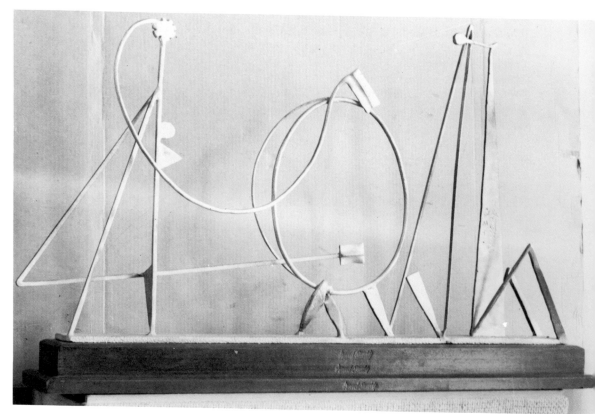

Figure 33. Alberto Giacometti. *The Palace at 4 A.M.* 1932–33. Wood, glass, wire, string, 25″ x 28¼″ x 15¾″. (The Museum of Modern Art, New York.)

rectangular canvas, and thus maintains the Cubist concentration of figural elements at the center and diffusion toward the outer limits of the framing shape. Smith, also because of his background as a painter, continues to stress contour, although in a more sculptural manner, and imposes the enframing edge upon the form itself.[30]

Smith's *Amusement Park* of 1938 (Figure 32) and *Interior for Exterior* (1939) are in fact the first manifestations in American sculpture of the combination of visceral Surrealist forms and a surrounding structural frame—a concept which will figure prominently later in the works of Lassaw, Grippe and Ferber. They derive in part from the transparencies of Lipchitz, but more specifically from Giacometti's *The Palace at 4 A.M.* of 1932–33 (Figure 33) where a spiral column and a skeletal bird are contained within a geometrical structure. *Amusement Park* also looks back to Picasso's work from the later twenties and early thirties, to such examples as *Woman in the Garden* (1929–30), where lines which do not actually serve as closed contours are juxtaposed with flat cloisonné shapes. But again in *Amusement Park* Smith's image is rendered with greater attention to the geometrical conception of the combined line and surface pattern.

Cubism and Constructivism predominate entirely in several of Smith's works from the late thirties, such as the blocky *Unity of Three Forms* (1937) and *Structure of Arches* (1939), and there are a number of pieces which relate closely to the graceful, rather elegant Surrealist constructions of Gonzalez. Smith's *Leda* of 1938 (Figure 34), for example, carries over the mannered contours and classical contraposto of Gonzalez' *Woman with a Mirror* (1936). At the same time, Smith's juxtaposition of perfect triangles and circles attests to his greater preoccupation with geometric form.

Smith considered his iron and steel sculpture a result of his experience as a metalworker even before he began to study at the Art Students League: "The equipment I use, my supply of material, comes from factory study and duplicates as nearly as possible the production equipment used in making a locomotive."[31] A similar application of industrial experience to sculptural technique occurs in the development of Theodore Roszak and José de Rivera.

25

Figure 34. David Smith. *Leda.* 1938. Steel, 29″ high. (Collection, D. Crockwell, Glens Falls, New York.)

The most pervasive influence for Roszak's work of the thirties was his trip to Czechoslovakia, made possible through a traveling grant in 1928. He had come to Prague at the time of the 1928 Exhibition of Contemporary Culture at Brno in which Czech industrial art had advanced the Bauhaus concept of collaboration between artist-designer, manufacturer, and consumer. His inclination toward Constructivism, and especially toward the kind of machine art developing within this Czech Bauhaus movement, was a sharp departure from his previous background, which involved little awareness of modern movements beyond the American Romantic Realist tradition of George Luks, George Bellows, Leon Kroll, and Eugene Speicher.

Roszak was born in Poland in 1902, and immigrated to Chicago with his family when he was two. In 1922 he began attending night classes at the Art Institute of Chicago, and in 1925 became a full-time painting student there. Later he studied at the National Academy of Design in New York with Charles Hawthorne, and privately with George Luks, while also enrolled in philosophy courses at Columbia University. In 1927 he returned to the Art Institute and, except for the tour he took to Eastern museums and the study of lithography at Woodstock, New York, in 1928, he remained in Chicago until his trip to Europe in 1929.

In addition to his exposure to machine art, Roszak responded in Paris to the Cubism of Juan Gris and the *scuola metafísica* of De Chirico. It was with a thorough exposure to this milieu that Roszak returned to the United States in 1931. A Tiffany Foundation Scholarship enabled him to spend two years at the foundation's Staten Island colony, where his dreams for a utopian collaboration

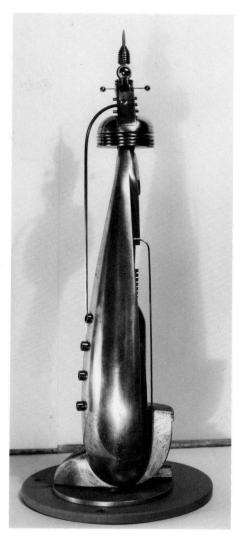

Figure 35 *(left)*. Theodore Roszak. *Fisherman's Bride*. 1934. Oil on canvas, 29″ x 27″. (Whitney Museum of American Art, New York. Photo: Geoffrey Clements.)

Figure 36 *(right)*. Theodore Roszak. *Air-port Structure*. 1932. Aluminum, copper, steel, brass, 14″ high. (Collection, Florence S. Roszak. Photo: Tadz.)

between artist and industrial society began to coalesce. He took courses in toolmaking and design and even established his own tool shop. By this time a Surrealist overtone was added to the romantic grounding of such earlier works as *Peasant Woman* (1928), and *Fisherman's Bride* of 1934 (Figure 35), which is strongly influenced by the perspective orientation of De Chirico's early paintings. Roszak also began sculpting in plaster and clay. In 1932 using machine processes he fabricated his first metal sculpture, *Air-port Structure* (Figure 36), which emulated aircraft engine components in the manner of the cast machines of the German Cubist Rudolph Belling. In the interim, Roszak was establishing critical recognition as a painter in New York in shows at the Whitney Museum beginning in 1932 and at the Roerich Gallery in 1935. Following a series of monolithic reliefs, he turned, around 1936, to three-dimensional constructions, although he would also continue to paint. At this time he became an instructor at the Design Laboratory in New York, which had been established by Moholy-Nagy with funds from the WPA.

Despite his ideological affinity with the Bauhaus, Roszak's machine sculpture departs significantly from their work. His constructions are generally beautifully engineered machines—sometimes imaginary and sometimes menacing—rather than geometric abstractions. They hold the potential of working, as his first welded piece,

27

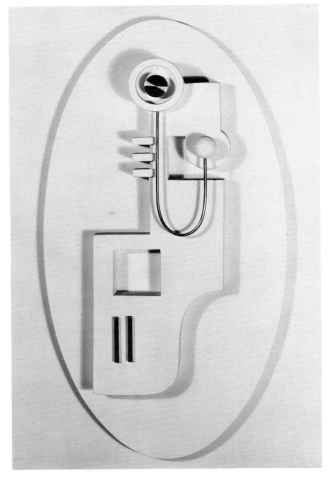

Figure 37 (left). Theodore Roszak. *Crescent-Throat Construction*. 1936. Sheet steel, brass, copper, 10″ high. (Collection, Florence S. Roszak. Photo: Tadz.)

Figure 38 (right). Theodore Roszak. *Forms within an Oval*. 1937. Wood, brass, 29½″ x 16″. (Collection, Sara J. Roszak. Photo: Tadz.)

the jigsaw-like *Crescent-Throat Construction* of 1936 (Figure 37). As "machinomorphic" symbols his work recalls the machines of Duchamp and Picabia. Duchamp had transformed human sexual anatomy into machines in his *Bride Stripped Bare*; Picabia frequently incorporated variations of actual machines into such of his paintings as the portrait of Paul Haviland, *Voilà Haviland*, of 1915 (here a portable electric lamp was taken from an ad which had appeared in a hardware dealers' magazine). Roszak's combination of objective and non-objective elements, moreover, ranges from the Cubist vocabulary of his *Forms within an Oval* of 1937 (Figure 38), to the organic Surrealism of Miró in his *Chrysalis* of 1937 (Figure 39) and *Harlequinade* (1938). The use of such associative titles denies the anonymity of Constructivism. Roszak's "content" escapes from the bounds of abstract, purely plastic relationships. His acceptance of the transition from "Muse to Production Manager," [32] as Roszak characterized his move toward Constructivism, did not, however, resolve what was a fundamental ambivalence: his romantic expressionist temperament, ever-present in his paintings and even in many of his constructions, would take precedence in his work of the next decades.

The sculpture of José de Rivera, on the other hand, remains closely allied to Constructivism in both theory and practice. Born in West Baton Rouge, Louisiana in 1904 as the son of a sugar mill engineer, De Rivera grew up on a plantation where he was trained in machine repairing. Like Roszak, he went to Chicago in 1924 and took a succession of jobs as a pipe fitter, die-caster and toolmaker. From 1928 to

1931 he was enrolled in evening drawing classes at the Chicago Studio School, where he began to experiment with sculpture as a result of encouragement by his teacher, John Norton. De Rivera's earliest works, including *Owl* and *Form Synthesis in Monel Metal* of 1930 (Figure 40), combine traditional sculptural form with industrial materials, permitting him to deal with an obsessive interest in the effects of light on polished surfaces. Already the influence of the Constructivists Naum Gabo and Antoine Pevsner is apparent in his *Bust* (1930), which has affinities to Gabo's 1915 *Constructed Head* and Pevsner's *Torso* of 1924–26.

After spending nearly a year in Europe in 1932, De Rivera returned home fully committed to sculpture. While in Europe he had seen the work of many advanced artists, including Mondrian and Brancusi, whose art he continued to observe through the intermediary of French art magazines. For a few years he alternated between abstract and figurative modes, but after a 1938 commission for a nine-foot cavalry monument in El Paso, Texas, he abandoned representation entirely. In the same year he made his first aluminum construction, *Red and Black (Double Element)* (Figure 41). In this and later constructions, the pattern was cut from a flat metal sheet and hammered into shape; the surface was smoothly polished and painted with primary colors. The flat metal bands with their continuous contours are close to the later works of Gabo, such as his *Spheric Theme* (Figure 42) and *Translucent Variation on Spheric Theme*, both of 1937, where sculptural space was defined in an essentially spheric form. Moreover, in his use of fluid shapes to create an inner volume rather than static form, De Rivera was working well within the scope of the 1920 Constructivist Manifesto and the Neo-plastic theories of Vantongerloo, who had asserted that, "if a point can move, it ceases to become a point and becomes a volume." The same problem of continuous planar forms had

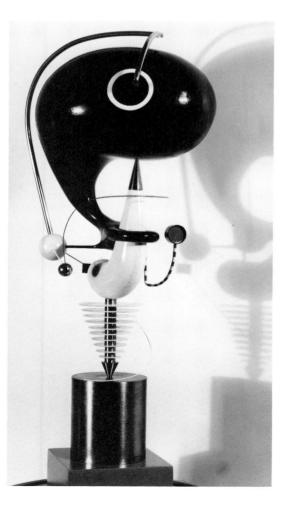

Figure 39 *(left)*. Theodore Roszak. *Chrysalis*. 1937. Wood, steel, brass, 20″ high. (Collection, Sara J. Roszak. Photo: Flair-Dordick.)

Figure 40 *(right)*. José de Rivera. *Form Synthesis in Monel Metal*. 1930. Monel metal, 18¾″ high.

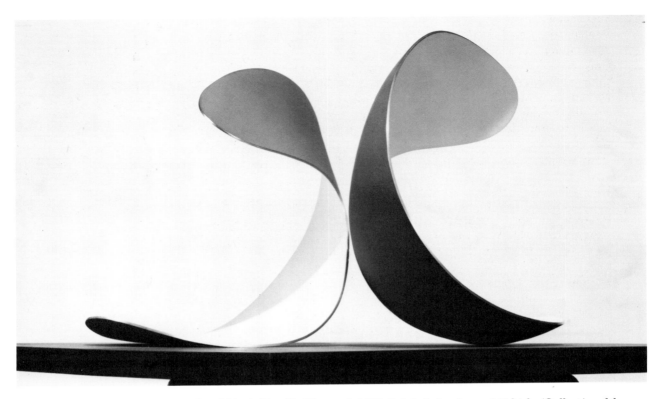

Figure 41 *(top)*. José de Rivera. *Red and Black (Double Element)*. 1938. Painted aluminum, 14″ high. (Collection, Mrs. Margarete Schultz.)

Figure 42 *(bottom)*. Naum Gabo. *Spheric Theme*. 1937. Bronze. About 39″ high. (Tate Gallery, London. Photo: E. Irving Blomstrann.)

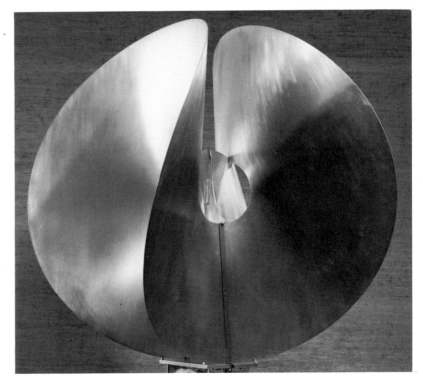

30

been dealt with by another member of De Stijl, Max Bill, who studied at the Bauhaus in Dessau. De Rivera's work at this time was markedly derivative, and his development appears to follow that of his sources. Gabo's transition from the *Constructed Head* to the *Spheric Theme*; Arp's progression from reliefs to such three-dimensional forms as *Star* (1931) was paralleled in De Rivera's development by the transition from the Cubist influence of his teacher John Norton to the Arp-like granite *Life* of 1939. The disparity between the individual influences, however, shows that De Rivera was not simply copying a group of models but rather was examining a variety of solutions to the problem of space and mass, and the complementary problem of appropriate materials.

The last of the pioneer abstractionists to fully emerge during the thirties was Ibram Lassaw, who was born in 1913 in Alexandria, Egypt and spent his first eight years travelling in Marseilles, Naples, Tunis, Malta, the Crimea, and Constantinople. Lassaw arrived in the United States with his parents in 1921. At the age of twelve he began sculpting and was enrolled in children's classes with Dorothea Denslow at the Brooklyn Museum the following year. From 1928 to 1930 he worked at what became the Clay Club, founded by Denslow, where he acquired a basic knowledge of modeling, carve-direct and casting techniques. Lassaw was first exposed to abstract art at the Brooklyn Museum's *Société Anonyme* show in 1926–27 where works by European Surrealists and Constructivists were on view, and he saw reproductions in European art magazines at the Beaux-Arts Institute of Design where he studied in 1930–31. At this time also he was particularly interested in Moholy-Nagy's *New Vision* and Buckminster Fuller's writings in *Shelter*. One of his first sculptures, *Torso* of 1931 (Figure 43), was cast in plaster and painted; this

Figure 43. Ibram Lassaw. *Torso*. 1931. Painted plaster. About 16″ high.

procedure was common in the thirties when bronze casting was beyond most sculptors' financial means. In later works, Lassaw became one of the few artists to allow the plaster to stand as a final medium. He reached full-fledged abstraction in his *Sculpture* of 1935 (Figure 44), made of natural plaster applied to a pipe and wire armature. The influence of biomorphic Surrealism becomes apparent here with reflections of Tanguy's shapes, Arp's cut-outs, and Picasso's anatomical forms;[33] the work previews as well the shapes of Smith's 1939 *Growing Forms* (Figure 45).[34] Lassaw's *Sculpture* of 1936 (Figure 46) also of plaster-coated pipe and wire—this time polished—is more angular, and reminiscent of Picasso's sculpture drawings with its knobby loops and bulbous projections. It parallels also a similar iconographic development in such works by David Smith as *Projection in Counterpoint* (1934) and *Interior* (1937). Although both worked in New York, Smith and Lassaw did not meet until 1936, after which they both showed in the American Abstract Artist exhibition of 1938 and 1939.

By 1937 Lassaw began working with sheet metal constructions assembled and brazed with solder. His brazed and painted iron and wood sculpture, *Sing Baby, Sing* (1937), is in the tradition of Calder's early constructions, again drawing on the organic perforated shapes of Arp as well as the non-continuous lines characteristic of Miró's compositions. These were not only reproduced in *Cahiers d'Art* in 1931, but also were exhibited in New York in the Museum of Modern Art's 1936 "Cubism and Abstract Art" exhibition. Earlier Lassaw had seen the work of Gonzalez in

Figure 44. Ibram Lassaw. *Sculpture*. 1935. Plaster on pipe and wire armature. About 36″ high. (Destroyed.)

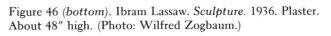

Figure 46 *(bottom)*. Ibram Lassaw. *Sculpture.* 1936. Plaster. About 48″ high. (Photo: Wilfred Zogbaum.)

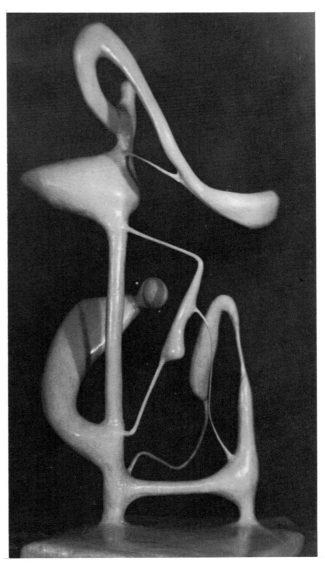

Figure 45 *(top)*. David Smith. *Growing Forms.* 1939. Cast aluminum, 28″ x 9″ x 6″.

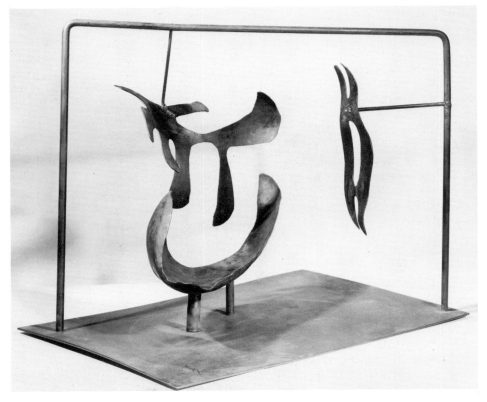

Figure 47 *(top)*. Ibram Lassaw. *Sculpture in Steel.* 1938. Steel, 18½″ high.

Figure 48 *(bottom)*. Ibram Lassaw. *Light Compositions within Two Shapes.* 1938. Painted sheet metal in electrically lighted shadow box, 30″ x 48″.

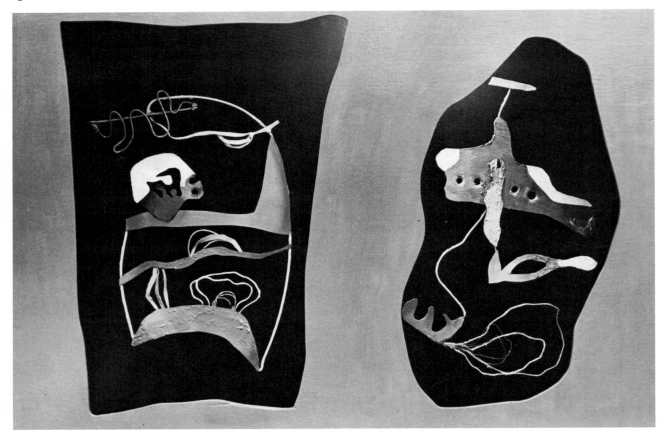

French magazines and bought a steel forge; in 1938 he produced his first welded work: *Sculpture in Steel* (Figure 47), a construction of Miróesque shapes suspended within a geometric framework. The static three-dimensional space of this piece indicates a common influence, along with Smith, of such prototypes as Giacometti's *The Palace at Four A.M.* (see Figure 33). Another work of 1938, *Light Compositions within Two Shapes* (Figure 48), a luminous sculpture anticipating Noguchi's *Lunars* of the forties, is composed of an electrically lighted wooden shadow box housing sheet metal shapes which repeat the forms of *Sing Baby, Sing*, but are now positioned within a rectangular frame.

Lassaw was the first American sculptor to sense the need for an organization that could bring together the ideas of the growing body of American abstraction-oriented artists.[35] A group of these artists, including Ilya Bolotowsky and Gertrude and Balcomb Greene, had been meeting at Lassaw's home; they joined with the painter Harry Holtzman, who had also been directing his efforts to this cause, to officially become in 1936 the American Abstract Artists.[36] In an essay "On Inventing Our Own Art" in the 1938 catalog of the Abstract Artists' show, Lassaw spoke for the pioneers of American non-representational art: "Certain artists have abandoned traditional . . . painting and solid, static sculpture. They are experimenting in the great fields opened up by the growth of modern physics, electricity and machinery, and are influenced by the recent discoveries in psychology and psychoanalysis. The new attitude that is being formed as a result of these searches is concerned with the invention of objects affecting man psychologically by means of physical phenomena. The artist no longer feels that he is 'representing reality,' he is actually making reality." [37] To Lassaw, at that time, this formula for creating a new sculpture—the formal fusion of vitalism and a rational, technological Constructivism—appeared to be "a new form of magic," especially when considered against the backdrop of the social realism of the Depression era. An unprecedented union of art, technology, and psychology was now in the hands of a nascent American avant-garde whose dependency on European models was rapidly diminishing.

NOTES

1. William A. Camfield, "The Machinist Style of Francis Picabia," *Art Bulletin* 48, nos. 3, 4 (September–December 1966): 309.

2. Lewis Mumford, "The American Milieu," *Art and Alfred Stieglitz* (New York: 1934), p. 46.

3. See Barbara Rose, *American Art Since 1900* (New York: Praeger, 1967), p. 50, for a more complete discussion.

4. I offered the dynamics of this in a College Art Association paper at the Walker Art Center in January of 1961, titled "Fusion in Modern Sculpture," and at the Museum of Modern Art in April of 1968 in a lecture titled "The Fusion of Constructivism and Surrealism in American Sculpture of the Forties and Early Fifties." For later comments on this subject see Dore Ashton, *Modern American Sculpture* (New York: Abrams, 1969), p. 20. For a different point of view, see Rosalind E. Krauss, *Terminal Iron Works* (Cambridge, Mass., M.I.T. Press, 1971), p. 3 *passim*.

5. Camfield, "Francis Picabia," p. 314.

6. Alexander Calder, *Calder* (New York: Pantheon, 1966), p. 73.

7. Michel Seuphor, *The Sculpture of This Century* (New York: Braziller, 1961), pp. 86–87.

8. James Johnson Sweeney, et al. "Alexander Calder," *Five American Sculptors* (New York: Arno, 1969), p. 19.

9. Calder, *Calder*, p. 113.

10. Alexander Calder, "What Abstract Art Means To Me," *Museum of Modern Art Bulletin* 18, no. 3 (Spring 1951): 8.

11. Peggy Guggenheim, ed., *Art of This Century* (New York: Arno, 1942), p. 96.

12. Katharine Kuh, *The Artist's Voice* (New York: Harper & Row, 1962), p. 42.

13. Calder, "Abstract Art," p. 8.

14. Calder had been puzzled by Miró's abstractions when he visited his studio in 1930; but by the time the two traveled to Spain in 1932, Calder relates that he had come to love Miró's paintings, his colors, and his personages.

15. Isamu Noguchi, *A Sculptor's World* (New York: Harper & Row, 1967), p. 17.

16. *Ibid.*, p. 18.

17. The utilization of land as a sculptural element will be explored further in the chapter on Earthworks.

18. Quoted in John Gruen, "The Artist Speaks: Isamu Noguchi," *Art in America* 56, no. 2 (March–April 1968): 31.

19. Isamu Noguchi, "A Reminiscence of Four Decades," *Architectural Forum* 136 (January–February 1972): 59.

20. Kuh, *Artist's Voice*, p. 221.

21. Sam Hunter, "David Smith," *The Bulletin of the Museum of Modern Art* 25, no. 1 (1957): 5.

22. *Ibid.*, p. 7.

23. David Smith, "Notes on My Work," *Arts* 34, no. 5 (February 1960): 44.

24. The waterfront metal work shop at 1 Atlantic Avenue in Brooklyn where Smith began welding.

25. Smith, "Notes on My Work," p. 44.

26. David Smith, "Gonzalez: First Master of the Torch," *Art News* 54, no. 10 (February 1956): 65.

27. *Ibid.*, p. 36.

28. Hunter, "David Smith," p. 7.

29. Smith has dated this piece 1935 (notebook of 1952, Archives III, item 1374); Edward Fry disputes the date in preference to 1940 (*David Smith*, New York, 1969, Cat. No. 20). I have a photograph of this piece which Smith gave me in 1956, on the back of which there is a date, 1941, in pencil (not in Smith's hand) crossed out by Smith and substituted with the date 1936. In my opinion this piece depends upon Ibram Lassaw, whom Smith met in 1936, and it is unlikely that it dates earlier than that.

30. These ideas and the sources I have cited in relating Smith's work to Picasso, Gonzalez, and Giacometti were given by me in summer session lectures at Harvard University in 1966 and in lectures at the Guggenheim Museum (1967) and the Museum of Modern Art (1968). Since that time they have entered into the literature on David Smith.

31. Hunter, "David Smith," p. 7.

32. Theodore Roszak, *In pursuit of an Image* (Chicago: Time to Time Publications, Art Institute of Chicago, 1955).

33. Earlier Lassaw had made a *Plaster Ring*, a clear plastic form suspended in a frame, in which he explored interior space recalling moon images from Max Ernst's *Forest* series, one of which was in the Brooklyn *Société Anonyme* show of 1926–27.

34. For further discussion of this relationship see Rosalind Krauss, *Terminal Iron Works*, p. 104, note 54.

35. The need to identify the American front of the abstractionist movement was felt by Lassaw's friend, Harry Holtzman, who in 1936 had been working on WPA murals with De Kooning, Stuart Davis, Balcomb Greene, and Ilya Bolotowsky; he had become friends with a number of European abstractionists and had discussed the problem of American abstract art with Jean Hélion in particular. Holtzman rented a loft next to De Kooning's studio and began rounding up work for an exhibition which was never realized because of ideological conflicts.

36. Their brochure, issued in January 1937, listed twenty-eight members, and their first exhibition was held in April of that year at the Squibb Gallery on Fifth Avenue. Lassaw was the sole exhibiting sculptor. The following year they staged a more extensive show at the Gallery of the American Fine Arts Society, which included sculpture by Lassaw and also David Smith's *Reclining Figure*.

37. Ibram Lassaw, "On Inventing Our Own Art," *American Abstract Artists: Three Annual Yearbooks* (New York: Arno, 1969), pp. 23–24. Reprint of a 1939 edition.

THE FORTIES

The absorption of Surrealism by American sculptors during the thirties was on a more formal than thematic level, involving the introduction of biomorphic shapes and visceral anatomies into a structured framework that depended, in turn, upon a generalized interpretation of Constructivism. It was only during the forties—the period of the Second World War—that American sculpture and painting began to reflect a more profound assimilation of Surrealist pictorialism.

Hard-core Surrealism had made its debut in America in 1936 with the Museum of Modern Art exhibition "Fantastic Art, Dada, Surrealism," but it took the migration of the major Surrealists to New York between 1939 and 1942 as a result of the war in Europe to bring about a wholesale shift of American painting and sculpture toward Surrealism. Matta came over in 1939; Max Ernst, Marcel Duchamp, André Masson, Yves Tanguy and André Breton, the prime energizer of the movement in Europe, followed. In 1941 the New School for Social Research organized a series of four exhibitions on the theme of Surrealism and its meaning in relation to art and life, featuring the works of De Chirico, Ernst, Matta and Tanguy.[1] These exhibitions signalled a new wave of European influence over American sculpture.

By 1942, in fact, New York had become the world center of Surrealist activity. The European Surrealists were at the center of the "artists in exile" group, which also included Jacques Lipchitz and Piet Mondrian, both of whom greatly influenced the character of American sculpture in the forties. Late in 1942, Breton organized a group exhibition of Surrealist art at the Whitelaw Reid Mansion in New York in which Calder was included. The installation was designed by Duchamp. Also during this year, Peggy Guggenheim's Surrealist-oriented Art of This Century Gallery opened with an environmental interior of curved walls and biomorphic furniture designed by the immigrant Surrealist-architect Frederick Kiesler.

Magazines featuring Surrealist art accompanied this activity. By late 1941 the periodical *View* had begun a series of special issues on the European Surrealists, and in 1942 a new magazine, *VVV*, was launched under the editorship of David Hare, with Duchamp, Tanguy and Ernst as advisors.

In the Surrealist Manifesto of 1924, Breton had defined Surrealism as: "Thought's dictation, in the absence of all control exercised by reason and outside all aesthetic or moral preoccupation."[2] Automatism, dream images, the recognition of the subconscious, all gave numerous American artists the means to reinvest Social Realism with a whole new vocabulary. The psychology of the Depression years with its accompanying themes of poverty, anguish, social violence and degradation, had begun to dissolve with the onset of the Second World War and the reclamation of jobs, patriotic ideologies and social cohesiveness. It rather easily gave way to Surrealism which offered new thematic material to reconstitute the moribund, conventionalized subjects of Social Realism as a fresh class of imagery, more

37

personal than journalistic, and more timeless, in the "fine art" sense, than topical or epic. Though most American sculpture would remain aggressive and often violent throughout the forties, the reasons are traceable more easily to thematic inventions than to social tribulations, and also to a kind of isomorphic interaction of their subject matter with new materials and new processes. David Smith, speaking of the beauty of steel attributable to "all the movements associated with it, its strength and function," added, "it is also brutal: the rapist, the murderer and death-dealing giants are also its offspring." [3]

Seymour Lipton, who emerged in the forties as this country's most powerful spokesman for "organicism" in sculpture has said about this transition and the new interaction of imagery and technique:[4]

In the late thirties I made wooden sculpture based on social themes. As I soon found social themes too limiting, . . . I left the human figure in about 1942 and began using skeletal forms—first in bronze, then in lead—constructions of horns, pelvis, etc., so as to convey a fierce struggle on a broad biological level. Gradually toward 1950, a sense of inwardness of struggle, growth, and of cyclical renewal led in part to an inside-outside sculptural form of an evolving entity: of a thing-suggesting process. This development was intensified by a search for new sculptural materials and ideas. Everyone had used solid forms, prefabricated forms, pierced forms. I felt the rightness of curved, convoluted sheets made in steel and covered with brazed nickel-silver or bronze as a new sculptural phraseology for what I was concerned with: the internal as well as the external anatomy of life and reality.

But not all of the artists of the forties were, or had been, indoctrinated Social Realists. Geometrical Abstraction had been the dominant American mode of painting since the late thirties. Although sustaining the trend of American abstract art that was already underway at the time of the Armory Show, it too was nourished by the immigration of European abstractionists to this country. The Nazi suppression of the Bauhaus school had brought many of the artist-teachers to the United States where they quickly established themselves in academic institutions. Josef Albers began teaching at Black Mountain College in 1933; Walter Gropius joined the Harvard faculty in 1937; László Moholy-Nagy established the Design Laboratory in New York in 1937 and the Chicago Bauhaus in 1939. An additional force in support of Geometrical Abstraction was, of course, the arrival of Mondrian in 1938. Strong groupings of Geometrical Abstraction artists became established in New York, Chicago, and Boston—their imagery based chiefly on compositions of both pure and modified elementary geometrical components: circles, rectangles, and triangles.

Although seemingly antithetical doctrines, and often in conflict, Surrealism and Geometrical Abstraction (Constructivism) could coexist in relative harmony, and also mix, hybrid-like, in the form of an organic-abstraction, as has already been seen in examples from the thirties. The question of their compatibility can be partially answered in terms of certain features that Surrealism and Constructivism had in common. Explicit in both was a rejection of traditional attitudes toward art on the part of the artist and the public. Constructivism, wrote Naum Gabo in 1937, "was the first ideology in this century which for once rejected the belief that the personality alone and the whim and the mood of the individual artist should be the only value and guide in an artistic creation." [5] Describing the foundation course he taught at the Bauhaus from 1923 to 1933, Albers wrote that the search for a "new contemporary visual idiom . . . led from an emphasis on personal expression and individualistic graphic and pictorial representation of material to a more rational, economic, and structural use of material itself . . . and so, to a more impersonal presentation." [6] At the same time, the Surrealist unconscious was vaunted as a collective one, leading to collaborative mechanisms like the "exquisite corpse" drawings of Tanguy, Man Ray, Breton, and others. Georges Hugnet, a literary member of the Surrealist group, reflecting upon the Surrealist object, observed that, "Nothing that the movement has produced is more authentic, more varied, more personal, and at the same time so anonymous. They [the Surrealists] have realized Lautréamont's saying that 'poetry must be made by all. Not by one.' " [7]

To a large extent the Surrealist idea of "impersonal presentation" was reflected in the variety of non-traditional materials that, by the late thirties, the Dadaists had long since incorporated into the larger scheme of Surrealism—found objects, "readymades," objects of everyday use, manufactured objects—the acceptance of all materials was a Dadaist doctrine that paralleled the Constructivist alliance with industrial materials which were also looked upon as impersonal. Just as the fresh psychological content of Surrealism and the formalized abstraction of Constructivism had offered new possibilities of imagery for a tired American representational school, the new attitudes toward materials, as expressed by the Surrealists and the Constructivists alike, authorized technical alternatives to the bronze, plaster, wood, and stone of the casting and carve-direct methods.

The war diverted the majority of American sculptors of the thirties from their art: Noguchi voluntarily interned himself in a relocation center for Japanese-Americans; Smith took a full-time defense job as a welder; Roszak worked for an aircraft corporation, and Lassaw and De Rivera both served in the armed forces. When they were able to return full-time to sculpture, however, it was almost uniformly with renewed strength. The emotional charge of Surrealism had already made itself felt in the Constructivist-inspired mobiles and stabiles of Calder, which by 1940 began to take on a menacing air quite different from the playful demeanor of his earlier work. The Surrealist notion of the artist's private myth was apparent in Lassaw's constructions as he became involved with Eastern philosophy; Roszak abandoned the machine aesthetic for organic abstractions intended as visual metaphors of subconscious associations. Only De Rivera appeared to remain aloof from a substantially Surrealist outlook; he continued in the formalist vein of his curved metal constructions throughout the forties.

Meanwhile, other American sculptors came into prominence in the forties: David Hare; Peter Grippe, whose work coincided for a time with Lassaw's in its fusion of organic and geometric form; Herbert Ferber and Seymour Lipton, who both developed a social realist idiom into a vitalistic abstraction along the lines of Roszak's powerful organicism; and Richard Lippold, who imbued Constructivist form with the romanticism of delicate materials.

Alexander Calder's attraction to the organic imagery of Arp and Miró throughout the thirties would continue to characterize much of his production in the forties. But some works from the second half of the thirties, like *Gibraltar* (1936), *Swizzle Sticks* of 1936 (see Figure 10, Chapter 1), and *Apple Monster* (1938), result as well from an expanding interest in materials, as directed toward the Dada-Surrealist metamorphosis of everyday objects. This was aptly summarized by Max Ernst on the back of his 1935 collage *Für Bieleny*: "The waste of the world becomes my art." If most of Calder's works of the late thirties and early forties continue along the playful lines of the circus—or of sculpture in a state of   39

Figure 1 *(top)*. Alexander Calder. *Black Beast.* 1940.
Stabile. Sheet steel, 105″ high. (Photo: Pedro E. Guerrero.)

Figure 2 *(bottom)*. Alexander Calder. *Constellation with Red Object.* 1943. Wood, steel wire, 25½″ high. (The Museum of Modern Art, New York.)

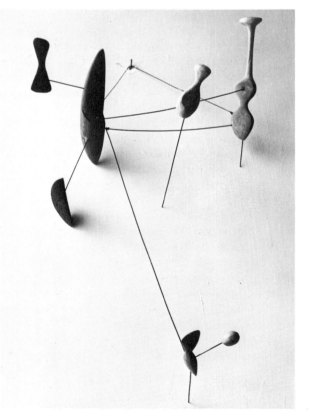

Figure 3. Alexander Calder. *Morning Star.* 1943. Stabile. Painted sheet steel, steel wire, wood, 79″ high. (The Museum of Modern Art, New York.)

performance—other works of the early forties show a turn toward greater emphasis on constructed form and heightened expressiveness. The titles *Snake and the Cross* (1940), *Thirteen Spines* (1940), *Black Beast* of 1940 (Figure 1), *Black Thing* (1942), and *Spiny* (1942) imply a new air of sobriety, as well as a strong current of aggression—maintained by the transition from brightly colored to simplified black shapes that recall the internal anatomy of visceral Surrealism. For all his lightheartedness, Calder was not immune to the outbreak of virulent Surrealism.

At the time of his first major retrospective, organized by the Museum of Modern Art in 1943, Calder was focusing his attention on two new sculpture groups, the *Constellations* of 1943–44 (Figure 2), and some small-scale, comparatively insignificant, carved and modeled works. The retrospective had made him feel the need for fresh ventures, at the same time that the war effort generated a severe metal shortage. Stimulated on both counts to seek new materials, Calder began experimenting with wood, wire, and plaster. The *Constellations* developed out of his geometric wire stabiles of the early thirties, the conventional base giving way first to wall-hanging and then to free-standing sculpture like *Morning Star* of 1943 (Figure 3). The generic title of the *Constellations* almost certainly derives from a series of paintings of that name executed by Miró between 1939 and 1942, while their combinations of wooden forms and wire connecting lines suggest further influence from the Romantic-Surrealist paintings of Tanguy. Tanguy's *Rendezvous of the Parallels* of 1935 (Figure 4) or *The Furniture of Time* (1939), are composed of both solid shapes and connecting lines to define spatial progression from foreground to background, all of which appear in Calder's *Constellations*.

Some of Calder's small works, like the plaster modeled *On One Knee* (1944), recall the anatomical, or bone drawings of Picasso in their playful distortion of   41

Figure 4 *(top)*. Yves Tanguy. *The Rendezvous of the Parallels.* 1935. Oil on canvas, 10½″ x 14″. (Kunstsammlung Basel, Oeffentliche.)

Figure 5 *(bottom)*. Alexander Calder. *Red Petals.* 1942. Mobile. Sheet steel, wire, sheet aluminum, 110″ high. (The Arts Club of Chicago.)

42

Figure 6. Joan Miró. *The Brothers Fratellini.* 1927. Oil on canvas, 51¼″ x 38″. (Collection, Lydia & Harry Lewis Winston.)

anatomy. Others display the graceful forms with menacing overtones characteristic of the period. Bronze casts of these sculptures proved to be too expensive and rather unexciting to Calder, and immediately after the war he returned to direct-metal sculpture, working on a larger than ever scale.

Calder's preoccupation with motion in the thirties gave way to renewed interest in sculpture at rest in the forties. His *Constellations* utilize the forms of the preceding decade to fashion what has been described as "mobiles immobilized." Other works like *Red Petals* of 1942 (Figure 5) although it recalls Miró's paintings—like *Brothers Fratellini* of 1927 (Figure 6)—or Calder's *Man Eater with Pennants* (1945), became standing mobiles where the moving forms were anchored to a standing base, while the stabiles, exemplifying full repose, prepared the way for the monumental standing constructions of the sixties.

Calder's brand of Surrealism was for the most part light-hearted, humorous, and elegant, but within his Constructivist framework his achievement was formally sound. As the post-war years passed, his work of the thirties and forties still looked fresh. After the war he continued to attract the attention of the best European artists and writers. Jean-Paul Sartre in the midst of post-war doldrums, described in 1946 a Calder mobile as "a little local merry-making, an object defined by its movement and which does not exist outside it, a flower which withers as soon as it is stopped, a pure play of movement . . ." Sartre continues of Calder that he:[8]

has not sought to imitate anything—because he has not wanted to do
anything but to create scales and chords of unknown movements they are at
once lyrical inventions, technical combinations almost mathematical and,
at the same time, the sensible symbol of Nature—this great vague Nature,

43

which throws pollen about lavishly and will produce brusquely the flight of a thousand butterflies, and of which one never knows if it is the blind chain of causes and effects or the timid development, ceaselessly delayed, thrown out of order, thwarted by an Idea.

More poetry than criticism, Sartre's words nevertheless count as a measure of Calder's post-war international popularity.

As the fifties approached, Calder was, in fact, the only American sculptor acclaimed in Europe. In 1946 he had had a successful exhibit at the Galerie Louis Carré in Paris; the following year he shared with Léger major shows in Berne and Amsterdam; in 1948 his new work appeared in Rio de Janeiro and Sâo Paulo, Brazil. He was equally acclaimed at home—Massachusetts Institute of Technology staged a full retrospective in 1950 on the heels of Calder's sustained success in Paris at the Galerie Maeght, and in 1952, he took first prize at the Venice Biennale.

Calder's stabiles and mobiles of about 1950, in contrast to those in the Museum of Modern Art's show in 1943, were more grand in scale. Significantly, they marked a further departure from the more suspended configurations of the thirties, when his thoughts were closer to painting and led him to set his mobile components within an actual pictorial framework or one which was implied by the limits of the mobile's movement. Appearing less often, also, after 1950, are stabile mobiles with wire extensions that, in reaching out, suggest tendrils, or stems with dangling flowers. As the light-hearted Miróesque Surrealism is reduced in his work, the emphasis shifts toward the monumental—as if increased size were essential to bring his production above the level of toy-making. Léger had forecast the change in 1950, in a perceptive statement in *Derrière le Miroir*:[9]

One cannot suppose a more contrasting image than that of Calder, the man, weighing 100 kilos, versus his work: airy, transparent, mobile. He is somewhat like a treetrunk on the march. He takes up a great deal of air, he stops the wind, he never goes unnoticed. There is an element of nature that, smilingly, curiously, balances. Set loose in an apartment, he is a danger to everything that is fragile. His place is rather outside, in the open air, in the bright sunshine. . . . Mobile sculpture was invented. It has existed for a while . . . Is it going to bring us something else?

Isamu Noguchi became an intensely Surrealist sculptor during the forties. Like Calder, his European experience had already exposed him to Arp and Miró; and at the same time, the emotional tenor of his work during the thirties when translated from representation to abstraction emerged as Surrealist content. By the late thirties Noguchi had returned to a formal idiom recalling Brancusi, and, to an even greater extent, Arp. Arp's late-thirties style of volumetric, rather soft plasticity[10] is apparent in works by Noguchi such as the *Hawaiian Spear Fisherman* (1938) and *Capital* of 1939.

Noguchi's preoccupation with social commentary during the thirties was only a prelude to his involvement in the struggles of the war, for as a Japanese-American he was a vulnerable participant. His anguish was conveyed outright in the Surrealist images of his wartime sculptures like *This Tortured Earth* of 1943 (Figure 7), a magnesite relief of ravished female anatomical shapes inspired by photos of a bombed African desert, or *Woman* (1944),[11] both of which derive formally from his *Contoured Playground* of 1940 (see Figure 21, Chapter 1). At the same time, however, Noguchi attempted to channel his emotion into positive gestures which were not limited to sculptural expression, continuing his drive to apply artistic

Figure 7 *(left)*. Isamu Noguchi. *This Tortured Earth.* 1943. Magnesite, 30″ long. (Photo: Soichi Sunami.)

Figure 8 *(right)*. Isamu Noguchi. *Monument to Heroes.* 1943. Magnesite wood, bones, string, 30″ high. (Photo: George Platt Lynes.)

means to utilitarian ends. For a few months early in 1942 he voluntarily entered the Japanese-American relocation center in Poston, Arizona to offer artistic contributions to the community there. During his stay, he designed park and recreation areas, an irrigation system, and a cemetery.

While the explicitly industrial or mechanical aspects of Constructivism were relegated to his various inventions and designs, the Constructivist principles of balance and structure remained implicit in all of his sculpture. "Everything I do," he commented in 1962, "has an element of engineering in it." [12]

Picasso's Surrealistic anatomical, or bone drawings (see Figure 28, Chapter 1) may have figured in Noguchi's formal vocabulary during the forties, but even more important was his contact with Tanguy, whose landscape idiom and sculptural illusionism were already compatible with Noguchi's concerns. As if in reaction to carve-direct sculpture, Noguchi began to fashion constructions out of wood, paper, bones, string, and rock, adding separate members together to enclose and penetrate space. *Monument to Heroes* of 1943 (Figure 8) or *I Am a Foxhole* of the same year, where string is used to connect the individual parts, resemble the figures of Tanguy's paintings. Also in 1943 Noguchi experimented with light sculpture, an idea growing out of his *Musical Weather Vane*, and made a series of self-illuminating pieces   45

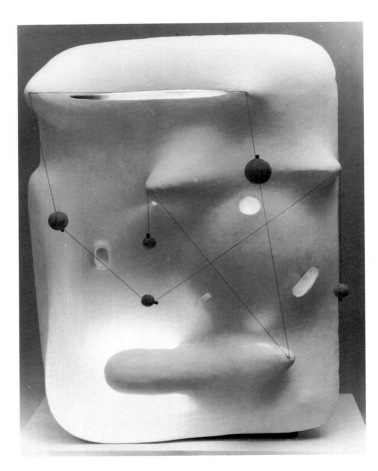

Figure 9 (left). Isamu Noguchi. *Lunar Landscape*. c. 1944. Electrified. Magnesite, cork, string, 33¼" x 24" x 7". (The Hirshhorn Museum and Sculpture Garden, Smithsonian Institution, Washington, D.C.)

Figure 10 (right). Isamu Noguchi. *Bird's Nest*. 1947. Wood dowels, plastic, 14" long. (Photo: Rudolph Burckhardt.)

called *Lunars*. Works like the *Lunar Landscape* of 1944 (Figure 9), carved in magnesite and illuminated with an imbedded light bulb, translate the illusionistic topography of Tanguy's paintings into relief sculpture based on Noguchi's earlier contour landscapes.

Noguchi's debt to Tanguy is related to that of Calder, whose *Constellations* are in fact quite similar to Noguchi's linear works, such as *Bird's Nest* of 1947 (Figure 10). Like Calder, moreover, Noguchi's adaptation of Surrealism always occurred within a larger context of rigid formal organization, a schema which finds literal application in the *Lunar Infant* of 1943–44 (Figure 11), a free form of magnesite suspended within a rectangular metal frame.[13] In the same manner, Noguchi's *Capital*, unlike Arp's sculpture *a-géométrique*, is given an architectonic form which is symmetrical and, as at least implied by the title, architectural. Similarly, in a work like the bronze *Cronos* (1947), individual formal elements remind one again of Picasso's bone figures, but these are given a sculptural coherence which is less evident in the drawings of Picasso.

46

Figure 11 *(left)*. Isamu Noguchi. *Lunar Infant.*
1943–44. Electrified. Magnesite, wood, metal
stand, 14″ high.

Figure 12 *(right)*. Isamu Noguchi. *Noodle.* 1943.
Botticino marble, 27″ high. (Collection, Joseph
E. Spinden, Houston, Texas.)

In 1944 Noguchi discovered a cheap source of carving material in the marble
slabs used for surfacing buildings. He was attracted to the combination of beauty,
delicacy and stability which the marble offered, and saw in it a means of pursuing his
own concerns with plane, space, and void while upholding the credo of materials
which was an inescapable part of his carve-direct heritage. Actually, Noguchi had
resumed stone carving after leaving the relocation center. His first piece, *Leda*
(1942), continued in the Brancusi manner of the thirties; in later works like *Noodle*
of 1943 (Figure 12) and *Time Lock* (1944–45), however, Noguchi imposed his own
sense of structure on the stone and developed an idiom of interlocking forms which
to him symbolized a fusion to resist erosion or decay.

When he began working in slab marble, he seemed again indebted to Tanguy.
The abstracted forms of human anatomy seen in paintings like Tanguy's *Rendez-
vous of the Parallels* (see Figure 4) or *The Doubter* (1937), were joined together by
Noguchi in actual interlocking constructions rather than the illusionistically   47

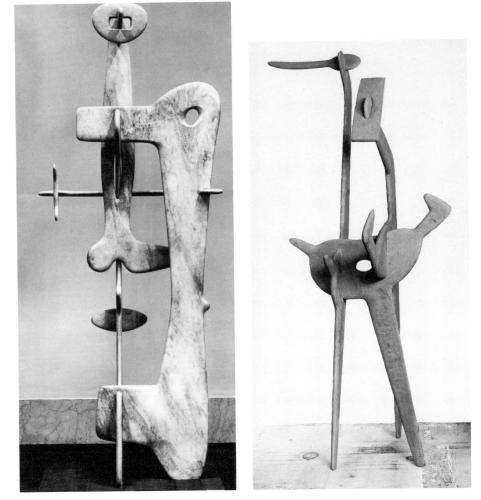

Figure 13 *(left)*. Isamu Noguchi. *Kouros*. 1945. Pink Georgian marble, 120″ high. (The Museum of Modern Art, New York.)

Figure 14 *(right)*. Isamu Noguchi. *Strange Bird (To the Sunflower)*. 1945. Green slate, 57″ high. (Photo: Rudolph Burckhardt.)

interwoven mass of his stone figures. The first of these new works, *Kouros* of 1945 (Figure 13), effectively summarized Noguchi's efforts to that point, bringing together the legacies of Surrealist form and Oriental calligraphy, carve-direct technique and the abstract constructions he had experimented with in his Paris brass works of the twenties. At the same time, with its explicit allusion to antiquity in the title and to archaic form in the vertical structure, *Kouros* previews his subsequent emphasis on permanence and continuity in art, which would be demonstrated in particular through the transformation of mythological themes, such as *Cronos, Gunas*, and *Avatar* (1947).

Noguchi's fusion of Surrealism and Constructivism, as in *Kouros, Cronos*, and other interlocking figures such as *Strange Bird (To the Sunflower)* of 1945 (Figure 14) and *Humpty Dumpty* (1945), constitutes a literal statement of his personal belief in the power of the artist to impose order upon a chaotic environment. "I say it is the sculptor who orders and animates space, gives it meaning," he wrote in the catalog of the *Fourteen Americans* show held at the Museum of Modern Art in 1946.[14]

Since the 1935 production of *Frontier*, Noguchi had been collaborating with dancer Martha Graham. Already in *Frontier* he was anticipating Tanguy's space-defining linear connectors with the use of a rope to bisect the void of the stage space so that, as he later explained: "Space became a volume to be dealt with sculpturally."[15] During the forties he worked on stage settings for *Herodiade* of

48

Figure 15 (top). Isamu Noguchi. *Herodiade*. 1944. Painted plywood. (Collection, Martha Graham. Photo: Arnold Eagle.)

Figure 16 (bottom). Isamu Noguchi. *Night Land*. 1947. Marble, 22″ high. (Collection, Mr. & Mrs. Arnold Maremont, Chicago.)

1944 (Figure 15), *Appalachian Spring* (1944), *Dark Meadow* (1946), and *Night Journey* (1947), drawing on the landscape idiom which dominated his sculpture of that period. The set for *Herodiade* in particular recalls Tanguy's *Rendezvous of the Parallels* (see Figure 4) with its disposition of non-functioning objects among which the dancers were to perform. Through these projects, he was able to work not with sculptural equivalents, but with the real space of the stage and the real movements of the dancers.

Noguchi's contemporaneous landscape environments and topographical reliefs like *Night Land* of 1947 (Figure 16), a table sculpture, translate the grossly Surrealist images of earlier works like *This Tortured Earth* of 1943 (see Figure 7) into a more 49

Figure 17 *(top)*. Matta. *Listen to Living.* 1941. Oil on canvas, 29½" x 37⅜". (The Museum of Modern Art, New York.)

Figure 18 *(bottom)*. Alberto Giacometti. *Project for a Square.* 1931. Plaster, 10¼" high. (Private collection, Paris.)

optimistic statement of life and survival. *Night Land* suggests associations with Tanguy's *Mama, Papa Is Wounded* (1927) and Matta's *Listening to Living* of 1941 (Figure 17), as well as to sculptures by Giacometti and Ernst: Giacometti's *Project for a Square* of 1931 (Figure 18) and *No More Play* (1932); Ernst's *The Table Is Set* (1944).[16] Like the interlocking figures, as *Kouros* (see Figure 13), that followed the images of destruction in his wood, bone and string constructions and wartime reliefs, the free-form components of Noguchi's landscape environments represent objects that have withstood erosion, and that, in their surviving state, show the durability of their original form, as do rocks eroded by water or hills by wind. They indicate the trend toward greater formalism—a stronger stance—which his work was to take in the next decade.

Figure 19 *(top)*. David Smith. *Elements which Cause Prostitution.* 1939. (Medals for Dishonor Series.) Bronze, 8⅝″ x 10½″. (Estate of David Smith. Photo: Rudolph Burckhardt.)

Figure 20 *(bottom)*. David Smith. *Food Trust.* 1938. (Medals for Dishonor Series.) Bronze, 7½″ x 14″. (Estate of David Smith. Photo: Rudolph Burckhardt.)

Like Noguchi, David Smith became actively involved in social protest in the thirties, and was drawn still further into the Surrealist arena during the forties. Smith had his first one-man show of welded iron constructions at the East River Gallery in 1938, but by this time he had turned to another series of works, the *Medals of Dishonor* which he produced in *ciré perdu* between 1937 and 1940. Exchanging the oxyacetylene torch for dentists' and jewelers' tools, he created fifteen bronze medals to commemorate themes such as *Elements which Cause Prostitution* (Figure 19), *Sinking Hospital* and *Civilian Refugee Ships*, and *Food Trust* (Figure 20). Smith became interested in intaglio seals, particularly Mesopotamian cylinder seals, during his visit to Greece in 1935–36, but immediate inspiration for the Medals of Dishonor came from some postcards of German war medallions which he bought in the British Museum during his European trip. He explained 51 these seals as follows: "medallions for killing so-and-so many men, for destroying so-and-so many tanks, airplanes, *et cetera*, . . ."[17] In another volume he added, "From a naturally anarchistic, revolutionistic point of view, the idea of 'medals for dishonor' became my position on awards."[18] The concern for shapes and contours apparent in his constructions manifests itself here in the distribution of solid forms over the surface of the medals. Fusing painting and sculpture in a low relief, Smith treated his subjects with emblematic representations, playing strongly on the juxtaposition of visual images and associations, in the manner of the Surrealist painters Salvador Dali and René Magritte.

While working on the Medals, Smith served on the Federal Arts Project of the WPA and also in the Section of Fine Arts at the Treasury Department. After a brief term as a machinist in Glens Falls, New York, he took a full-time defense job as a welder of M-7 tanks and locomotives in Schenectady in 1942. He had moved to Bolton Landing, New York in 1940, working in a studio which he named after the Terminal Iron Works in Brooklyn and living in virtual seclusion from the New York art scene. The decade which followed was for Smith a period of experimentation, of departure from the formative aesthetic of Picasso and Gonzalez, and of the development of a uniquely personal style.

The propagandizing depictions of social evils in the Medals of Dishonor mark a reversal of Smith's earlier tendency toward abstraction and constitute the first phase of his "social Surrealism," which took on pointed vehemence during the war years with works like *Widow's Lament* (1942), *Atrocity* (1943), *War Landscape* (1945), and *Aftermath Figure* of 1945 (Figure 21). A new aggressiveness becomes apparent in pieces like *The Rape* of 1945 (Figure 22) where a fallen woman, ambiguously shown inviting her attack, is about to be violated by a phallic cannon.[19]

Taking up the theme of war in more abstract terms than the Medals of Dishonor, several bronze pieces, including *Aftermath Figure* and *Figure of Greed* (1945), continue the visceral Surrealism of Picasso and Giacometti. A group known as spectres which include *Spectre of War* (1944), *False Peace Spectre* (1945), or *Spectre of Profit* (*Race for Survival*) of 1946 (Figure 23) project a still greater sense of movement and change in terms of silhouette and line rather than mass.

Figure 21. David Smith. *Aftermath Figure.* 1945. Bronze, 14½" high. (Estate of David Smith.)

Figure 22 *(top)*. David Smith. *The Rape*. 1945. Bronze, 9″ high.

Figure 23 *(bottom)*. David Smith. *Spectre of Profit (Race for Survival)*. 1946. Steel, stainless steel, 18⅜″ high. (Collection, Mr. and Mrs. Nathan Allen, Greenwich, Connecticut.)

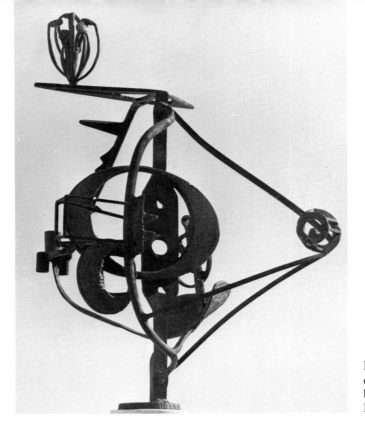

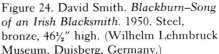

Figure 24. David Smith. *Blackburn–Song of an Irish Blacksmith.* 1950. Steel, bronze, 46½" high. (Wilhelm Lehmbruck Museum, Duisberg, Germany.)

Throughout the second half of the forties Smith pursued alternate modes of sculpture—the Constructivist-oriented open constructions with great formal contrasts, like *Cello Player, Oculus* (1947), or *Blackburn-Song of an Irish Blacksmith* of 1950 (Figure 24), and fanciful images of Surrealist content displaying themes generally associated with paintings—like the genre interior *Home of the Welder* of 1945 (Figure 25) or the still life *Pillar of Sunday* (1945) and *Construction with Cheese Clouds* (1945). The influence of Smith's early training as a painter, his continual preoccupation with drawings, and his intaglio work on the Medals, are apparent in the pictorial orientation of his new constructions. As he explains, "I belong with painters, in a sense. . . . I never conceived of myself as anything other than a painter because my work came right through the raised surface and color and objects applied to the surface." [20] Detail is absorbed more thoroughly into the overall structure, and forms individually conceived, primarily in two dimensions, are related along strong directional axes. But these retain their sculptural identity through a continuous emphasis on surface and materials rather than contour and figure-ground relationships. Narrative content reaches its extreme with the *Home of the Welder*, a three-dimensional Dutch interior carried to the present, perhaps through the intermediary of Miró's *Dutch Interiors.* A wife-figure which metamorphosizes into a menacing plant, a wheel and chain as symbols of burden, a fanciful goose juxtaposed with paintings of a reindeer and a Venus are all used to comment on the domestic life of the welder—further alluding to the extremes of welder as laborer and as artist, merged in the person of Smith himself.

Toward the beginning of the fifties, Smith, too, lightened the Surrealist load of his previous imagery and embarked on a new discipline of form. Although very much in consequence of his works of the late thirties, such as *Interior for Exterior* (1939), Smith's form by the early fifties, seen in *Australia* of 1951 (Figure 26) or *Hudson River Landscape* (1951), is more firmly resolved and his imagery less literal, recalling the precision of Gonzalez' constructions, which distinguished the Spanish welder's work from that of Picasso in the thirties.

54

Figure 25 *(top)*. David Smith. *Home of the Welder.* 1945. Steel, bronze, 21″ high. (Estate of David Smith.)

Figure 26 *(bottom)*. David Smith. *Australia.* 1951. Painted steel, 79¾″ high. (The Museum of Modern Art, New York. Photo: John Stewart.)

The Constructivist aesthetic was to some extent reasserted among American painters and sculptors with the arrival of Mondrian in New York in 1938. The influence of the Neo-plastic painter, however, was already apparent in the works of Ibram Lassaw, whose concern for deep space within a sculptural framework—seen in his 1938 *Sculpture in Steel*—came to dominate subsequent work, where in fact the free forms of Miró and Arp were abruptly replaced with the strict geometry of Mondrian. Lassaw's enthusiasm for Mondrian may have been instigated by his fellow-student at the Beaux-Arts Institute of Design in New York, Harry Holtzman, who later became a pupil of Hans Hofmann at the Art Students League. Holtzman saw Mondrian's paintings at the Museum of Living Art in 1934, promptly sought him out in Europe, and began to emulate him. Lassaw's conversion is evident in the appropriately-titled *The Mondrian* of 1940 (Figure 27), a steel and plastic construction of austerely interlocking rectangles that generate cubic space. Lassaw had already absorbed the influence of Gabo and Pevsner, and turned to the metal construction as a means of creating Constructivist-inspired space not possible with plaster.

After his discharge from the Army in 1944, however, he undertook a synthesis of the Mondrianesque construction with his earlier Surrealist vocabulary of the late

Figure 27 *(left)*. Ibram Lassaw. *The Mondrian*. 1940. Steel, plastic. About 36″ high.

Figure 28 *(right)*. Ibram Lassaw. *Arachnide*. 1944. Steel, wood, plastic, 25″ high.

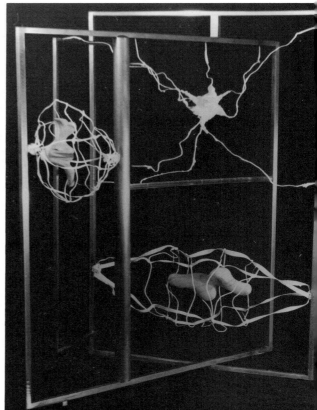

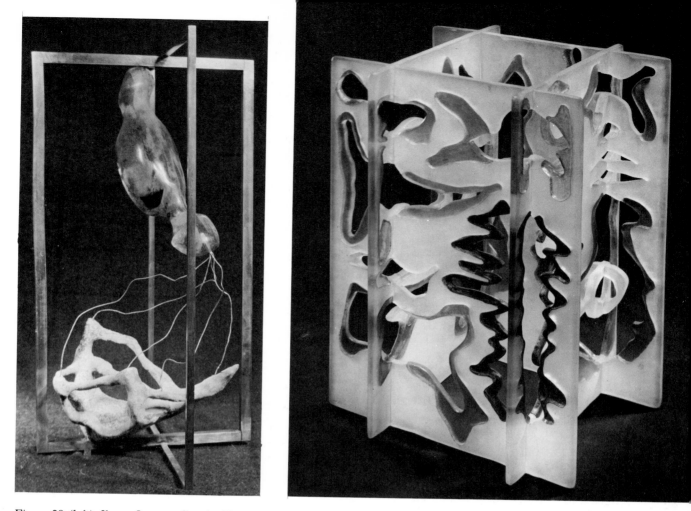

Figure 29 *(left)*. Ibram Lassaw. *Gravity Tension*. 1945. Metal, lucite, 19″ high.

Figure 30 *(right)*. Ibram Lassaw. *Mandala*. 1949. Polychromed plastic, 16″ high. (Photo: Peter A. Kozack.)

thirties. In the first of these works, *Arachnide* of 1944 (Figure 28), crafted in a variety of new materials, wooden forms are suspended in a plastic "cobweb" within a geometric frame of rounded steel columns which was not only a supporting structure but which created also a sense of enclosure. This framework was perhaps inspired by the cobweb cage of a Miró self-portrait etching of 1938 and published in 1944.[21] The spider form itself is not unlike the familiar Miró sunburst figure that recurs throughout Miró's works. The steel frame departs from the strict geometry of *The Mondrian* to form an organic enclosure suggestive, as the title implies, of natural life. Although he later insisted that his constructions were not meant to "express, symbolize, or represent anything"[22] Lassaw's works of the late forties evoke a subjective content that is not so evident in his earlier, more formal works.

Lassaw's series of sculptures like *Gravity Tension* of 1945 (Figure 29), *Uranogeod* (1946), and the references to stars, like *Fragment from Aldebaran* (1947), *Mandala* of 1949 (Figure 30) and *Star Cradle* of 1949 (Figure 31) all suggest a preoccupation with the cosmos—a mystic strain no doubt resulting from Lassaw's growing involvement with the Eastern philosophies of Taoism, Vedanta, and Zen Buddhism. Surrealist elements also are dominant; for example in *Uranogeod* (Urano-sky, Geodes-earth), the stainless steel, cubic enframement contains a strange, earth-like morphology. In the cast-metal *Fragment from Aldebaran*, as in the early constructions of David Smith, the frame is eliminated entirely, and the

57

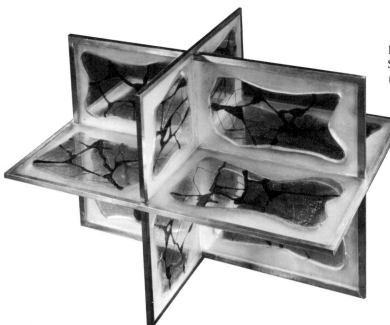

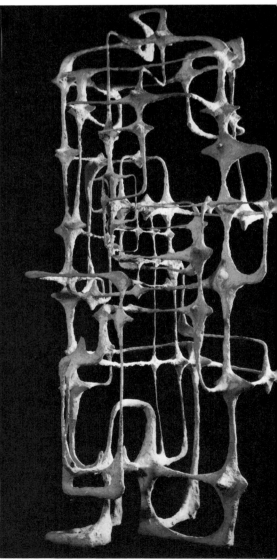

Figure 31 *(top)*. Ibram Lassaw. *Star Cradle*. 1949.
Stainless steel, plastic, 12″ high.
(Photo: Peter A. Kozack.)

Figure 32 *(bottom left)*. Ibram Lassaw. *Albescence*. 1948.
Plastic. (Destroyed.)

Figure 33 *(bottom right)*. Ibram Lassaw. *Milky Way*. 1950.
Plastic composition on metal armature, 52″ high.
(Photo: Peter A. Kozack.)

interior organic mass becomes structural. In *Somewhere Window* (1947), poly-chrome plastic triangles with amorphous bases are fitted into the corners of a stainless steel armature to create an effect of translucent color planes, like a stained glass window. This use of plastic in a structured network soon gave way to an inverson of Lassaw's characteristic solid-void relationship. In *Albescence* of 1948 (Figure 32) the familiar Arp-like shapes of Lassaw's earlier works are cut out of two intersecting sheets of transluscent plastic; *Mandala* is a variant of the shadow box format of the earlier *Light Compositions within Two Shapes*, with four intersecting sheets of articulated plastic creating an interior void. *Star Cradle* (see Figure 31) introduces a horizontal sheet which bisects two intersecting planes, recreating with its metal-trimmed contours the geometric framework of *Uranogeod*.

With *Mandala*, Lassaw began to dye sections of the cut-out biomorphic shapes and set them back into position. In *Star Cradle*, he filled in the open spaces with transparent plastic on which a darker, liquid plastic had been dribbled, overtly referring to the paintings of his friend Jackson Pollock. The dripped plastic represents an adaptation of Pollock's technique of producing a surface pattern of interconnected nuclei as in *The Cathedral* of 1947. At the same time, however, Lassaw's drip sculpture is consistent with his earlier experiments in altering the surface of his materials, from the early polished plaster and painted wood through the dyed plastic. This new development in Lassaw's style, moreover, led to what became his ultimate resolution of the Surrealist-Constructivist, organic-geometric dichotomy which pervades his work throughout the forties. With *Milky Way* of 1950 (Figure 33), he returned to an architectonic wire framework—this time coated with the dripped plastic. The result is not limited to a space-defining sculpture, but goes beyond pure form to create what he sees as a metaphor of universal existence. An avid student of astronomy, biology, and cosmology, Lassaw developed his own view of the universe as a continuum, within which his sculptures were not meant to be microcosmic symbols of the whole, but rather, analogical fragments taking on a dual aesthetic and religious significance.

One year older than Lassaw, Peter Grippe (b. 1912) came to New York from his native Buffalo in 1939 to work on the WPA as well as to observe the latest trends in art. In Buffalo he had been part of a rebellious group called "The Seven," which included the painter William Seitz, who later would become a curator at the Museum of Modern Art. This group was formed to demonstrate opposition to the *retardataire* teaching at the Buffalo Art Institute from which Grippe was finally expelled due to his outspoken support of abstract art. Working principally in terra cotta, he experimented briefly with steel welding in the early forties but found that it lacked the tactile freedom of clay; he was also dissuaded from its use by Lipchitz who looked upon welding as a cheap substitute for bronze casting. The influence of the European master, who was in New York at that time, is apparent in the stacked planes and cubic masses of Grippe's early semi-figurative works—like the *Man with Barrel* of 1939 (Figure 34). Equally important to his development, however, was the impact of the East Indian sculpture that Grippe saw in the mid-thirties at the Albright-Knox Gallery in Buffalo, envisioning it as "a dance of segmented parts moving architecturally around the figure in an endless movement." [23] From this example arose Grippe's preoccupation with movement which was to dominate his work throughout the forties, as would a continuing influence of Lipchitz's style of "transparent" sculpture.

While Grippe was teaching in the Federal Arts Project in New York, he made his first sketches for the *City* series. Here, the effect of simultaneous movement, of shifting parts radiating about a central core, which is characteristic of East Indian sculpture, led him to experiment with what he called "dancing architecture," in the

59

Figure 34 *(left)*. Peter Grippe. *Man with Barrel.* 1939. Plaster, 30″ high.

Figure 35 *(opposite page, top)*. Peter Grippe. *The City #1.* 1941. Terra cotta, 9½″ high. (The Museum of Modern Art, New York.)

Figure 36 *(opposite page, bottom)*. Peter Grippe. *The City #2.* 1946. Terra cotta, 26″ high. (Collection, Washington University, St. Louis, Missouri. Photo: Adolph Studley.)

form of the *City*. For what he termed a "wedding together" of figures and buildings, Grippe drew on pre-Columbian architecture and Mayan art—the objects of widespread interest at that time among carve-direct sculptors. These same sources contributed decorative motifs, images and pictographs which Grippe applied to the surface of *City #1* of 1941 (Figure 35) in the manner of the annotated Cubist and Futurist paintings. The solid construction and multiple viewpoints of the *City* are derived from Grippe's earlier Cubistic sculpture, while the angular, dissected figures and decorative harlequin patterns and musical notes attest to his familiarity with Picasso's *Three Musicians* (1921), acquired by the Museum of Modern Art in 1940. At the same time, however, the inscriptions on *City #1*—the dates of the Declaration of Independence, the French Revolution, and the First World War—expressed Grippe's reaction to the war, his fear for the future. The postdated inscriptions of *City #2* of 1946 (Figure 36) and *City #3*, on the other hand, were intended to convey his ultimate faith in the survival of man. The city format was significant for Grippe in that it reflected the urban image of man in his environment, as well as his loneliness and social dependency:[24]

60

Figure 37. Peter Grippe. *Growth After Destruction.* 1944. Terra cotta, 12½″ high. (Willard Gallery, New York. Photo: Soichi Sunami.)

> *The City* is a result of the people becoming the buildings . . . becoming the pavements . . . becoming the walking feet. They are the faces against faces . . . figures moving together in the subway, out of the factory, down the streets. They are the movement and energy of the cities. Movement is our machine age . . . churning energy and motion. It is our factories . . . our buildings . . . our homes . . . people moving . . . becoming the buildings . . . the houses . . . becoming the vehicles . . . becoming the machines . . . becoming the streets.

Unlike most of his contemporaries, Grippe continued working with terra cotta during the forties, building up architectural frameworks in slabs—a technique to be associated with the form-building of Neo-plasticism. His surfaces were often enhanced with applied pellets of clay, as found in Mayan statuary, common to Lipchitz, and certainly reflected carve-direct techniques which preserved evidence of the tool in the surface of the sculpture.

In *Dance of Fear* (1943), as well as later *City* sculptures, Grippe introduced what he called sculptural transparency: the figure is separated from and occupies the space within the architectural framework, just as in Lassaw's contemporary steel, wood, and plastic constructions. Like Lassaw, Grippe acknowledged his debt to Mondrian for the architectonic framework of the *Cities*, and as his tribute, comparable to Lassaw's *The Mondrian*, incised the name *Piet* into the surface of *City #2* (see Figure 36).

In a 1944 statement Grippe explained that his primary concern was architectural movement, that transparency and the slab construction were means of escaping the confines of gravity and the solidity of architectural form, but that he

Figure 38. Peter Grippe. *Symbolic Figure #4*. 1946. Bronze, 17″ high. (Newark Museum, Newark, New Jersey. Photo: Adolph Studly.)

refused to limit himself to any one approach to the problem of virtual movement. The influence of Surrealism appeared also in his work around this time, simultaneously reappearing in Lassaw's *Arachnide* (see Figure 28). Grippe's terra-cotta *Growth After Destruction* of 1944 (Figure 37), while recalling the concurrent subject matter of Noguchi, maintains the textured surface of the *Cities* but introduces the organic forms which were to characterize his later *Symbolic Figure* series. The bronze *Symbolic Figure #1* (1944) suggests such influences as Lipchitz's *Rape of Europa* (1938) in its organic structure and pelleted surface; but whereas Lipchitz concentrates on organic movement, Grippe is again stressing the transparency or detachment of his figures within their architectural framework. *Symbolic Figure #4* of 1946 (Figure 38) marks the apex of this development. Lassaw would later call this "the best sculpture Grippe ever did." Here an animated organic figure is placed within a cage-like armature, constituting an adaptation of Giacometti's imagery of cages (see Figure 57) and the fusion of Surrealism and the Neo-plastic structure of Mondrian's paintings. Like Lassaw, and as Giacometti had done much earlier, Grippe used the cage construction to create space for the interior forms, rather than to act as a mere foil for them.

Around 1944, Grippe also began working with lost-wax casting to create "Space Figures," as he called the transparencies which, in contrast to the terra cottas, were devoid of details and symbols and rather were inspired by sketches from streets, parks and subways. Grippe devised special means for one-piece casting which combined aesthetic and technical needs with a minimum of allowance for process, 63

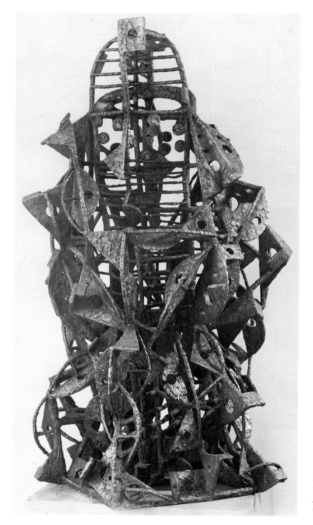

Figure 39. Peter Grippe.
Modern Benin. 1946. Bronze,
32″ high. (Photo: Oliver Baker.)

at a time when this method had been all but abandoned for welding. *Modern Benin*
of 1946 (Figure 39)—a monument to the Nigerian bronze casters who were
massacred by the British in 1897—is an early example of the large, complex
transparencies that were cast in one piece.

In the early thirties, the paintings of Theodore Roszak had gradually
subordinated romantic content to structural abstraction. This style was first
introduced, as Harvey Arnason has explained, through the Cubist geometry of Juan
Gris, as exhibited in Roszak's *Self-Portrait* of 1934; it was extended through Stuart
Davis and Max Weber as in *42nd Street* (1936), finally arriving at such Purist-
inspired works as *Pierced Circle* of 1941 (Figure 40).[25] Similarly, his constructions
were purged of their remaining associative images along with their descriptive titles
during the thirties. Angular forms arranged in symmetrical compositions with a
maximum emphasis on neat contours and smooth surfaces characterized Roszak's
style during the first half of the forties, as in *Bipolar Form* (1940), *Spatial
Construction* (1943), or *Vertical Construction* (1943).

Roszak suddenly embraced organic Surrealism in the mid-forties, however. In
1945 he abandoned the machine constructions in favor of a new, free-form sculpture

which he later described as "an almost complete reversal of ideas and feelings." [26] Overtaken by his concern for humanity in the aftermath of the Second World War, Roszak sought a more personal statement than was possible within the Constructivist aesthetic. The interaction of art and life, which was a basic premise of Constructivism, meant for Roszak that technology had to govern art, a situation which he felt forced the artist to ignore vital areas of human structure. Pure form alone, he realized, could not suffice for content. Human experience, for him the substance of art, had to be expressed in images.[27]

Roszak's exposure to experiments with welding and brazing in New York at this time, as well as his work in an aircraft factory during the war, had introduced him to new possibilities for surface effects. Soon the non-associative, geometric shapes of his most orthodox constructions gave way to suggestive metal forms, which were animated with tactile surface variations and contrasting spatial orientations. The organic forms which played a secondary role in his early machine constructions were now developed as "reminders of primordial strife and struggle." [28]

Roszak had engaged in an extensive program of self-education from 1931 when he returned from Europe to the early forties. This led him from the philosophy of Plato to that of Nietzsche, Kierkegaard, Goethe, Croce, and Focillon. The wealth of American literature, and especially the writings of Herman Melville, acted as a catalyst for the ideas and imagery which found visual expression in his post-war sculpture. Paralleling the work of David Smith, Roszak channeled his energies into dramatic themes of despair and violence, explicit in titles like *Anguish* (1946), *Surge* (1946), *Scavenger* (1946–47). The menacing force of the welding process is implicit

Figure 40. Theodore Roszak. *Pierced Circle.* 1941. Plastic, wood, wire, 24″ high. (Collection, Sara J. Roszak. Photo: Flair-Dordick.)

65

Figure 49. Herbert Ferber. *Labors of Hercules*. 1948. Lead, 36″ high. (New York University, New York.)

tragic comment on an individual caught in the brambles of his own making where, as the title of another 1949 work indicates in an allusion to Abstract Expressionism, *The Action Is the Pattern* (1949). The *Portrait of Jackson Pollock II* is closely related to Giacometti's 1929 *Reclining Woman*, exhibited in a retrospective at the Pierre Matisse Gallery in 1948, but the general form was suggested by the George Washington Bridge, as seen from the roof of Ferber's apartment on Riverside Drive. Like the Giacometti, the portrait consists of two horizontal layers connected by vertical bars, effectively separating the sculpture from its base. Ferber had already experimented with this device in the *Labors of Hercules* of 1948 (Figure 49), where a club-like form is barely supported by semi-circular shapes. Roszak's *Spectre of Kitty Hawk* (see Figure 41) had dealt with a similar problem in balancing a cumbersome network of arm-like projections on a few points. Roszak's piece, in turn, relates to Ferber's *Manifestation II* (1949), where a monumental spider-like form rests on legs that taper to barely visible points.

In the mid-forties Ferber was associated with the Surrealists and Peggy Guggenheim's Art of This Century Gallery, but by the end of the decade his affinities had clearly shifted to a more formal approach—that of his expressively vertical *Flame* of 1949 (Figure 50), *He Is Not a Man* of 1950 (Figure 51), and *Horned Sculpture* (1949). Each of these works comes to its base on a single point and can be swiveled, creating a sculptural pattern through the movement of either the observer or the sculpture itself. The internal agitation of *The Action Is the Pattern* is greatly diminished in these works, which attain a classical contrapposto in their stance.

72

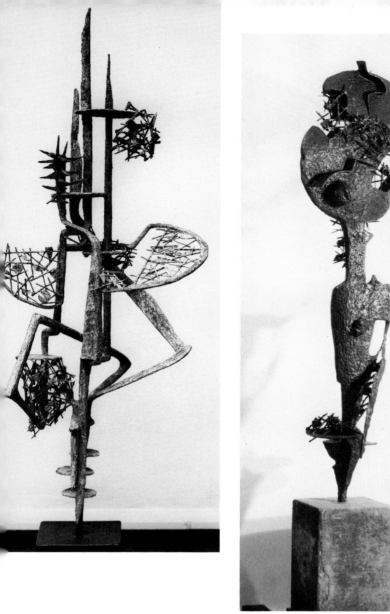

Figure 50 *(left)*. Herbert Ferber. *Flame*. 1949. Brass, lead, soft solder, 65½″ high. (Whitney Museum of American Art, New York. Photo: Oliver Baker.)

Figure 51 *(right)*. Herbert Ferber. *He Is Not a Man*. 1950. Bronze, 72″ high. (The Museum of Modern Art, New York.)

Here again Gonzalez, whose *Head* of 1935 (Figure 52) Ferber saw at the Museum of Modern Art, stands out as the catalyst for the reorientation of much of American sculpture from the Surrealism of the forties to a more formal Constructivism around 1950. In Ferber's case, the space-engaging scale and movement inherent in his earlier works developed into environmental sculpture in the fifties.

Seymour Lipton's early history parallels in many ways that of Ferber. Born in 1903 in New York City, he too received a degree in dentistry from Columbia in 1927. Although he had no formal training as a sculptor, he had a period of "aesthetic studies" devoted to El Greco, Ruskin, Bosch, Barlach, Gothic bestiaries, and primitive art. His earliest small sculptures were modelled in plaster and plasticene, but his strongest inclination was an association with the carve-direct movement of the thirties. *Lynched* (1933), his first wood carving, was, like Noguchi's *Death* of the same year, a literal representation of a murdered Negro in which special emphasis is on a textured uniformity of the minutely-faceted surface. Other

73

Figure 52. Julio Gonzalez. *Head.*
1935. Wrought iron, 17¾" high.
(The Museum of Modern Art,
New York.)

pieces of the thirties maintained overt social references while stylistically evoking
the expressionism of Barlach and Zorach, as seen in the hunched pose of *Soldier and
Mandolin* of 1940 (alluding to the Spanish Civil War) or that of Wilhelm
Lehmbruck in the elongated forms of *Cold Man* (1938). Cubism, and the sculpture
of Lipchitz in particular, introduced him to open-form abstraction and to the
combination of organic and inorganic shapes. At the same time, however, the
influence of Henry Moore, whose work he first saw in 1938, was already contributing
to a geometrical simplification of plane and line, drawing Lipton even further away
from representation. By the early forties this influence can be seen in such works as
Lipton's *Folk Song* (1941) and *Clown* (1942) with their interpenetration and
openness of parts and curvilinear forms characteristic of Moore's *Reclining Woman*
(1932) or *Reclining Figure* (1939).

In *Sailor* (1937) Lipton had contrasted the roundness of the torso with the
planar representations of the face and hands, where the forms of rope and man were
actually fused into one. During the early forties he continued to develop the idea of
contrasts of plane and volume to achieve what he called "Planal Dynamism,"
exemplified in *Blues Player* (1942)—a tribute to Louis Armstrong in which the
Moore-like pose is coupled with the planar quality of Lipchitz's work of the thirties,
like the series of *Woman Leaning on Elbows* of 1932–34.

This concern with planar surfaces became even more pronounced when Lipton
found casting—which he experimented with intermittently throughout the forties—
not only too expensive but too impersonal. The sheet-metal technique with which
he began experimenting in 1942, on the other hand, not only enhanced the planar
qualities, but the material was cheap and the process direct. For several years until
1951 he worked with lead sheeting and then turned to Monel metal sheeting which
he surface-textured with brazing alloys such as brass, nickel-silver and bronze.[32]

Lipton's retreat from representation, which paralleled that of Ferber, continued through this period, reaching a peak of abstraction soon after the war when he, too, began to deal with highly-charged themes that were conveyed through a new vocabulary of non-objective forms.

The influence of Surrealism, and of Miró in particular, becomes apparent in his *Dissonance* of 1946 (Figure 53), where a fairly literal presentation of the face and limbs of a human figure are fused with a Surrealist torso which recalls the skeleton and internal organs of Miró's *Seated Woman* of 1932 (Figure 54). Surrealism

Figure 53 *(top)*. Seymour Lipton. *Dissonance*. 1946. Sheet lead, 24″ long.

Figure 54 *(bottom)*. Joan Miró. *Seated Woman*. 1932. Oil on canvas, 18″ x 15″. (Private Collection.)

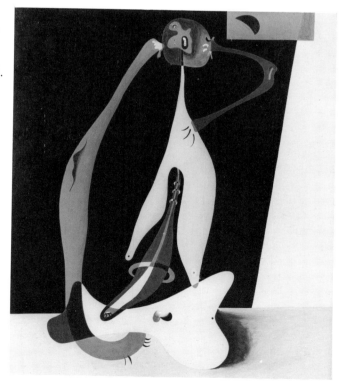

introduced Lipton to the process of free association and surrounded him with themes and images of destruction as did the impressions of South American ritual objects he saw in 1945 at the Museum of Natural History in New York. The sharp and penetrating shapes evident in the clawing hand of *Dissonance* came to dominate Lipton's sculpture in the post-war period beginning with the *Moloch* series (*Moloch #1, #2, #3*) executed in 1945–46 (Figure 55). These three sculptures, with their poised, threatening imagery, express "the sheer horror and malevolence" and the "harsh tensions [which are] a basic reality in man." [33] The title, *Moloch*, refers to the ancient Hebrew king-god to whom children were sacrificed by fire. The series emphasizes as well Lipton's concern with social commentary, manifested by freely associated metaphor, described by Albert Elsen as "correspondences . . . in mood, feeling, or gesture that uniquely join together aspects of seemingly unrelated objects." [34] For the *Moloch* pieces, Lipton turned to Paleozoic reminiscences of thorns, bones, tusks, teeth and jaws which make up the vocabulary of Aztec and Mayan death ritual sculpture. "The dinosaur and its bones have come alive to me," he wrote in 1947. "The bud, the core, the spring, the darkness of earth, the deep animal fountainhead of man's forces are what interest me most as the main genesis of artistic substance. The old bones are moving again in a new body, a new organism." [35]

The theme of spiritual conflict dominates other of Lipton's works like *Invocation* (1948) and *Travail* (1949), while the same thrusting forms of the *Moloch* series are carried over to the *Moby Dick* series (1946), and also to *Wild Earth Mother* (1947), *Firebird II* (1949), and *Horned Dancer* (1947). To expose what he called the "underneath in man," [36] Lipton developed further the relationship of interior and exterior parts and gave sculptural form to the cyclical life process of organisms in which inside feelings and outside appearances would become fused in a

Figure 55. Seymour Lipton. *Moloch #3*. 1946. Sheet lead, 24″ high. (Photo: Walter J. Russell.)

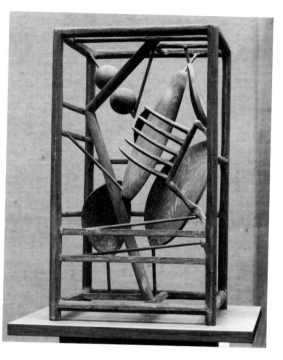

Figure 56 (right). Seymour Lipton. *Imprisoned Figure*. 1948. Wood, lead, 80″ high. (The Museum of Modern Art, New York. Photo: Geoffrey Clements.)

Figure 57 (left). Alberto Giacometti. *Cage*. 1930–31. Plaster, 17⅜″ high. (Galerie Maeght, Paris.)

renewal procedure of growth, death and rebirth. As had Giacometti, who thought of the "interior" as frightening, mysterious and irrational, in contrast to the "rational exterior"—carried out literally in his *Palace at 4 A.M.*—Lipton set himself to the task of giving visual form to the "dark inside, the evil of things, the hidden area of struggle." [37] This statement echoes the carve-direct tenet that apparently continued to influence Lipton—for that matter also Lassaw and Grippe, and later Ferber—as evidenced by their caged sculptures. In these constructions the idea of the image impressed in the stone called out for release to the sculptor. More generally its influence is related to the idea of sculpture as an expanding form constrained by a tight skin. "Sculpture," Lipton later explained, "is used by me to express the life of man as a struggling interaction between himself and his environment." [38] *Imprisoned Figure* of 1948 (Figure 56), one of Lipton's first constructed pieces, depends on Giacometti's *Cage* of 1930–31 (Figure 57). It involves a sense of interior space, and was inspired by the post-war disclosures of genocide and the fate of prisoners of war; it uses the cage concept to convey the sense of the prisoner striving for freedom. [39]

Perhaps in his imagery—the most aggressive and violent of the Surrealist-inspired American sculptors in the post-war era—Lipton also approached a more positive statement toward the end of the forties with pieces like *Deliverance* (1948), *Metamorphosis* (1949) and *Renascence* (1950) as the emotional energy of the *Moloch* series, *Wild Earth Mother* and other pieces was channeled into the more formal concern of the development of form in space.

77

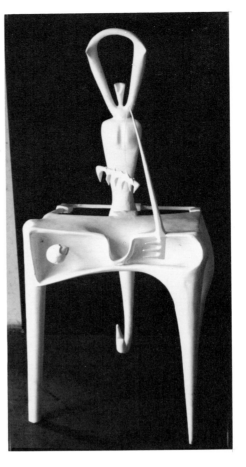

Figure 58 *(left)*. Seymour Lipton. *Cloak.* 1951. Bronze on steel, 96″ high. (Collection, Nelson Rockefeller. Photo: Oliver Baker.)

Figure 59 *(right)*. David Hare. *The Magician's Game.* 1944. Bronze, 44″ high. (The Museum of Modern Art, New York.)

With *Cloak* of 1951 (Figure 58), Lipton makes his entrance into the new sculptural sensibility of the fifties. Appearing almost simultaneously with Lassaw's first structural galaxies and Ferber's *Flame*, this piece marks a clear break with Lipton's style of the forties in the direction of a stable, monumental idiom out of which will develop his "personage" image: the anonymous figure that stands for the human presence.

In the last International Surrealist Exhibition held in Paris in 1947, the participating Americans were Calder, Noguchi, and Hare. David Hare stood out as the most authentic Surrealist sculptor America had produced, perhaps because, unlike Calder and Noguchi, he had turned to sculpture only in the forties, and unlike Lassaw, Ferber, Grippe, and Lipton, he had arrived at his sensibility not through the American carve-direct or social commentary phases, but from intimate association with the exiled Surrealists in New York.[40]

78

David Hare was born in New York City in 1917, where he earned a degree in analytical chemistry in 1936; he then embarked on various careers as a commercial artist, portraitist, and color photographer.[41] A one-man show of his photographs in 1939 included a number of well-known political and social personalities; later his subject matter shifted to the Indians of New Mexico and Arizona. About 1941, however, Hare began experimenting with "heatages," an abstract photographic technique used by the French Surrealist photographer Raoul Ubac in which the image was transformed by heating, melting and distorting the gelatine of a photographic negative after it was developed. At this point Hare came into contact with Breton, Miró and other leading Surrealists, becoming the editor of the review *VVV* in 1942. Later that same year, his photographs were included, along with the works of the most prominent international artists identified with the movement, in "The First Papers of Surrealism" exhibition.

By 1944, Hare had turned from photography to sculpture, and his success was almost instantaneous: he had a one-man show at Peggy Guggenheim's Art of This Century Gallery that year. His earliest sculpture, such as *Fat Young Girl*, echoed Calder's mobiles, with plaster and wire figures suspended from the ceiling. Hare's Surrealist bent was evident from the start, however, in the brittle hybrid forms and smooth distorted anatomies of *Lady of Waiting* (1944), and *The Magician's Game* of 1944 (Figure 59). He was not particularly involved in the theoretical aspects of Surrealism, but like Picasso, whom he knew quite well, he focused on the transformation of appearances. He wrote in 1946 in the Museum of Modern Art's *Fourteen Americans* catalog, "In order to avoid copying nature and at the same time keep the strongest connection with reality . . . it is necessary to break up reality and recombine it, creating different relations which will take the place of relations destroyed. These should be relations of memory and association." [42] By 1947 his human-animal figures like *Suicite* of 1946 (Figure 60), *Floater* (1947), and

Figure 60. David Hare. *Suicite*. 1946. Bronze, 32″ long. (Chicago National Bank, Chicago.)

Goat Looking Man (1948) were drawing heavily on erotic, violent imagery reminiscent of Matta's painting. By using intricate compositions, humorous visual puns, and literary networks of overlapping images he was creating those relations he had himself prescribed: "It all goes back to Freud. . . . *Suicite* is a masculine gesture, that of suicide, performed by a woman. The gesture is the driving into the ground . . . a sexual fantasy with the front element suggesting a horn, nose, sword, trumpet, clitoris." [43]

In 1946 the American critic Clement Greenberg had already characterized Hare's Surrealism as going beyond the doctrines of the movement; ten years later critic Robert Goldwater's retrospective assessment concurred:[44]

> Hare is not doctrinaire. He works with no set vocabulary of "subconscious" images, and with no dream symbols. Therefore his work (with the possible exception of some of his earliest pieces of 1944–45 whose smooth and polished surfaces have a surgical glow) is altogether without that breathless, vacuum-like, scrubbed cleanliness which is so much a part of some of the subtlest (Tanguy) and also some of the most banal (Dali) of the Surrealist creations. Nor does his *oeuvre* as a whole evolve within a closed and self-sufficient system. Hare is a stranger to both the poignant and the blatant extremes of Surrealist narcissism. . . . His whole purpose is to allow himself to wander freely through what he has called "the spaces of the mind," to work in such a way that the program of what he is doing is never a closed program, but always open to the apparent impulse.

Near the end of the forties, Hare began working with cast metals. In the early fifties he became a late convert to the Constructivism of Gonzalez.

Among the last of the major figures to emerge during the forties was Richard Lippold (b. 1915), whose work stands in marked contrast to that of David Hare—each represents an opposite pole of the Constructivist-Surrealist synthesis. Like De Rivera, Lippold spent his formative years as an artist in the New Bauhaus environment of Chicago. He studied industrial design at the Chicago Art Institute and the University of Chicago from 1933 to 1937 and then worked for four years as a professional designer. In 1940 he began to teach industrial design; the following year, while teaching at the University of Michigan, he made his first wire constructions, later described by Lawrence Campbell as "semi-automatic scribblings in cubic space." [45]

His earliest works, like *Hysteria of Pomposity* (1942) use thin wire to create intricate patterns of loops and curves and exist largely in two dimensions. Later constructions, including *The Bud Knows All* of 1943 (Figure 61), *Winter Thoughts* (1945), and *Tragic Baroque* (1946) incorporate varying thicknesses of wire and sometimes small glass beads to enhance their fragile beauty. More significantly, however, their patterns are developed in the third dimension so that the wire focuses attention not on itself but on the negative space it encloses, relating perhaps to the space modulator exercises Lippold carried out as a design student. These three-dimensional forms became more regular in subsequent works, like *Act for Two* (1946) and *New Moonlight* (1946), which are far more structured in their geometric shapes, in their symmetry, and in their orientation to a base. With *Primordial Figure* of 1947–48 (Figure 62) and *Departure* (1947), the earlier sense of free-hand drawing in space is completely transformed according to Bauhaus principles of design. Loops and curves are brought into closed contours which make up regular circles and squares, and additive relations among separate parts replace the organic composi-

Figure 61 *(left)*. Richard Lippold. *The Bud Knows All.* 1943. Steel, iron, brass wire, 12″ high including base. (Collection, Mrs. W. R. Valentiner.)

Figure 62 *(right)*. Richard Lippold. *Primordial Figure.* 1947–48. Brass, copper wire, 96″ high. (Whitney Museum of American Art, New York.)

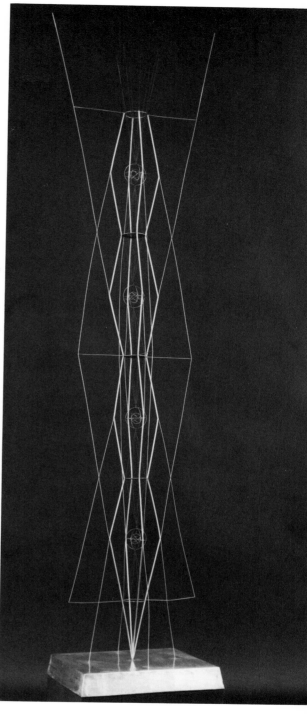

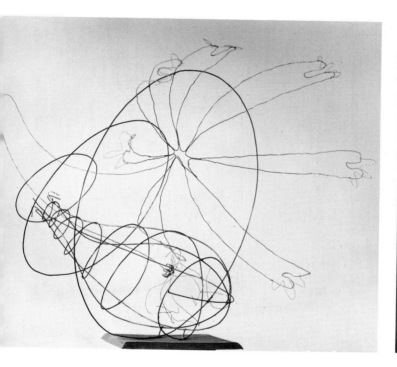

tions of the earlier constructions. *Devotion* (1948) introduces the concept of modular units, suggested to some extent in Lippold's constructions of 1946–47, where cones and spheres within a hexagonal framework are mounted in a vertical composition of four units.

In 1947 Lippold began a series of *Variations on a Sphere*; he continued these well into the fifties. The first five spheres were created for the composer John Cage, who had taught experimental music at the New Bauhaus in Chicago and was familiar with the theories of Moholy-Nagy. After his 1945 arrival in New York,

Figure 63. Richard Lippold. *Variation #7: Full Moon.* 1949. Brass rods, nickel-chromium and stainless steel wire, 120″ high. (Museum of Modern Art, New York.)

Figure 64. Sidney Gordin. #3. 1950.
Steel, silver brazed, 35″ high.

however, Cage had become interested in Eastern philosophy, which was *au courant* among artists at that time. The influence of Zen principles of variation and continuation fitted into the scheme of Bauhaus exercise in Lippold's *Variations on a Sphere.* The series is an experiment in composition, using as its basic unit the double cone found in *Primordial Figure.* Lippold spent an entire year working on *Variation #7: Full Moon* of 1949 (Figure 63)—a basic construction of concentric cubes that expands from a central core at eye level to architectural scale extending from ceiling to floor. The precise, symmetrical handling of the brass framework and the wire webbing again points to Lippold's Bauhaus orientation. Yet at the same time, and equally characteristic of all his work, the precision of technique and technology are used as means to a highly romantic vision, and in his own words, "a prophetic center of activity, uniting diversity, sanctioning solitude (even its own), and pulsating as the very heart of a newly co-ordinated totality." [46]

Sidney Gordin was the most tenacious of the young sculptors who adhered to Constructivist tenets in the forties. Born in Russia in 1918, Gordin studied at Cooper Union with the abstractionist painters Morris Kantor, William Harrison, and Leo Katz. His earliest works show similarities with the New Bauhaus "Light Modulators" of the type Moholy-Nagy had constructed in 1938, and with the French Neo-plasticist Jean Gorin. Like Lippold's work, Gordin's constructions often combined flat, planar elements with wire continuities. It was, in general, more severely rectangular, composed of contrasts, either of the curved with the flat, or the horizontal with the vertical as in #3 of 1950 (Figure 64). More architectural than   83 decorative in his imagery, he was aligned with the Neo-plasticism of Mondrian, Vantongerloo, and the influential American painter-sculptor Burgoyne Diller who was teaching at Brooklyn College in the company of the Neo-plastic, Abstract Expressionist painters, Ad Reinhardt and Mark Rothko.

Gordin exhibited steel and bronze constructions, some of which were painted black and red, at the Peter Cooper Gallery in 1951. By the mid-fifties he abandoned strict Neo-plasticism, and came largely under the influence of gestural painting and related sculpture in this country. (Diller and Biederman, on the other hand, continued their strict structuralist styles into the sixties.) Gordin's works at this time often had brazed surfaces and joints with exposed, or unchased welds that challenged the technical tenets of the dogmatic structuralists, who insisted on the strictest technique. This aligned him—however slight in degree—with Lassaw and Lipton, who were welding and brazing in a manner that made the technical process a visible quality of the form.

Diller's reliefs and free-standing polychromed sculptures were conceived as three-dimensional "color structures," painted in the manner of Mondrian, in reds, blues, and yellows, set off by whites and blacks (Figure 65). Along with the arch-structuralist Charles Biederman, Diller was the only true Neo-plasticist among American artists. He was, in fact, the one who encouraged Holtzman to look at Mondrian's paintings at the Museum of Living Art in 1934, and thus was indirectly responsible for Mondrian coming to New York.

Diller's influence as a teacher was strong in the late thirties and throughout the forties. Although he had not formulated a new aesthetic, his faithful adherence to Neo-plasticism kept Mondrian and Vantongerloo consistently in view as an alternative to Surrealism. Unlike the evangelistic Biederman, who retired to the Mid-West, where he preached the promises of salvation through Neo-plasticism while castigating all art being produced in New York, Diller was a viable catalyst in the on-going art of this country. As early as 1932 he had exhibited in an "Abstract Art in America" show at the Art Students League (along with Holtzman). With a Cubist background to his early work, he was also an ardent admirer of Cézanne and Georges Seurat; in 1934 he advanced to the general style of the De Stijl artists, to which he would faithfully adhere until his death in 1965. In the sixties both he and Biederman will be re-evaluated by younger sculptors and painters who will see them as having sustained the viability of pure abstraction.

It was Diller's concern in the forties to point out the pervasive weakness of painting that still adhered to illusionistic references, even when the illusions were composed of abstracted shapes, and at the same time the potential of sculpture to be real, that is non-illusionary. As had Mondrian, Diller came to abstraction with the eye of a landscape artist who composes, in the open space of nature, complementary objects, planes, and lines, which play with and against each other in certain orders and rhythms, while color and contrasting values establish sensation of volume. Moreover, his cool, detached manner was an effective antidote, as was Mondrian's direct reference, for excesses of both Expressionism and Surrealism.

Allied with Diller in this respect was De Rivera; they shared a show at Harvard University in 1945. De Rivera had effectively abandoned his semi-realist style after 1937 and emerged around 1940 with sculpture conceived in controlled, free-form metal sheet beaten into shapes simultaneously concave and convex. In *Yellow Black* of 1946–47 (Figure 66), De Rivera held to the severe restrictions of Neo-plasticism while at the same time sharing the general Surrealist tenor of the time: the continuous contour that encloses the surfaces evidences a debt to the anatomical free-form sculpture of Arp, while the holes that punctuate his form have precedent

84

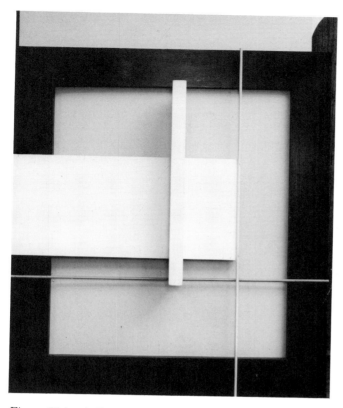

Figure 65 *(top)*. Burgoyne Diller. *Construction #16.* 1938.
Painted wood, 32″ high.

Figure 66 *(bottom)*. José de Rivera. *Yellow Black.* 1946–47. Painted aluminum, 22″ high.

in the work of Miró. And the inside-outside contrasts that De Rivera stressed were in line with the "interior-exterior," or the penetrating idioms of the other Americans, notably Smith, Grippe, Lassaw, and Lipton.

By the end of the forties Abstract Expressionist painting and the parallel movement in sculpture were already in a second phase: the pioneer painters—Jackson Pollock, Robert Motherwell, Hans Hofmann, Adolph Gottlieb, William Baziotes, Mark Rothko, and Clyfford Still—had been joined by Willem de Kooning, Franz Kline, Philip Guston, Bradley Walker, Jack Tworkov, and Esteban Vincente. There was at last a self-sufficient American idiom in art; as Clement Greenberg wrote: "the first phenomenon in American art to draw a standing protest at home and the first to be deplored seriously, and frequently, abroad." [47]

The format for painting expanded and sculpture became larger and more vertical as radical abstract tendencies and more formal concerns overtook the private and chimerical obsessions that characterized much Surrealist-oriented painting and sculpture of the preceding years. Important in the mass transition away from direct European linkages were Ferber with *Flame* (see Figure 50), and *He Is*

Figure 67. David Smith. *The Hero.* 1952. Painted steel, 73¹¹⁄₁₆″ high. (The Brooklyn Museum, New York.)

86

Not a Man (see Figure 51), Lipton with *Cloak* (see Figure 58), and David Smith with *The Hero* (Figure 67).

The concept of the mysterious totem or personage distinguished by its undefined sense of presence emerged in the late forties in American sculpture. The sense of presence, or of personal power implicit in the way a person or the image of a person appears, is historically bound to the Archaic Greek Kouros. In the mid-forties Noguchi's *Kouros* (see Figure 13) and Lippold's *Primordial Figure* (see Figure 62) responded to the personage idea that Ferber, Lipton, and Smith would develop at the turn of the decade. Infused with the Surrealist concept of the undifferentiated and the undefinable—the power of the unconscious and the dream—the totemic personage idea proliferated among American sculptors, incorporating the sense of loneliness and alienation that had been conditioned by post-Second World War psychology. This notion marked an apparent return to the idea of heroic imagery—or sculpture as statue—but the concept of heroism was unlike anything that sculpture had addressed itself to before. The whole idea of what heroism now meant, considering the nature of modern warfare, had shifted the emphasis to the unknown person. Heroes were no longer specific, nor for that matter were the vanquished. The "Unknown Political Prisoner" international sculpture competition sponsored in London in 1953 was a collective metaphor of the personage concept, just as the frequent images of anguished anatomies within geometric frames or cages were the sculptural equivalent of the Second World War spectre of concentration camps and prisoner-of-war compounds. With the personage concept of the figure, the literalness of most sculptural imagery of the forties became subordinated to a formal generalization of a pervasive mood, generated by a sense of presence rather than emotional display.

NOTES

1. See "Surrealism and its meaning in relation to art and life," *Art Digest* 15, no. 9 (February 1, 1941): 29.

2. André Breton, *What Is Surrealism?* David Gascoyne, trans. (London: Faber & Faber, 1936), p. 59.

3. Quoted in Elaine de Kooning, "David Smith Makes a Sculpture," *Art News* 50, no. 5 (September, 1951): 40.

4. From a letter to the author (February 12, 1958).

5. Naum Gabo, "Art and Science," *Gabo* (Cambridge, Mass.: Somerset, 1937), p. 180.

6. George Rickey, *Constructivism: Origins and Evolution* (New York: Braziller, 1967), p. 46.

7. Georges Hugnet, "Dada and Surrealism," *The Bulletin of the Museum of Modern Art* 4, nos. 2–3 (November–December 1936): 30.

8. Jean-Paul Sartre, Essay in catalog of the Calder exhibition at Galerie Louis Carré (October 25–November 16, 1946).

9. Fernand Léger in *Derrière le Miroir*, no. 31 (July 1950).

10. See Arp's *Human Concretion* (1935) in the Museum of Modern Art. Included in *Art in Our Time* (New York: Museum of Modern Art, 1939), cat. no. 319; Noguchi's *Capital* is cat. no. 322.

11. This work was exhibited in the last International Exhibition of Surrealism in Paris in 1947 and illustrated in the catalog, "Le Surréalisme en 1947," p. 136.

12. Quoted in Katharine Kuh, *The Artist's Voice* (New York: Harper & Row, 1962), p. 175.

13. This work bears a strong resemblance to Lassaw's experiments from 1940–45 with illuminated organic forms within a geometric steel frame. See for example *Arachnide* (Figure 28, Chapter 2) and *Gravity Tension* (Figure 29).

14. Isamu Noguchi in *Fourteen Americans*, ed. Dorothy Miller (New York: The Museum of Modern Art, 1946), p. 39.

15. Isamu Noguchi, *A Sculptor's World* (London: Thames and Hudson, 1967), p. 125.

16. Giacometti, too, designed furniture and lamps; his "tabletop" sculptures had developed out of his plaques or reliefs of 1927–28, like *Woman* and *Head*, which Noguchi seems to have looked at closely.

17. David Smith, *David Smith* (New York: Holt, Rinehart & Winston, 1968), p. 174, note 32. Dorothy Dehner, Smith's wife, says Smith saw actual satirical medals made to be given to the Germans for their war feats.

18. Kuh, *Artist's Voice*, p. 222.

19. For an analysis of the cannon image in Smith's work, see Rosalind E. Krauss, *Terminal Iron Works* (Cambridge, Mass.: M.I.T., 1971), Chapter Two. For an early statement and another aspect of this imagery see Stanley Meltzoff, "David Smith and Social Surrealism," *Magazine of Art* 39, no. 3 (March 1946): 98–101.

20. Smith, *David Smith*, p. 106.

21. Miró's etching is illustrated in Sam Hunter, *Joan Miró–His Graphic Work* (New York: Abrams, 1958), p. 23.

22. Robert Motherwell and Ad Reinhardt, eds., *Modern Artists in America* (New York: Wittenborn Schultz, Inc., 1951), p. 14.

23. Peter Grippe, "Notes on my Work." Original manuscript in my files.

24. Peter Grippe, "Enter Mephistopheles with Images," *Art News* 59, no. 6 (October 1960): 45–47, 56–57.

25. H. H. Arnason in his introduction to the catalog of the Theodore Roszak exhibition at the Walker Art Center, Minneapolis (December 16, 1956–January 20, 1957), p. 18.

26. Theodore Roszak, *In Pursuit of an Image* (Chicago: Time to Time Publications, Art Institute of Chicago, 1955).

27. *Ibid.*

28. *Ibid.*

29. The references to representational imagery come from a taped interview with the artist by James Elliott on February 13, 1956. The theme *Thorn Blossom* is from Yeats's "Prayer for my Daughter."

30. From my taped interview with Ferber conducted in conjunction with the retrospective exhibition I organized at the Walker Art Center (April 15–May 27, 1962).

31. *Ibid.*

32. For a careful analysis of Lipton's development during these years see Albert Elsen, *Seymour Lipton* (New York: Abrams, 1970).

33. Seymour Lipton, "Some Notes on my Work," *Magazine of Art* 40, no. 7 (November 1947): 264.

34. Albert Elsen, "Seymour Lipton: Odyssey of the Unquiet Metaphor," *Art International* 5, no. 1 (February 1, 1961): 39.

35. Lipton, "Notes," p. 264.

36. *Ibid.*

37. Quoted in Andrew Carnduff Ritchie, "Seymour Lipton," *Art in America* 44, no. 4 (Winter 1956–57): 14.

38. Albert Elsen, "Lipton's Sculpture as Portrait of the Artist," *College Art Journal* 24, no. 2 (Winter 1964–65): 113.

39. In a letter from Lipton to the author (April 24, 1969).

40. See Irving Sandler, *The Triumph of American Painting* (New York: Praeger, 1970), p. 33. Very few Americans actually became active participants in the Surrealist group in New York—most notable among those who did were Robert Motherwell, William Baziotes, Arshile Gorky, Peter Busa, Gerome Kamrowski, and David Hare.

41. Hare also worked for two years as a surgical photographer in hospitals.

42. David Hare, in *Fourteen Americans*, p. 24.

43. Albert Elsen, *The Partial Figure in Modern Art* (Baltimore: Baltimore Museum of Art, 1969), p. 67.

44. Robert Goldwater, "David Hare," *Art in America* 44, no. 4 (Winter 1956–57): 18–20.

45. Lawrence Campbell, "Lippold Makes a Construction," *Art News* 55, no. 6 (October 1956): 64.

46. Richard Lippold, "On Hanging, Seeing and Maintaining *Variation #7: Full Moon.*" Typed manuscript in my files.

47. Clement Greenberg, " 'American-Type' Painting," *Partisan Review* 22, no. 2 (Spring 1955): 180.

THE FIFTIES IN NEW YORK   III

New Directions

Recognition of the legitimacy of an American-style abstraction was publicly demanded by a large group of painters and sculptors who picketed the Metropolitan Museum of Art in 1951.[1] The solidarity demonstrated on this occasion had been established by a series of events in 1949 and 1950 when groups of artists began to organize formally through meetings, open lectures, and discussions aimed at consolidating their efforts on a common professional ground. Eighth Street was the geographical focus of these avant-garde activities. The Cedar Street Tavern, in the neighborhood of De Kooning's and Kline's studios, was the social center.

In the late thirties the Eighth Street area was the center of WPA art projects; it was also the location of the Hofmann School and the Annual American Abstract Artists shows. The Subjects of the Artist School at 35 East Eighth Street, organized by Baziotes, Rothko, Motherwell and Hare in 1948 (all of the founders, including Barnett Newman, who soon joined the faculty, had uptown galleries) was the first formalized activity of the Eighth Street artists. Friday evening lectures by respected figures—including Jean Arp, Richard Huelsenbeck, Willem de Kooning, and John Cage—brought a large number of artists together on a regular basis and cohered what had been, during the forties, a heterogeneous grouping.[2] Eighth Street was also the location of what was called "The Artists Club," founded in the fall of 1949 in a loft at Number 39. The charter members were largely from the "Waldorf group"—a loose association of about eight artists who had met nightly during the war at the Waldorf Cafeteria at Sixth Avenue and Eighth Street. The group included sculptors Phillip Pavia, Landes Lewitin, Aristo Kaldis, and occasionally James Rosati.[3] Pavia and Rosati, along with Grippe and Lassaw, became very active in The Club.

The Club had been founded on the premise of informality with no exhibitions and no manifestoes.[4] A closed group of artists united solely by their sense of alienation from the mainstream, bonded by common aspirations, the members were generally unwilling to do anything which might agitate internal rivalries: "The gods could be named (Picasso and Matisse mostly)," wrote critic Robert Goldwater, recalling the spirit of the Club, "and so could the demi-gods (Pollock and De Kooning, mostly). But no ordinary mortals—artists, that is, who might be present or have friends [at the meetings]."[5] Many of the artists in The Club shared a general concern that only certain of the vanguard were successfully exhibiting and achieving recognition in the uptown galleries—Peggy Guggenheim's Art of This Century, Betty Parsons, Samuel Kootz, and Charles Egan. In view of this, calls for Club-sponsored shows to establish its own audience occasionally arose. These were quickly shouted down, as many members feared that Club sponsorship would result

89

in internal conflicts over who was to be included, since the members did not constitute a collective style; rather, they shared a kind of common culture and a certain sensibility, of which aesthetics was but a part.[6] The conflict was resolved in 1951, however, by the dealer Leo Castelli who volunteered to organize a collective exhibition with the founding members as jurors. Among those exhibiting were several sculptors, notably Grippe and Rosati. The show was held in a vacant store on Ninth Street next door to the studios of Franz Kline, Conrad Marca-Relli and John Ferren, and was a great success. Precedent was set for what would become a viable downtown gallery scene as artist cooperatives soon appeared in the neighborhood.

More than anyone else the sculptor Phillip Pavia shaped the character of The Club. Pavia had been working as a sculptor since 1930, but during the fifties he devoted most of his time to The Club, administering its program of panel discussions and lectures of a diverse cultural range characterized by Jack Tworkov in 1952 as constituting "an unexcelled university for an artist." [7] Pavia understood, most importantly, that an authentically original statement in American abstract art could not be made until the restraints of European Surrealism were overcome, and he was dedicated to keeping The Club experience neutral and open-ended to foster eventual artistic autonomy: "I think that when we broke the stronghold of Surrealism in America, we discovered something very rich in the plastic arts . . . the French were not able to break with Surrealism and they were left in shackles."[8]

Since his days as an art student in Paris in the late thirties, Pavia had had a strong distaste for Surrealism, particularly its heavy literary and political flavor, its obsessiveness with dogma and manipulative exhibitionism. His attitudes were reinforced when he encountered the immigrant Surrealists in New York in the forties. He regarded the American sculpture most influenced by Surrealism as painterly and linear—epithets for a sculptor who was deeply committed to mass and volume and a carve-direct ethic.[9]

Still others rejected Surrealism as the fifties wore on. By 1956, Clement Greenberg, who had heralded the potential of modernist sculpture in this country in the late forties,[10] singling out Smith, Roszak, Hare, Ferber, Lipton, Lippold, Lassaw, Noguchi, Grippe, Diller and the Californian Adaline Kent, would extricate only Smith from the overwhelmingly Surrealist-oriented group which he concluded had "succumbed epidemically . . . to 'biomorphism' and the fanciful and decorative improvisation of plant, bone, muscle and other organic forms." [11] Greenberg felt that David Smith had continued to develop in the fifties "with the energy of a young artist," sometimes elaborating his work beyond the point to which the momentum of his inspiration had carried it—afraid that the result might not look enough like art and surrender to artiness, but always able to steady himself in the final process of realization. "Wherever else Smith may fail," Greenberg concluded, "he remains direct." [12] But Greenberg, by this time, had narrowly refined his own sensibility along the Cubist line; he favored the trued and faired Cubist look of Smith's sculpture, its classical stance as opposed to the baroque look of so much American sculpture of the forties—including much of Smith's.

By 1956, however, the proliferation of direct-metal sculpture in this country had so thoroughly confused the issue of what the early fifties work of Ferber, Lassaw, and Lipton, for example, was all about, that it was difficult for most critics to sustain a supporting interest in their production. By about 1952 the radical developments of Roszak, Grippe, Ferber, Lassaw, De Rivera, Hare, Lipton, and Lippold had begun to settle into a steady production with little innovation, as if the energy that they had expended in the assimilation of the old and the creation of the new had become dissipated in their solutions. Moreover, the spirit of the forties had wavered by the early fifties; the most critically innovative phase of American art, timed precisely with the crisis of the Second World War and the upheaval of the

90

European art world brought about by the massive geographical redistribution of artists, was essentially broken—the fervor had passed. Direct-metal sculpture had become a vogue, and in the hands of hundreds of practitioners who were not in on the innovative first stage, the technique became rapidly an "applied" one. To many it appeared to have forfeited its *raison d'être* to become just a way of making sculpture.

Beyond those who had established the new media and its parallel techniques before 1950, there were few exceptional sculptors. As a result, direct-metal sculpture lapsed into either a gross expressionism or a mannered decorativeness, following the route of carve-direct sculpture when the *way* of carving became more important than the *matter* of why. By the mid-fifties it became necessary to justify the sculptors' use of iron, steel and other metals worked directly into form with the welding torch or other industrial machinery. In the catalog of the "Irons in the Fire" exhibition assembled in Houston in late 1957, Sam Hunter, then Associate Curator of the Museum of Modern Art, would write: "traditional sculptural forms no longer can tell us enough about the texture and sensations of modern experience. The very use of metals, with their industrial associations, puts the artist in a direct relationship with his actual environment." [13] But such exhibitions, for all their high aspirations to demonstrate the broad stylistic and geographical spread of sculpture constructed by the welding process as well as claims that this process stood for the industrial age—uniting the very best work with the most banal—only proved, in the final analysis, that quality lies outside the parameters of materials and technique, as it has throughout the histories of both art and technology.

The academic center for the direct-metal mode of sculpture in New York was the Sculpture Center—a combination workshop and gallery located at 169 East 69th Street. As associate director since 1938, Sahl Swarz, who adopted direct-metal in 1944 after military service in Italy, where he learned welding, was most responsible for the proliferation of the welding technique at the Center. Originally the Center was the Clay Club, a school founded by Dorothea Denslow in Brooklyn in 1928. In 1932 the Clay Club moved to New York, first to West Fourth Street, a year later, to 4 West Eighth Street in the Village near the old Whitney Museum where Sahl Swarz, Lassaw, Harry Holtzman and Gabriel Kohn were among the first students.

The move to 29th Street came about in the late forties with an inaugural exhibition in January 1951; in February of that year, Swarz assembled a show of twenty-six pieces of direct-metal sculpture. Included were Smith, Roszak, De Rivera and Calvin Albert, along with the Sculpture Center contingency of Swarz, Juan Nickford, Barbara Lekberg and Ruth Vodicka. Toward the end of the year Swarz's second show of sculpture featured forty-six exhibitors, many working in direct metal. In 1953 the Center's twenty-fifth anniversary show included Calder, Smith, Lassaw, Roszak, Lipton, Lippold, De Rivera, Gordin and the Californian welder, Bernard Rosenthal. Louise Nevelson was represented with a piece in painted plaster; Noguchi with one in wood.

The success of the Center and the popularity of direct-metal sculpture fostered a coterie of young welders. Nickford, Lekberg, and Vodicka achieved notoriety in *Art News* reviews, but by the mid-fifties, as the formal achievements of the older direct-metal sculptors were focused, the significance of the second wave of practitioners rapidly diminished. The essential difference between competent craftsmanship in direct metal and the character of the results became clear. Welded sculpture, like most carve-direct sculpture before it, had become a tour de force in craftsmanship, while the themes it translated into spiky, threatening, frenetic forms were seen as contrived to justify the technique that produced them: preying insects, primordial fantasies, mad dogs, apparitions, screaming mothers, weird and menacing

Figure 1 *(left)*. Juan Nickford. *Running Dog*. 1954. Steel, 23″ long.

Figure 2 *(right)*. Barbara Lekberg. *Prophecy*. 1955. Welded steel, 34″ high.

creatures (Figures 1, 2). David Smith's and Roszak's spectres, Lipton's and Ferber's images of internal conflict manifested in forms that struggled with themselves, lent sculptural credence to a monstrous production of expressionistic sculpture that seemed to justify itself by a literal interpretation of the violence inherent in the process of forming sculpture with the intense heat of an oxyacetylene torch.

More essential to the transitional phase of the early fifties, and to the direction of American sculpture after 1955, was the work of Louise Bourgeois, Louise Nevelson and Richard Stankiewicz. In 1949 Bourgeois introduced her first three-dimensional works at the Peridot Gallery (Figures 3a, b). A number of tall, austere, life-size images standing without bases were grouped together to surround the viewer. These organic wooden forms, abstract and totemic in ambience and uniformly painted in red, black or white, were conceived at a time when the advanced sculptors with whom Bourgeois was in touch were working in direct metal.[14]

By the time she began sculpting, Bourgeois had already established herself as an abstract painter represented at the Museum of Modern Art. Born in Paris in 1911 and educated at the École des Beaux-Arts and the Académie Ranson, she later worked with Robert Wlérick and Fernand Léger. She emigrated to the United States in 1938. Caught up in the Surrealist current in New York, her first exhibitions in 1945 and 1946 consisted of emotionally-charged paintings which drew upon Surrealist pictorial and abstract symbolic imagery rendered with a French taste for *matière*. By 1947, however, she had evolved a more restrained imagery. Her move to sculpture passed first through a group of engravings entitled *He Disappeared into*

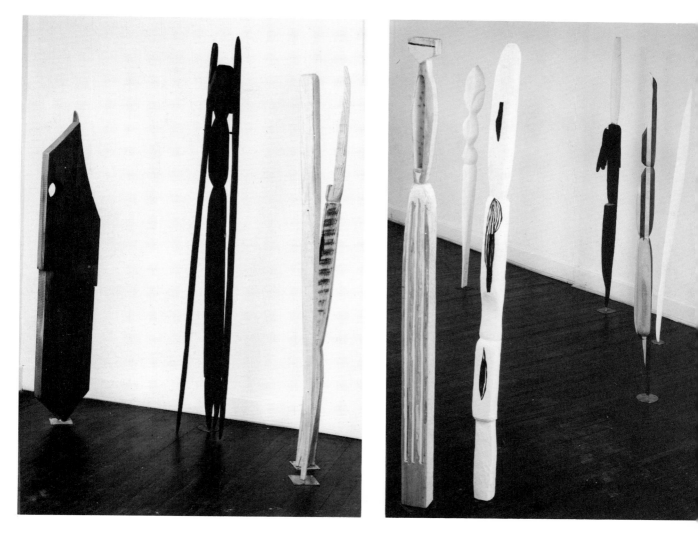

Figure 3a, b *(left, right)*. Louise Bourgeois. *Installation.* 1949.

Complete Silence which illustrated parables narrating the difficulties of interpersonal communication—a theme which would become the main content of her sculpture. In these engravings, people were represented as architectural forms, simplified vertical structures in isolation and defined by irregular striations and occasionally a small aperture; they functioned as metaphors for ostracism. In her sculpture these became transformed into elemental anthropomorphic, yet still architectonic-like forms, which Bourgeois later described as "blind houses without any openings." [15] The architectural structure "contained" the emotional content. To this extent, therefore, Bourgeois's concept paralleled that of other sculptors in the forties who had built imagery of organic forms contained within a geometric framework or enclosure.

In *Attentive Figures* of 1949 (Figure 4) and *Witnesses* (1950), recalling Ernst's *Lunar Asparagus* of 1935 (Figure 5), paired forms, articulated with window-like hollows, lean tensely toward one another; the subtle rhythms of the contours of internal variations suggest restrained interpersonal relationships. The emotion is generalized and controlled—compelling but without specific literary or mythological allusions of the kind that become associated with Surrealist art. The *Blind*   93

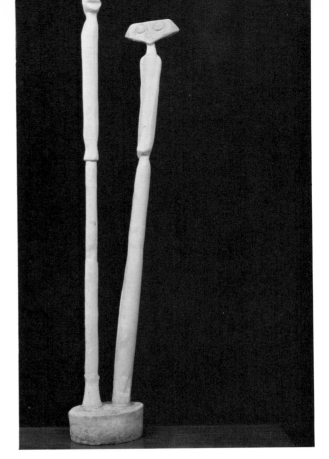

Figure 4 *(top left)*. Louise Bourgeois.
Attentive Figures. 1949. (Detail.)
Wood, 80″ high.

Figure 5 *(top right)*. Max Ernst.
Lunar Asparagus. 1935. Plaster,
65¼″ high. (The Museum of Modern
Art, New York.)

Figure 6 *(bottom)*. Louise Bourgeois.
The Blind Leading the Blind. 1949.
Painted wood, 69″ high. (Photo:
Peter Moore.)

94

Leading the Blind of 1949 (Figure 6), another piece from her first Peridot Gallery show, was one of the earliest examples of what would later be called environmental assemblage. Most of Bourgeois's works from this period, however, were conceived as individual or single pieces as opposed to multiple arrangements of parts to construct a unique work; the environmental relationships among the pieces were achieved solely by their arrangement in the gallery space. These early concepts would culminate in multiple arrangements of moveable parts forming a single sculpture as in *Quarantania I* (1948–53), *Garden at Night* of 1953 (Figure 7), and *One and Others* (1955).[16]

Coming as they did in 1949, Bourgeois's "personages" reflected the larger dissociation of specific identities and meanings as well as the sense of isolation that characterized the times. In a statement in *Design Quarterly* in 1954, Bourgeois traced her development to this point:[17]

> My work grows from the duel between the isolated individual and the shared awareness of the group. At first I made single figures without any freedom at all. . . . And then I began to develop an interest in the relationship between two figures. . . . Now the single work has its own complex parts, each of which is similar, yet different from the others. But there is still the feeling with which I began—the drama of one among many.

Closely related to the earlier work of Louise Bourgeois were the mid-fifties wood constructions of Louise Nevelson: *Black Majesty* of 1955 (Figure 8) and *Formation* (1956) are blocky, frontal compositions of matte black shapes, coupling Cubist geometry with a light, romantic nostalgia. They establish a personal idiom which Nevelson would soon develop into large-scale environmental sculpture.

Nevelson was born in Kiev, Russia in 1900 and came to the United States as a

Figure 7 *(left)*. Louise Bourgeois. *Garden at Night.* 1953. Painted wood, 45" high.

Figure 8 *(right)*. Louise Nevelson. *Black Majesty.* 1955. Wood, 20" high. (Whitney Museum of American Art, New York.)

Figure 9. Louise Nevelson. *Fertility.* 1940. Terra cotta, 22″ high. (Photo: Jeremiah W. Russell.)

Figure 10. Louise Nevelson. *Ancient City.* 1945. Wood, 36″ high. (Birmingham Museum of Art, Birmingham, Alabama. Photo: A. C. Kelly Studio.)

child. She attended the Art Students League in 1929–30, studied painting with Hans Hofmann in Munich in 1931, and returned home in 1932 to rejoin Hofmann at the League and to become an apprentice, along with painter Ben Shahn, to the Mexican artist Diego Rivera, who was then working on murals for the New Workers School in New York. The European trip left her strongly impressed with the order of Cézanne, the "purity" of Picasso, and to similar qualities in the African and Egyptian sculpture that she had seen in the Musée de l'Homme and the British Museum.[18] Her first sculptures of the thirties and early forties were primitive Cubist-inspired animal and anthropomorphic figures in polychrome wood, plaster or terra cotta, like her 1940 *Fertility* (Figure 9). In the mid-forties, Nevelson also produced works in bronze and marble, maintaining in these pieces an abstract Cubist idiom which would be further strengthened in the late forties by her exposure to the pre-Columbian art during trips to Mexico and Central America.

Going beyond the multiple environment situations that Bourgeois had set up with her sculpture groups, Nevelson set about to compose unified environments through the subordination of individual pieces to a single theme. Her first solo show of etchings in 1950, "Moonscapes," had been collectively titled, and she had precociously staged an environmental exhibition some years before, in 1943, at the

Norlyst Gallery. Within a specific thematic framework titled "The Circus, The Clown Is the Center of His World" she had arranged in a gallery space, decorated with a group of old circus posters, block-like animal figures assembled from scraps of wood, metal, cloth and glass; some pieces were set up on furniture casters, others were elaborated with multi-colored lights. Sharing a wry wit with Calder's early circus pieces, these works predated by almost a decade the satirical junk personages and groupings of Richard Stankiewicz.

Nevelson continued experimenting through the mid-forties with assembled constructions. *Time to Spare* (1944) and *Ancient City* of 1945 (Figure 10), were composed solely of wood—architectural and furniture parts, duck decoys and bowling pins. Although reminiscent of the "table landscapes" of Giacometti, the mood of these arrangements was softer and much less fantastic. But for all their originality they were part of a larger picture of the Surrealist assemblage of the forties. At this time the architect Frederick Kiesler was designing "decors" for group exhibitions; a rash of Surrealist-inspired commercial window displays in New York City had quickly followed. The idea of the Surrealist tableau had taken a strong hold on the ways in which gallery installations were designed.

The undercurrent of a soft romanticism in Nevelson's wood sculpture dominated the formal restraint of the terra-cotta pieces and evoked themes that would be carried further in such etchings as *The Sunken Castle* (1949) and *Night Figures* (1952) in which shadowy images, textured with patterned fabrics, are barely relieved from total darkness. Following her work in graphics at Atelier 17 in 1953, where she studied under Peter Grippe, Nevelson decisively entered her "black period," although she had occasionally painted individual wood pieces black since the early forties, no doubt suggested by Calder's stabiles. Alluding to kings, queens, chiefs, moon gardens and unlighted cathedrals, the black sculptures of 1955–58 were emotionally evocative but carefully controlled structures. Uniform black paint generalizes the parts and unifies the whole while at the same time suppressing the identity of the "ready-made" or "found-object."

In 1955 at the Grand Central Moderns Gallery in New York, Nevelson had her first solo show: wood constructions painted black, terra-cotta pieces, and etchings. The show was titled collectively "Ancient Games and Ancient Places." The director of the gallery recalls the exhibition as resembling a miniature Stonehenge: "wooden pieces of found objects that seemed isolated; linked only by the base." [19] In 1956 a new grouping, including some pieces from the 1955 show, *Royal Voyage* (Figure 11), was installed at Grand Central Moderns. This show established the "sense of place" toward which Nevelson had been working in constructing earlier exhibitions. The mood of Surreal fantasy that pervaded her dream-world environment was subordinated now to a controlled environmental scheme. Totemic king and queen figures, reminiscent of earlier Bourgeois pieces, were surrounded by ritual gift-pieces and subterranean seascapes of driftwood enclosed in plexiglass cases.

With *The Forest* (1957) Nevelson firmly established an "architectural" format of pedestal-sculpture combined with "cabinet sculpture"; the "cabinets" served as light-controlling and order-enforcing enclosures. An expansion of the cabinet pieces in turn led to the monumental wall construction, *Sky Cathedral*—stacks of crates and boxes filled with furniture parts, mouldings, and other wooden house ornaments, game sets, lumber, and wood scraps were brought together into a single façade. Shadow boxes on the walls, standing crates, and half-open closet-like enclosures completed the environment. The uniform blackness, fully exploited with controlled lighting, granted an obscurity of both form and physical identity to the otherwise disparate array of societal debris. "This is the Universe," she explained, "the stars, the moon—and you and I, everyone." [20]

Nevelson followed *Moon Garden Plus One* with *Sky Columns–Presences* at   97

Figure 11. Louise Nevelson. *Royal Voyage*. 1956. Exhibition at Grand Central Moderns Gallery.

Figure 12. Louise Nevelson. *Sky Columns–Presences*. 1959. (Photo: Oliver Baker.)

Figure 13. Louise Nevelson. *Dawn's Wedding Feast.* 1959. (Photo: Rudolph Burckhardt.)

the Martha Jackson Gallery in 1959 (Figure 12), introducing wood-encrusted columns that stood on the floor and hung from the ceiling. Her reputation now established with black Gothic ruins, she broke with it to venture into the drama of white-on-white in *Dawn's Wedding Feast* of 1959 (Figure 13). This ensemble was presented in the "Sixteen Americans" exhibit at the Museum of Modern Art and consisted of a sixteen-foot wedding chapel and wedding cake. Disappearing along with the mystery of black shadow was pictorial ambiguity, as the interior forms of the constructions became more articulate and the architectural framework containing them became not only more pronounced but also more geometrically regular. This would continue with the all-golden *Dawn* of 1962, in which interior arrangements were simplified, and the counterpoint of contained and containing shapes was replaced by a harmony of interior verticals and exterior grid. Nevelson later commented that "cubism has never left, even if you accept or deny it, . . . that [Cubism] gave us the structure." [21] With these works the implicit geometry of the early environmental pieces was rendered explicit, making apparent the preciously neglected fact that in her development Nevelson had anticipated the general trend that much of American sculpture was to follow in the sixties.

A reference in Nevelson's assemblages to Kurt Schwitters was noted by Jean Arp in a poem to her which appeared in *xxe Siècle* in March 1960: [22]

> . . .
>
> *Louise Nevelson a un grand-père sans probablement le connaître:*
> *Kurt Schwitters.*
> (Louise Nevelson has a grandfather, probably without knowing it:
> Kurt Schwitters.)

99

Figure 14. Kurt Schwitters.
Merzbau. 1920.

Arp had in mind Schwitters's *Merzbau* of 1920 (Figure 14), a monumental interior space made of scrap wood, conceived as if it were the interior of a huge collage. Like Nevelson's wall environments, the *Merzbau* involved a physically defined, but shallow and non-delimitable, third dimension surrounding the viewer.

Nevelson's "boxes" would depend much more, however, on the boxes of the American Joseph Cornell, who was already affiliated with Surrealism in the early thirties; his European soul-mates included Dali, Ernst, Man Ray, and also Moholy-Nagy; his earliest work in collage was strongly influenced by Ernst's *La Femme 100 Têtes.* Cornell's first show of "boxes" was at the Julian Levy Gallery in New York in 1932, and he was included in the Museum of Modern Art's "Fantastic Art, Dada, Surrealism" show of 1936. The rectangularity of the box containers Cornell used was not, however, a commitment to Constructivism; rather, it grew out of the "two-dimensionally" framed collage into a three-dimensional container in which collage objects were placed. Nonetheless, unlike related surrealist assemblages, Cornell's works were structured geometrically, and the collage elements compartmentalized somewhat along the lines of De Stijl constructions, or even of Mondrian's paintings. Cornell's 1946 *Multiple Cubes* (Figure 15) approaches total geometric abstraction in the manner of Mondrian and even borrows his colors: white with accents of yellow and blue. Beyond Cornell's influence on Nevelson's work the geometrical, box-like divisions of the canvas that several painters, including Adolph Gottlieb, were employing during the forties had somewhat of a tradition. Peter Grippe, with whom Nevelson had studied at Atelier 17, often employed this structuring device in his etching. More practical as an explanation, perhaps, is the common use of produce crates for book cases and shelving during the late forties and fifties. Nevelson used such crates in her studio for storing her sculptural elements and the assembly of the crates suggested to her the idea of a sculptural

100

Figure 15. Joseph Cornell.
Multiple Cubes. 1946–48.
Construction, 14″ x 10⅜″ x 2¼″.
(Collection, Mr. and Mrs.
E. A. Bergmann, Chicago.)

wall. The transition from studio to gallery environment was thus a very short step.

Blanche Dombek's life-size wood abstractions of the mid-fifties like *Silence* (1955) and *Figure* of 1956 (Figure 16) were generally associated with the "personage" tradition—especially the totemic spirit of Bourgeois and Nevelson. With an eye sensitized to the possibilities of rough-hewn as well as meticulously smoothed forms, Dombek sometimes added her own incisions and openings to the penetrating cracks of weathered blocks. Her formal language, precedented by Brancusi, was dominated by an attitude of biomorphism; often figural associations were overt. Born in New York in 1914, she had studied sculpture with Leo Amino, a follower of Noguchi, in the forties. In the late forties, she was represented in Whitney Annuals with her simplified expressionist-figurative statements in hard, smooth woods. The bulging volumes, sinuous contours and dramatic use of light on these works was later tempered by a restraint characteristic of the transitional sculpture of the early fifties. It never assumed the vigorous spirit of the action aesthetic.

Richard Stankiewicz was another figure who eased the transition from Surrealism. In his welded junkyard sculpture, primarily assembled from ready-made machine castoffs—rusty pipes, bolts, boiler plates, gears, ratchets, etc.—he amplified the innovations of David Smith's industrial found-object constructions, concentrating on a light-hearted and witty play on visual and verbal associations. Drawing more from a Dada than a Surrealist heritage—in which Schwitters especially had validated the junk aesthetic—Stankiewicz, like Smith, accepted the romantic potential of materials' past functions. However, he abruptly turned away from any direct comment either on their social implications or on their past functions. In this way he is aligned with Nevelson in their shared sense for the undefined nostalgia value of social detritus—a value that depends upon the found object's loss of   101

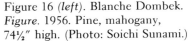

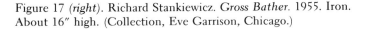
Figure 17 (*right*). Richard Stankiewicz. *Gross Bather*. 1955. Iron. About 16" high. (Collection, Eve Garrison, Chicago.)

identity but retained character. Whereas Smith could incorporate a metal tool into a piece of sculpture (the tool used because of its shape but also because, in romanticizing the industrial process, tool and product *can be* fused), both Nevelson and Stankiewicz would reject any such associative meaning. When an architect-client identified certain elements in Nevelson's sculpture as toilet seats, which indeed they had once been, Nevelson replied sharply: "Isn't the halo around the Madonna a toilet seat? Mine are images, not toilet seats." [23]

Stankiewicz was born in Philadelphia in 1922 and moved to Detroit in 1927. During a six-year-period in the Navy from 1941 to 1947, he was stationed for a time in Seattle where he met a number of artists including Mark Tobey and Morris Graves, who exposed him to the Abstract Expressionism of the Pacific Northwest. After his discharge, he pursued Abstract Expressionist painting at the Hofmann School in New York in 1948–49, where he met Jean Follett (who later also gained recognition for her sculpture). Her ideas, Stankiewicz admits, reinforced his own sense of formal discipline. In 1950–51 they went to Paris together to study first with Léger and then at the Atélier Zadkine, where Stankiewicz began to work seriously in terra cotta and plaster. He had his first one-man show at the Hansa Gallery in 1953, which included delicate human and insect figures articulated with plaster and such found objects as shredded rope, buttons, and sections of metal tubing. These works not only elicited humorous commentary close in spirit to the European wit of Picasso, Miró or Klee, but stressed a Constructivist ethic of empty volumes and implied planes.

During the following year, while he was working as a construction engineer, Stankiewicz abruptly turned to welding in order to assemble the array of metal junk he had begun to collect. In a later interview, Stankiewicz told of his sudden cognizance of old pieces of rusted metal which he had found in his studio courtyard:[24]

My glance happened to fall on the rusty iron things lying where I had thrown them, in the slanting sunlight at the base of the wall. I felt, with a real shock—not of fear but of recognition—that they were staring at me. Their sense of presence, of life, was almost overpowering.

Attracted to the shapes and surfaces of various discarded objects, he developed the analogies he had sensed between mechanical and organic form. Capitalizing on De Kooning's flirtation with common imagery in an Abstract Expressionist context, and his own experiences—such as his brief stay with Léger (who had always responded to metal machine parts) and earlier experiments with found objects at the Hofmann School—Stankiewicz began to construct his junk "personages." Early pieces like *Secretary* (1953), a typewriter set on a steel drum, and *Gross Bather* of 1955 (Figure 17), tend to focus on the objective identity of the materials as transformed; others, like *Flower Sculpture* (1956) and *Kabuki Dancer* of 1955 (Figure 18), become a familiar object made with junk components, recalling such antecedents as Picasso's *Bull's Head* of 1943, made from a bicycle seat and handle bars.

Figure 18. Richard Stankiewicz. *Kabuki Dancer.* 1955. Steel, cast iron. About 84″ high. (Whitney Museum of American Art, New York.)

Although fantastic imagery and chance relationships associated with Dadaism and Surrealism were part of his aesthetic, Stankiewicz's work always displayed a formal precision that could carry the viewer beyond superficial responses to his wit and unorthodox materials. In 1959, the critic Hilton Kramer, who had been following Stankiewicz's development closely, lauded a new sophistication in Stankiewicz's sculpture: "What might have been a mannerism—the continuing adherence to 'junk' materials—became a kind of guarantee of seriousness." [25]

Stankiewicz moved completely away from his satirical figurative pieces by the late fifties; like Nevelson, he gradually reduced the found object to a neutral, geometric element, distilling explicit content into a lyrical statement of open-form relationships.

Nevelson and Stankiewicz most effectively bridged the fifties, but the situation in this decade was extraordinarily more complex and non-linear than the progress of their sculpture indicates. By the time the importance of these sculptors was being felt, most of the older sculptors, especially those working in direct metal—but excepting Calder, Noguchi, and Smith—were falling into disfavor among both critics and younger sculptors. At the same time a great many sculptors who had passed through the forties but who had resisted Surrealism were coming into the foreground. The mid-fifties was an era of proliferation in which options were varied and open-ended; for several younger sculptors it was a cushion between the mature achievements of the older generation and the need to find their own way.

Proliferation

By the mid-fifties the remarkable diversities which constituted Abstract Expressionism were being generalized and codified by art criticism; the situation in the forties and its continuity in the early fifties was rapidly becoming art history. "American-type painting," the title of a major article by Clement Greenberg published in 1955,[26] was now clearly separated from the School of Paris. To some of the younger artists, Abstract Expressionism had even become the Establishment style. New directions were being sought to avoid the inevitability of a derivative manner; and the work of a number of older artists, especially sculptors, was being re-appraised. Just as the consolidation of Abstract Expressionism by critics was limiting the scope of the new art, it was also clearing the field for alternatives to be more sharply defined. Originality and freshness would come to depend less now on the fitness of one's style to the mainstream than on uniqueness as such.

The mid-fifties was a period of intense excitement as the parameters of artistic possibility widened as much for older as for younger sculptors. Young sculptors entered the art scene with fresh ideas, but there was also a shift of attention to a second group of sculptors who had been around since the thirties but who had not taken up the styles that constituted the vanguard of American sculpture in the forties.

Most of the mid-fifties action took place on East Tenth Street, where an alternative to the uptown gallery situation was established with the organization of cooperative, artist-run galleries. But the shift from Eighth Street represented more than a change of location. The early, low-keyed sobriety of Eighth Street where, as Irving Sandler recalls, "lower middle-class colorlessness became a protective coloration" [27] became on Tenth Street a tourist attraction which advertised its bohemian character. A lack of substance seemed to pervade the area which concerned itself, as Greenberg was to say in 1957, with the "trappings" and "forms" and "labels" of the Eighth Street culture; "the respectability of culture was what was sought rather than its substance." [28] After the dissolution of the Tenth Street scene in the late fifties, critics began speculating on the reasons for its demise. John Canaday compared Tenth Street to a "second-rate Madison Avenue" which was, he said, unlike off-Broadway "a parasite on rather than supplement to well-established, uptown commercial galleries." [29] Earlier, Robert Goldwater had placed the blame on the attitude that was already basic to The Club: "The assumption was that everyone knew what everyone else meant, but it was never put to the test. Communication was always entirely verbal . . . It amounts to giving up the critical faculty, a refusal to make distinctions of quality." The misunderstandings, he felt, had resulted in the "strange stylistic associations one sees these days in the Tenth Street galleries." [30] Clement Greenberg isolated the problem in terms of American dependency on the School of Paris as a hindrance to new solutions. Greenberg believed that the Tenth Street embracement of Arshile Gorky, Willem de Kooning, Bradley Walker Tomlin and Franz Kline—whose basic philosophy depended upon the continuation of a European sensibility—in preference to people like Jackson Pollock, Adolph Gottlieb and Mark Rothko—who recognized the need for American artists to boldly state their independence from European roots—led to the degeneration of both the Eighth and Tenth Street schools.[31]

The Club's Ninth Street show in 1951 had confirmed the financial potential of artist-sponsored exhibitions downtown. Although a few similar ventures had existed there before, the concept of a cooperative gallery, run by artists, was initiated in the

Village by the Tanager group—four painters and sculptor William King, who were not affiliated with The Club but who were impressed by the independent and inexpensive yet successful character of the Ninth Street show. Opening first in 1953 on Fourth Street, again with the help of Leo Castelli, who became their influential ambassador, the Tanager Gallery moved in 1954 to Tenth Street and assumed the leadership in a group of small artists' cooperatives which came to include the Camino, March, Cedra, Grimaud, Fleischman, James Nonagan, and Image.

During the most active years of the Tenth Street cooperatives, sculptors William King, David Slivka, James Rosati, George Spaventa, Sidney Geist, Israel Levitan, Gabriel Kohn and Raymond Rocklin, became known as representatives of the Tenth Street style of sculpture, even though there was remarkable diversity in their works (Figure 19a, b).

Figure 19a. "Sculptors Selected by Painters." Group exhibition installation, Tanager Gallery, New York. 1956. (Photo: O. E. Nelson.)

Figure 19b. "Sculptors Selected by Painters." Group exhibition installation, Tanager Gallery, New York. 1956. (Photo: O. E. Nelson.)

William King was one of the first sculptors of the fifties to eschew Surrealism and European linkages by turning to earlier American art. He developed a style involving witty figurative interpretations of American folk genre, tempered formally by the modernist sensibility of Elie Nadelman. An incisive study of individual personalities through gestures and mannerisms, rather than expressions of interior states of mind, came to characterize his work and establish it as American-style figurative art. King (b. 1925) had studied architecture at Cooper Union before going to Rome on a Fulbright scholarship in sculpture at the *Academia dei Belli Arte* in 1949–50. On returning, he resumed a teaching position at the Brooklyn Museum Art School from 1953–59 and was included in Whitney Sculpture Annuals throughout the fifties. He was a founding member of the Tanager, but his relationship with the gallery was tenuous; though participating in the group shows, he exhibited mainly with the Alan Gallery uptown. In the early stages of his career he worked predominantly in wood and clay, creating pseudo-primitive, subtly humorous and narrative social commentaries drawn from everyday experience as in

Figure 20 (left). William King. *Sheba.* 1950. Bronze, 24″ high.

Figure 21 (right). William King. *Fitzie.* 1953. Pine, wire, 15″ high.

Sheba of 1950 (Figure 20). King's work in the mid-fifties satirically reinterpreted the American Gothic archetype: stylized contemporary social commentaries, often life-size, illustrating such commonplace subjects as tennis players, boxers and bathing ladies executed in carved and painted wood, sometimes elaborated with metal attachments (Figure 21). His essential concern with attitudes and poses to explore conventional social stereotypes would become important for the sixties as further developed by Escobar Marisol, Ernest Trova and George Segal.

David Slivka gained some recognition in the fifties through his inclusion in group exhibitions at the Tanager. Born in Chicago in 1914, he had studied at the Art Institute from 1927–31. During the thirties he lived in California where he attended the Beaux Arts Academy in San Francisco and executed many stone figures and reliefs commissioned by the WPA. After the war, Slivka settled in New York, where he began experimenting with direct-wax techniques in a manner related to Abstract Expressionist painting. Working rapidly with sheets of hot wax, Slivka modeled fragile organic abstractions which were then cast in bronze. Thoroughly immersed in the problem of achieving spontaneity in sculpture he evolved his wax process toward retaining that quality in the finished bronzes, challenged, as he was, by the possibility of using a traditional material to state contemporary ideas. Throughout the fifties Slivka worked and reworked his wax pieces, developing controls and techniques and restating his concern with process. In *Young Flower* of 1958 (Figure 22) a lyrical organic spirit is embodied in a vertical configuration that reproduces all the decisions of its wax model. It was not until 1962, however, that Slivka finally had a one-man show uptown at the Graham Gallery.

108

James Rosati would also figure in the East Tenth Street community, where he was close to many Abstract Expressionist painters. Although he had some success with direct welding and open-form constructions in the early fifties, his temperament was suited to a cultivated monolithic expression, and the atmosphere of alternatives culled by the downtown scene fostered his development in that direction and away from Surrealism.

Rosati had turned to sculpture from music in 1932 when he was twenty years old. He apprenticed for four years in the Pittsburgh workshop of Frank Vittor, where he was exposed to the craftsmanship of the Italian workmen who were employed there. In the latter part of the thirties he was involved in Pittsburgh WPA projects, experiencing stonecutting, modeling, and casting. He came East during the war and worked in an airplane factory where he learned to weld; in 1943 he settled in New York, becoming a participant in Pavia's Waldorf group. In 1954 Rosati had his first one-man show at the Peridot Gallery after being included in Whitney Museum Annuals in 1952 and 1953; he had also shown in the 1951 Ninth Street Exhibition.[32] Many of his early pieces like *The Bull* of 1954 (Figure 23) were small, open-form animal studies or human heads in metal and revealed his preoccupation with the Surrealist-inspired ethos of the direct-metal sculptors. There was, however,

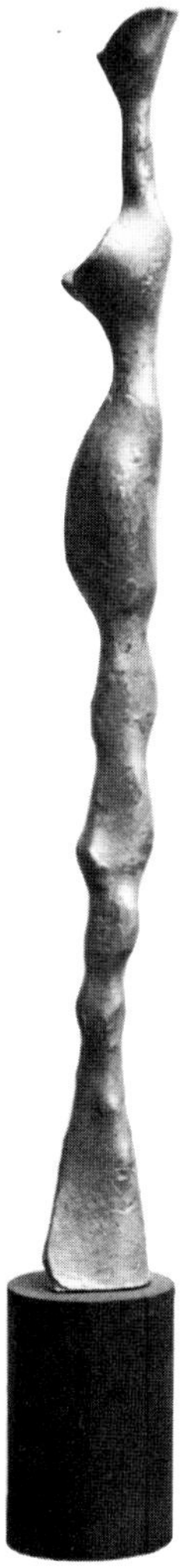

Figure 22 *(left)*. David Slivka. *Young Flower*. 1958. Bronze, 14″ high. (Collection, Mr. and Mrs. Harold Rosenberg, New York.)

Figure 23 *(right)*. James Rosati. *The Bull*. 1954. Bronze, 30″ high. (Photo: Rudolph Burckhardt.)

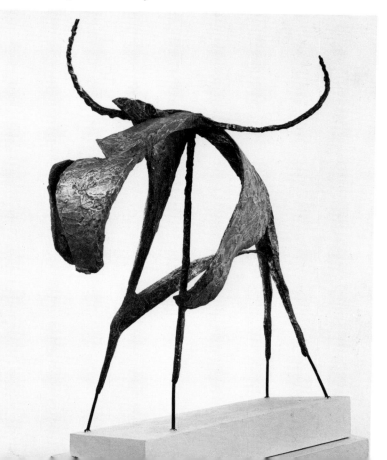

in these works an aura of intimacy and quietude that anticipated his later style. After 1954, Rosati returned to the monolithic tradition, shaping his masses after Brancusi and Arp. Considering the medium itself secondary to the organic presence he wished to assert, Rosati carved in stone and modeled in wax and plaster for bronze casting. In works like the bronze *Torso* (1954) and the marble *Hamadryad* of 1957–58 (Figure 24), lyrical and sensuous qualities are conveyed through undulating contours and a sensitivity to the play of light which Dore Ashton calls his "thoughtful, infinitely subtle endeavor to make stone into a viable contemporary medium." [33] In *Head* (1956) and *Portrait of the Poet Stanley Kunitz* (1957), Rosati sought to describe what he referred to as "the mystery of personality" [34] in the bulging masses that suggested volcanic energies inside, and that were precursors to his abstractions of the early sixties. In the late fifties, Rosati also worked on a *Heroic Galley* series (Figure 25). Multiple forms with vestigial anatomical reference were interlocked in a vertical relief procession which has been related by Hilton Kramer to Matisse's series on *The Back*.[35] More severe than any of his earlier work, the series pointed to the more formalist direction Rosati's work would take in the sixties.

The sculpture of George Spaventa, who worked in the Tenth Street area and showed sporadically in group exhibitions there throughout the fifties, had its roots in Giacometti's post-Second World War multiple figure landscapes. Like Slivka, Spaventa relied on traditional media for bronze casting to execute his small-scale sculptures, which also strongly depend upon the physical act of handling the

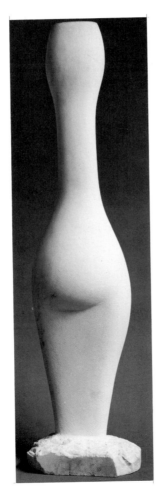

Figure 24. James Rosati. *Hamadryad.* 1957–58. Marble, 35″ high. (Photo: Rudolph Burckhardt.)

Figure 25. James Rosati. *Heroic Galley.* 1959. Bronze, 55″ high. (Photo: Rudolph Burckhardt.)

material. Spaventa used a tableau format to explore spatial relationships, and modeled single figures as well in clay, wax, or plaster.

Spaventa was born in New York in 1918 and studied at the Leonardo da Vinci Art School and the Beaux-Arts Institute of Design, but it was not until he joined a large group of Americans at the Académie de la Grande Chaumière under Zadkine that he began to develop a personal idiom. During his stay in France from 1947–50 his main preoccupation was with Giacometti-like images of man's spiritual isolation and anxiety that Spaventa "saw everywhere in the streets" [36] rather than Zadkine's bombastic Cubism. Even before the war, Spaventa had been interested in expressionism, studying Rodin, Rosso and Lehmbruck. When he returned to New York he concentrated on a reconciliation of his European experiences with the exuberant vitality of the Tenth Street milieu, captured in his *Tenth Street Allegory* (1958). Like Giacometti, Spaventa often responded to real-life situations as an impetus for his sculpture, which he then imbued with a mystical presence: "I came upon situations in life that have a symbolic character, a meaning larger than their actuality. The moments are so intense and total that I have to make sculpture of them, sculpture which is biographical and ought to be dated." [37] *The Studio* of 1958 (Figure 26)—a posthumous tribute to Jackson Pollock in which the artist is realistically portrayed walking away from his studio, takes on the intense psychological character of an arrested moment. More abstract in imagery, *The Sculptor's*

111

Table of 1957 (Figure 27), continues the Surrealist tradition of Giacometti's "table-top sculptures" with specific allusions to Max Ernst's *The Table Is Set* of 1944 (Figure 28). In his single and group figure pieces as well, many of which were exhibited in his first one-man show at the Poindexter Gallery in 1964, Spaventa continued to work on a modest scale. His gesture became more vigorous, his figures more specifically defined and a positive attitude of interrelatedness replaced a Giacometti-like existentialism. His impetus came from the Tenth Street mood of what he called "spirited quests," [38] and a commitment to making the human figure meaningful in contemporary terms.

Sidney Geist (b. 1914) participated in the woodcarving revival of the fifties and often exhibited at the Tanager Gallery. He studied with Zadkine in Paris in 1949–50, but his propensity for wood was established in the early forties when he worked under William Zorach and José de Creeft in New York. At that time he was making small abstract constructions of varied wooden shapes stressing three-dimensional spatial relationships as in *Landscape* of 1940 (Figure 29), which anticipated Bourgeois's gallery arrangements of the forties and Nevelson's wood pieces of the mid-fifties. When he returned to New York, Geist had his first one-man show at the Hacker Gallery early in 1951, exhibiting forty-two works of a variety of types and media, several of them still concerned with arrangements of multiple pieces on a single base. After a trip to Mexico in 1951–52 Geist responded to the rapid changes that had occurred in New York between 1949 and 1951, when the sculpture of Noguchi, Ferber, Lipton, and Smith had become vertical and totemic, and he began concentrating on frontally-oriented, more vertical forms. His work of the mid-fifties

Figure 26. George Spaventa. *The Studio.* 1958. Plaster for bronze casting, 11″ high.

Figure 27. George Spaventa. *The Sculptor's Table*. 1957.
Bronze, 9″ x 11″ x 11″. (Massachusetts Institute of Technology, Cambridge, Massachusetts.
Photo: Peter Sramek.)

Figure 28. Max Ernst. *The
Table Is Set*. 1944. Bronze,
11″ high. (Collection, D.
and J. de Menil, Houston,
Texas.)

Figure 29. Sidney Geist. *Landscape.* 1940. Wood, nails, 12¾″ high.

retained the sensual expandedness of carve-direct sculpture that he continued to admire in the work of Brancusi (Figure 30).[39]

The duality of artistic sensibility prevalent in the fifties was reflected in Israel Levitan's wood monoliths. Involving a system of deeply-cut, interpenetrating planes carved from a single block, his vertical abstractions, totemic in the manner of Bourgeois and Nevelson, like *Fugue #3, Nofretete,* and *Macrocosm* of 1953–54 (Figure 31), ascribe to the Cubist formalism he had mastered at Zadkine's atelier in 1950–51. At the same time, however, the introduction of robustly handled curves and arabesques, while also reminiscent of Zadkine, not only suggested vague anatomical references but a passion for psychological revelation current on Tenth Street. Unlike most of the artists who worked in wood during the fifties, Levitan had been a painter for many years (since 1938). Born in 1912 in Lawrence, Massachusetts, he was enrolled in Hans Hofmann's classes from 1947–50, where his experiments in sculpture began. While he was in Europe in 1950–51 he was exposed to the tradition of Western sculpture. In 1952 Levitan visited Mexico and lived for a time in the American Southwest. Like the carve-direct sculptors he came to admire, John Flannagan in particular, Levitan was attracted to textures and variegations of natural materials; but in the idiom of the newly-evolved interest in urban detritus, he chose discarded railroad ties and beams whose cracks and imperfections often suggested the ultimate forms of his pieces. Levitan sometimes increased the natural virility of his surfaces with gestural chisel marks, which contrasted to cleanly cut planes as in his *Queen* (1959). By the end of the fifties, Levitan was responding to a more ascetic trend, in pieces like *Helix* of 1959 (Figure 32) where the Baroque exuberance of his earlier work was tempered by a architectonic system.

In 1954 Gabriel Kohn developed a unique style and technique in his wood sculpture that incorporated the current gestural attitude into a Constructivist-based aesthetic that further signalled the approaching shift toward Primary Structures in

Figure 30. Sidney Geist. *Figure.* 1953. Wood. About 60″ high.

Figure 31 *(left)*. Israel Levitan. *Macrocosm*. 1953–54. Wood, 38″ high. (United Jewish Appeal.)

Figure 32 *(right)*. Israel Levitan. *Helix*. 1959. Wood, 24″ high. (Collection, Anasuya Devi, Key Largo, Florida.)

the sixties. Kohn was born in 1910 and studied at Cooper Union, doing conventional works from Renaissance casts, and at the Beaux-Arts Institute of Design in 1930–34 assisting academic sculptors on architectural commissions. From 1934 until he joined the Army in 1942, Kohn worked on his own, mainly in terra cotta, but achieved no recognition. He studied with Zadkine in Paris in 1946–47 before the ingression of most of his compatriots; he then moved to Rome for a while, and was included in group exhibitions in both cities. Kohn was also one of the American prize winners in the 1953 "Unknown Political Prisoner" International Competition. The diversity of influences in Kohn's work during this period is reflected in the bronze bust portrait, *Girl with Ribbon* (1949), a stylized response to Degas's *Little Ballet Dancer* (1880)—or to French sculptor Charles Despiau's *Paulette* (1910)—and *Genesis*, which interprets the conventions of Romanesque relief sculpture in terms of a Cubist-inspired interest in planes. By the time Kohn returned to New York in 1954, however, he was experimenting with small, open-form vertical structures on blocky supports, which were reminiscent of the work being produced in Zadkine's atelier after the war. Kohn began showing consistently on Tenth Street galleries in group and one-man exhibitions after his return. In *Monument to Thomas Wolfe*, exhibited at the Sculpture Center in 1955, and in *Cathedral* (1956) there was a new concern with surface detail evident in the incised tracery and applied paint. At the same time, Kohn was motivated to 115 continue some experiments in wood which he had begun while still in Europe. Finding it difficult to obtain single blocks for carving, he began to assemble odd pieces of wood. His first wood sculpture, *Memorial to A* of 1956 (Figure 33), exhibited in the 1956 New Talents show at the Museum of Modern Art, in many ways was still committed to the considerations of his earlier architectural terra cottas, but the emphasis on arrangement of part to part became Kohn's major preoccupation. Kohn's mature personal expression evolved with *Object of the Sea* of 1957 (Figure 34). Developing a carpenter's vocabulary of doweling, laminating, and joining, Kohn engineered precisely-cut and angled wood planks into blocky masses that thrust into space in a restrained but gestural manner. His earlier interest in applied texture was now satisfied by combinations of woods, wood grains, and lamination patterns, which added variety to, but did not detract from, the purity of the forms. His improvisational working method of beginning with a single unit and adding elements intuitively without preliminary designs enhanced the fluency of the works and related him more, in the last analysis, to the Abstract Expressionist ethos than to the doctrinaire modernism of Primary Structures in the sixties.

Raymond Rocklin was a latecomer to the Tenth Street scene, joining the Tanager Gallery in the mid-fifties. Born in Connecticut in 1922, he graduated from Cooper Union in 1951, and after a period of study at the Skowhegan Art School, he traveled to Italy on a Fulbright. About 1955 the aggressive, tortuous imagery of his early-fifties sculpture in bronze and terra cotta gave way to personages, evocations, and cloud-like forms constructed of curvilinear metal shapes welded together around a steel armature as in *Clouds* of 1956 (Figure 35). The interplay of the concave and convex in these pieces, combined in a kind of fluttering configuration, was a fairly widespread formal motif of the mid-fifties.

Figure 33 *(left)*. Gabriel Kohn. *Memorial to A.* 1956. Wood, 43″ high.
(Private Collection, New York. Photo: Soichi Sunami.)

Figure 34 *(right)*. Gabriel Kohn. *Object of the Sea.* 1957. Wood, 62″ high.

Figure 35. Raymond Rocklin. *Clouds.* 1956. Brass, 34″ high. (Collection, Mr. and Mrs. Edwin Bergmann, Chicago. Photo: Soichi Sunami.)

Some of the older sculptors who had resisted Surrealism and Constructivism during the forties—who had held on, rather, to carve-direct and modeling techniques into the fifties—were now either adjusting to the new directions of American sculpture or being reevaluated as a result of the shift in art criticism away from European models. Foremost among these were Raoul Hague, Reuben Nakian, Turku Trajan, Day Schnabel, Calvin Albert, and Peter Agostini.

When curator Dorothy Miller included Hague's gigantic sensual abstractions in the 1956 "Twelve Americans" show at the Museum of Modern Art, he became one of the most talked about sculptors in New York. Hague had been working in wood since the mid-forties and before that in stone as a carve-direct disciple since 1928. Of Armenian descent, he had arrived in America from Turkey in 1921. He attended Iowa State College and later the Art Institute of Chicago. In 1925, he moved to New York City and enrolled in the Beaux-Arts Institute of Design. By 1927 he had begun making sculpture under the tutelage of Zorach. About this time he met John Flannagan, who taught him to appreciate the inherent beauty of found stones— they often gathered them together in the fields of Long Island. Throughout the thirties Hague worked in stone, influenced primarily by Diego Rivera's stylized realism and by oriental and primitive sculpture. He was included in Holger Cahill's "American Sources of Modern Art" at the Museum of Modern Art in 1938, and like most artists in New York in the thirties, he participated in the WPA art projects. In the forties, Hague began to work in wood as well as in stone, at first because it was an accessible commodity in Woodstock, New York, where he had moved permanently. His forms gradually became more simplified, evolving into monolithic torso fragments that frankly admitted their tree source. *Chestnut Torso* (1946), one of his earliest wood pieces, which was shown in the 1948 Whitney Sculpture Annual,

117

Figure 36. Raoul Hague. *Mount Marion
Walnut.* 1952–54. Wood, 31⅜" high.
(Albright-Knox Gallery, Buffalo, New York.)

exhibited a classical containment and incipient contrapposto that evoked his Mediterranean heritage.

Hague's mature statements did not fully emerge, however, until he shifted exclusively to wood around 1947. With increasing complexity he cut deeply into the massive logs he had hauled from the woods, shaping the parts into dynamic, biomorphic volumes which retained only vague associations with human parts in reclining or standing poses as in *Plattekill Walnut* (1952) and *Mount Marion Walnut* of 1952–54 (Figure 36). His approach, unlike that of most of the woodcarvers of the forties, remained cool and restrained, and his attraction to wood was highly cultured. He worked slowly, sanding and polishing the sculpture surfaces until they were saturated with light, sometimes spending four to five months on a single piece.

Although Hague was closely associated with Bradley Walker Tomlin and Philip Guston during the forties and had been friends with Gorky and De Kooning since the late twenties, there is little of their gestural or expressionist character in his work. Rather, as he moved into the fifties, Hague represented a continuation of the Brancusian ideal. His methodical, technical procedures, his innate respect for materials and idealization of surface which suppressed impulse and gesture, emphasized his conservatism; Hague owed much of his critical acclaim to the eclectic permissiveness in taste of the mid-fifties.

Like Raoul Hague, Reuben Nakian was concerned with a contemporary expression of the continuation of ideals he identified with the classical past. When he was well over fifty years old, Nakian reappeared on the New York scene with heroic sculptures based on allusions to Greek and Roman mythology. His attitude was cultivated by some first-generation New York School painters and in the mid-fifties developed for a time a Constructivist syntax. It was a dramatic embarkment for a sculptor who in earlier years had been recognized as a mature

Colorplate 1. John Chamberlain. *Dolores James*. 1962. Welded auto metal, 79″ high.
(The Solomon R. Guggenheim Museum, New York).

Colorplate 2. George Sugarman. *Inscape*. 1963. Polychrome laminated wood, 108″ x 144″.

Colorplate 3. Jeremy Andersen. *Early Morning Hours.* 1966. Enamelled redwood, fruitwood, 35′ high. (Photo: Henry Segall).

Colorplate 4. Kenneth Price. *S. D. Green.* 1966. Painted clay, 5″ high x 9½″ long. (Photo: Robert Kays).

professional in the academic tradition, and his versatility was another example of the climate of options that the fifties engendered.

Born in New York in 1897, Nakian had served as an apprentice to Paul Manship in 1916 when Gaston Lachaise was Manship's chief assistant. From 1920 to 1923, Nakian and Lachaise shared a studio. During the 1920's Nakian frequently exhibited stylized animal sculptures in cast bronze and stone, and he was sponsored by the Whitney Studio Club until 1928. Nakian's circle of friends at that time included Zorach and Hague, and he met and helped Brancusi install his exhibition at Brummer Gallery, New York, in 1926. In the thirties Nakian, like Noguchi, earned a reputation as a portrait sculptor.

In 1936 he moved to Staten Island, where for the next ten years, he experimented in an expressionist mode drawn from such disparate sources as Tanagra figurines, Jean Antoine Watteau, Jean-Honoré Fragonard, Rodin, and Rosso. The potency of this mix was amplified by his association with Gorky and De Kooning, who shifted Nakian's attention to European art. The forties was a period of study, re-evaluation and reflection; two bronze busts, one *Marcel Duchamp* (1943), the other titled *Ecstacy* (1946–47) and some semi-abstract plaster configurations are among the few works Nakian executed during that time.

In 1947, while he was teaching at Newark School of Fine and Industrial Arts, Nakian began a series of wet brush drawings and small-scale terra-cotta plaques and statues depicting the more Baroque aspects of mythological themes—abduction, seduction, and rape. His attraction to these motifs provided a format for his preoccupation with sensuality and eroticism, exhibited as much in his method of incising lubricious slashes into the wet clay as in the explicitness of his subjects. His goddesses of Mediterranean lore were invested with the modern energy of the women of De Kooning and Lachaise,[40] and were glazed in pale rococco colors; they were first exhibited at the Egan Gallery in 1949. With the execution of a large, abstract terra cotta *Voyage to Crete* (1952), a variant on the Europa theme he had employed many times, Nakian reached the limit of scale possible in terra cotta.

By 1948 he had moved to Stamford, Connecticut where he had found a more suitable studio. Inspired by ancient leather shields he had seen in the Metropolitan Museum of Art, and utilizing certain standard sculpture techniques in a fresh way, he started draping sheets of glue-stiffened burlap over chicken wire supported on a welded pipe armature, then covering the whole with quick-setting plaster. This process forced him to work quickly to simulate the surface vitality of his earlier terra cottas. The models were meant to be cast in bronze, and the technique would later be developed by Peter Agostini. In *The Emperor's Bedroom* of 1953–54 (Figure 37),

Figure 37. Reuben Nakian. *The Emperor's Bedroom*. 1953–54. Bronze, 70″ long. (Photo: Seymour Rosen.)

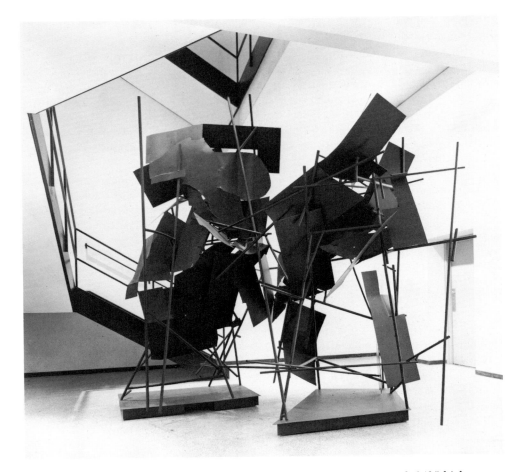

Figure 38. Reuben Nakian. *The Rape of Lucrece*. 1955–58. Painted steel, 141″ high.
(The Museum of Modern Art, New York. Photo: Thor Bostrom.)

a free-standing mass of organic shapes loosely based on the reclining nude theme, Nakian arrived at his own formal language. With his new technical means, he not only captured the buoyancy of his earlier work on a heroic scale but was able to open up his forms. From his tentative acquaintance with direct-metal welding in the armatures of *The Bedroom* and then *Hecuba on the Burning Walls of Troy* (1954)—which he destroyed later that year—Nakian executed three major open-form welded constructions of painted steel sheets and rods: *The Rape of Lucrece* of 1955–58 (Figure 38), *The Duchess of Alba* (1959) and *Mars and Venus* (1959–60). In each example, an armature of thin, criss-crossing rods supports a proliferation of irregular broken and bent flat steel sheets, which are set at a variety of angles to emulate the energy and sensuousness of the earlier *The Bedroom*, recalling the spatial interaction of steel shapes of Calder's stabiles. In the sixties, however, Nakian returned to his plaster-wire-burlap technique, creating several monumental works that were variations on his mythologically-inspired themes of the fifties; in 1966 he was granted a retrospective at the Museum of Modern Art.

Nakian's poetic visions, based on the classical tradition, were shared by Turku Trajan, another sculptor whose career had spanned most of the first half of the century. Unlike Nakian, Trajan had minimal public exposure, with only one major exhibition in 1944 at the Valentine Gallery when he was fifty-six years old. Until his

120

Figure 39. Turku Trajan. *Kneeling Figure.* 1958–59. Plaster, 28″ high. (Photo: John A. Ferrari.)

death in 1959, he worked in almost total obscurity, being included occasionally in group shows at the Tanager, Whitney, or Stable Gallery Annuals, and admired by a small coterie of artists and critics, including Jacques Lipchitz, Lyonel Feininger, and art historian Meyer Schapiro. Sentiment for his work was publicly aroused by Hilton Kramer's "An Apology to Trajan" in *Arts* magazine,[41] and he enjoyed posthumous recognition comparable to that of so many artists in the fifties who never before seemed to fit into the mainstream.

Trajan had immigrated to this country from Hungary in 1908 and studied at the Art Institute of Chicago and in New York at the Beaux-Arts Institute and Art Students League. Throughout his life, he remained consistent in his vision regardless of the current attitudes. The primacy of material that was a tenet of carve-direct sculpture had no meaning for him; he was more interested in capturing the spiritual expression, almost religious in intensity, that he found in much ancient art. From the twenties on, Trajan worked from the figure, modelling classically-inspired nudes and reliefs like *Birth of Isis* (1944), *Fallen Angel* (1944), and *Kneeling Figure* of 1958–59 (Figure 39) in plaster or cement which he then colored. He was one of the first twentieth-century American sculptors, after Nadelman, to conceive of sculpture in terms of color, which he applied contrapuntally, not as an adjunct to form but as a refractor of light much as in Impressionist painting. His method of modeling also was surface-oriented and did not convey any sense of internal structure. The presence of the artist's touch—in Trajan's case expressed most strongly through color—offered a tension between the poise and calm traditionally attributed to classical form, and earned him a niche in the sensibility of the fifties.

Day Schnabel was born in Vienna in 1905. After studying painting at the Vienna Academy of Fine Arts, and architecture and sculpture in Holland, Italy, and France, she came to New York during the war. Her first solo show was at Betty Parsons Gallery in 1947. While in Holland Schnabel was influenced by the lingering De Stijl movement; in Paris she studied with Gimond and Malfray; on settling in New York she continued her studies with Zadkine. More than any of the other sculptors of the American forties and early fifties, she remained internationally oriented; her style often fluctuated, and her lack of geographical identity undercut the recognition that her work might otherwise have received. She had solo shows at Betty Parsons in the fifties (1951, 1957), and was regularly included in the Whitney Museum Annuals; in 1955 she was included in the Stable Gallery Annual. Her sculpture of the late forties was animistic; in the early fifties, as in *Forms Within a Cube* of 1952, the carve-direct tenet of the image contained within a block, complemented by a De Stijl orientation, combines in a quasi-architectural sculpture that only by its subtle angles and slight curves maintains continuity with her work of the forties. In 1954 she turned to welding for a year—in *Galleon* (1954), only to abandon it in favor of lost-wax casting as in *Woman Entering a Temple* of 1956 (Figure 40). Her sensibility at this time was linked to the intuitive technique of Abstract Expressionism; although rooted in fantasy it was free of Surrealist mythology.

Figure 40. Day Schnabel. *Woman Entering a Temple*. 1956. Bronze. (Photo: Hans Namuth.)

Figure 41. Calvin Albert, *Moment of Precision*. 1957. Lead alloy, stainless steel, 12″ high x 28″ long.

Calvin Albert was another sculptor who came into prominence in the mid-fifties. Albert was born in Michigan in 1918; his early studies were in Chicago with Moholy-Nagy, and he taught for a while at the Chicago Institute of Design. Albert came to New York in 1947, and turned to sculpture that year under the influence of Roszak, Ferber, and Hare; after a year of futile efforts at welding, he began experimenting with lead in 1948. Albert credits Ferber with motivating him to search for new technical approaches to metal sculpture; Ferber credits Albert for discovering the use of metal foil, crumpled, shaped, and lead-coated, which in conjunction with metal armatures, could bypass the need for expensive castings. The technique was also in keeping with the tradition of modeling; the foil-lead alloy could be shaped with a soldering iron.

Albert experimented in metals for the next several years. After considerable research and advice from metallurgical manufacturers, he developed Modalloy—a metallic material in sheet or powder form that later, in a plastic base, became known as Sculp-metal. For the first time in the history of sculpture, metal became a modeling medium, like clay, seen, for example, in Albert's *Mathematician* of 1956 .[42] His interest in arresting motion by retaining the effect of molten metal in his pieces of the mid-fifties was in line with action-painting, as practiced by the followers of De Kooning (*Moment of Precision* of 1957 Figure 41). The general attitude Albert had pioneered would be extended by Peter Agostini and John Chamberlain, both of whom came to the foreground in the late fifties. Agostini would extend such explorations further into the manipulation of materials and the evidencing of their characteristic forms and traces.

123

Agostini was one of the members of the WPA generation who did not enter into the mainstream until the late fifties. Through Conrad Marca-Relli, his teacher in the thirties at the Leonardo da Vinci Art School where he was a pupil with Spaventa, Agostini became friends with Franz Kline, Willem and Elaine de Kooning, Milton Resnick, and Phillip Pavia; working on the WPA, he met Jackson Pollock, Lee Krasner, Arshile Gorky, and Jean Xcéron. His work from the forties included Medardo Rosso-like portrait busts and a series of small human figures reminiscent of Nadelman and Giacometti as well as of Tanagra figurines. Working as a casting specialist, he made plaster models for bronzes. The air of independence on Tenth Street combined with Agostini's solid knowledge of conventional techniques to encourage him to avoid the prevailing open-form mode, striving instead for a personal statement in the monolithic tradition. Dealing with themes of movement and following Nakian's precedent, he manipulated surfaces into spontaneous swirling networks of ridges and grooves analogous to the gestural brushwork and automatism of the action painters. "The only way I can find any truth to anything," he would later say, "is through accidents." [43]

After his first show at the Tenth Street Grimaud Gallery in 1959, where eleven pieces devoted to figural and sea themes were exhibited in the intermediary model state, Agostini focused his attention on the intrinsic properties of plaster. He abandoned the idea of plaster as a cast for bronze and began to cast the plaster instead. He first modeled the plaster as it set inside plaster bags, but seeking a means of working on a larger scale, began to pour thin layers into molds made from crumpled sheets of aluminum and then modeled the exposed surface. The speed with which he had to work before the plaster dried necessitated a physical activity which Agostini himself compared to Pollock's drip painting.[44] Apart from the technique, however, Agostini was preoccupied with natural phenomena in his early work, and began with specific themes which directed his execution, such as *City Fragments* of 1956–60 (Figure 42) or *Hurricane* (1959–60).

Later his imagery became more literal and his experiments with plaster-coated rags, string, and other materials led to the use of white casts made from real objects, including beer cans, egg cartons and tire tubes, precedented by Jasper Johns's replications in the mid-fifties. These "albino twins," as Max Kozloff refers to them,[45] were then assembled in Surrealist-tinged tableaux like *The Clothesline* (1960), or *The Table* of 1962 (Figure 43), or in abstract assemblages like *Zeppelin Through Summer Clouds* (1961–62), an ovoid object coated with plaster castings from melted wax. The plaster medium was no less transformed than the objects whose form and surface it recreated, and in the dual process, otherwise ephemeral phenomena like the fluttering of drapery, the spattering of hot wax, or the bobbing of a balloon were preserved in hard white plaster, while at the same time having the appearance of being soft and light. Out of his attempt to materialize an invisible nature came a preoccupation with detail comparable to Giacomo Manzu's bronze sculpture, but otherwise it was confined to painting.[46]

The work of Agostini and many of his contemporaries on Tenth Street was characterized by a "private mythology, of which the principal ingredient is the myth of the artist's own creative process." [47] Central to this intermediary period was the revelation of the inherent possibilities of various materials, conditioned in turn by the aesthetic of Abstract Expressionism and its preoccupation with capturing action and elusiveness. The direct-welding process that achieved currency during the forties was essentially a technical adjunct to already developed styles and traditional techniques. Even though Agostini's unique use of plaster has some precedent in the preliminary fashioning of armatures for plaster sculpture—the wrapping of armatures with plaster-soaked strips of cloth—it emerged in his work as a technique that was equivalent to the brushwork of such Action Painters as De Kooning.

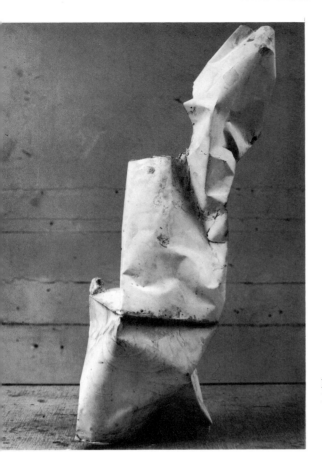

Figure 42 *(top)*. Peter Agostini. *City Fragment.*
1956–60. Plaster, 17″ high.

Figure 43 *(bottom)*. Peter Agostini. *The Table.*
1962. Plaster, 52″ high.

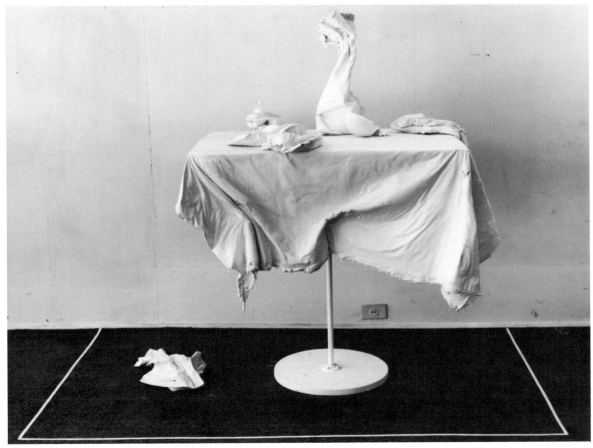

A similar attitude toward material prevailed in the work of John Chamberlain, Chuck Ginnever, Mark di Suvero, George Sugarman, and David Weinrib, who were central to the final group of sculptors to emerge from the fifties—and the only group to which the term Abstract Expressionism can be generally applied. None of them owed a debt to the carve-direct mode, nor had any one of them been involved in the reassessment of American sculpture during the mid-fifties.

The breakthrough in John Chamberlain's development came with his exploitation of the sculptural possibilities of crushed auto bodies. Chamberlain was born in Indiana in 1927, and was a painting student at the Art Institute of Chicago from 1950 to 1952. While there he met Joseph Goto, who had just begun making welded sculpture, and he saw one of David Smith's *Agricolas* and also a painting by De Kooning. After a year at Black Mountain College, Chamberlain was drawn to New York by the lure of Abstract Expressionism—the imprint of De Kooning and David Smith had remained indelible.

Figure 44. John Chamberlain. *Wildroot.* 1959. Welded, painted steel, 68⅞″ high. (Collection, Karl Ströher, Darmstadt, Germany. Photo: Rudolph Burckhardt.)

In 1957 while visiting Larry Rivers in Easthampton—and primed by a desire to get into new sculptural materials—Chamberlain's thoughts settled on parts of a '29 Ford that Rivers had lying around in his back yard. From these Chamberlain made his first scrap metal sculpture, *Shortstop* (1957).[48] Scavenging for heavy metal in auto graveyards from that time on, he was attracted to the battered fenders, bumpers, hoods, and other portions of wrecked automobiles that had been cut off by junk dealers to get at the iron framework. With the switch to the new materials, his sculpture soon imitated the powerful style of action painting—shown in the turbulence of De Kooning's brushwork. In pieces like *Wildroot* of 1959 (Figure 44) and *Johnnybird* (1959), the crumpled and dented sheets of metal, retaining their original automobile colors, contributed to a strong pictorial effect which was complemented with calligraphic accents of metal strips and pipes. Gradually Chamberlain also began to develop the suggestion of mass and volume in the collage-like organization of overlapping planes. Billows of metal over-extending from a non-existent core generated a "redundant" volume far greater than the physical structure warranted.[49] Cascading forms like those of *Dolores James* of 1962 (see colorplate 1) were used to activate the surrounding space just as the Abstract Expressionist brushstroke tore up the canvas surface.

Motivated by a singular concern for the traditional elements of mass and volume, Chamberlain himself was not involved with the popular associations of the crushed auto parts he used in his sculpture. Rather, he dealt with found materials, not with found objects, and in this way sustained a stronger body of work than the imitators who mistakenly subordinated formal coherence to the shock value of implied violence.

Beginning around 1959, color became increasingly important in Chamberlain's sculpture as an enhancement of formal contrasts. In the early sixties he did a series of all-black and all-white pieces, further extending the limitations of the found materials. During a visit to California in 1964, he began to spray the metal with auto lacquer, effectively transforming not only color but also surface to move away from the roughness of action-painting toward the polish of the hot-rod aesthetic.

Mark di Suvero's style was similarly molded by the combination of urban materials and Abstract Expressionist ideology. He was born in Shanghai, China, in 1933 and came to New York from California in 1957, after graduating from the University of California, Berkeley, with a degree in philosophy. While there he had enrolled in sculpture courses. In 1958 Di Suvero became interested in Gabriel Kohn's constructions and turned to wood himself when he discovered a supply of timber in a downtown Manhattan lumber factory. By the time of his first one-man show in New York at the Green Gallery in 1960, he was making giant constructions out of wood salvaged from the Fulton Street area. The canted beams of pieces like *Hankchampion* of 1960 (Figure 45) recreated in three dimensions and on an environmental scale the thrusting forms of Franz Kline's paintings that had impressed Di Suvero as early as 1953.

In 1960 Di Suvero was critically injured in a freight elevator mishap. Resuming work after a miraculous recovery, he began to move away from the basic Kline imagery and to concern himself more and more with the intricacies of construction based on principles of geometry and structural design: networks of I-beams, railroad ties, logs, and tree-trunks were maintained in precarious states of balance, setting up physical and psychological tension (Figure 46). Around 1963, he began to include rubber tires, hammocks, and other devices capable of supporting passengers in the constructions themselves. From the modest six-foot scale of *Love Makes the World Go Round* (1963), which projects two tires from a simple vertical core of steel, Di Suvero expanded his scope in a succession of outdoor pieces culminating in the 127

Figure 45. Mark Di Suvero. *Hankchampion.* 1960. Wood, iron, 84″ high. (Whitney Museum of American Art, New York. Photo: Rudolph Burckhardt.)

twenty-two-foot-high *Elohim Adonai* of 1966 (Figure 47), a mobile tetrahedron of logs, steel pipe, and steel cable.

Since 1960 Di Suvero has been widely acclaimed for the singular nature of his sculptural vision. In the formative stages of his development before the Green Gallery show, however, he was actively engaged in dialogue with two other Californians who had recently migrated to New York: Peter Forakis and Chuck Ginnever. Forakis was born in 1927 in Wyoming, and graduated from the California School of Fine Arts in 1957. He came to New York in 1958 as an Abstract Expressionist painter, but having little money, began to work with the cast-off building supplies he found around the city. He fashioned boxy geometric constructions out of wooden boards and covered over their rough surfaces with paint. Vacillating between painting and sculpture throughout the early sixties, Forakis did not approach Di Suvero's dynamic stance as a sculptor, and once he ceased to paint in 1964, channeled his sculpture in the direction of Minimal Art.

Figure 46 (*opposite page, top*). Mark Di Suvero. *Tom.* 1961. Wood, steel, 8′ x 10′ x 10′.

Figure 47 (*opposite page, bottom*). Mark Di Suvero. *Elohim Adonai.* 1966. Iron, wood, 264″ high. (City Art Museum, St. Louis, Missouri. Photo: John D. Schiff.)

128

Figure 48. Charles Ginnever. *Project 2*. 1959–61. Steel, railroad ties, 120″ high x 25′ long.

Closer to Di Suvero's work, though preceding it in form and spirit, were the sprawling constructions of Chuck Ginnever. Born in 1931 in San Mateo, California, he was educated at the California School of Fine Arts, and at Cornell. As early as 1957 Ginnever was making large-scale Pollock-influenced constructions, and then, like Di Suvero, drew closer to Kline in works of the late fifties—like *Project 2* of 1959–61 (Figure 48), recreating the characteristic calligraphy with huge railroad ties. Ginnever's constructions of this period were less architectural than Di Suvero's, however, and like Forakis, he was using paint to transform the surfaces of his materials, eventually making color his major concern.

The structural function which color began to assume in sculpture, seen already in the work of John Chamberlain, significantly parallels its changing role in painting over the same period of time, from the pictorial mode of Abstract Expressionism to color field painting, geometric abstraction, and Minimal Art. In sculpture, the use of color served to clarify three-dimensional structure without, however, reinstating the traditional relationships of part to whole that were abandoned under the influence

130

of Abstract Expressionism. In the early sixties, George Sugarman and David Weinrib also began to explore the possibilities of polychrome sculpture in this manner.

In 1958 Sugarman began to make inconspicuous appearances in group shows with open-form sculpture and reliefs made out of laminated wood. Born in New York City in 1912, he studied at City College, and resided in Paris from 1951–56, where he studied with Zadkine. In Paris also he met Chuck Ginnever, and retained a trace of Cubist geometry behind the organic forms of his early constructions. Sugarman made his first venture into polychrome sculpture in 1960 with *Yellow Top* (Figure 49), a compressed assemblage of free-form wooden slabs. Subsequent pieces such as *Blue, Black and White* of 1961 (Figure 50) and *Spiral Sculpture* (1961) developed the forms of Léger, Arp, and Stuart Davis in three dimensions, using color to emphasize their discontinuity. He began to activate the previously static forms, finally adopting the sequential format of a horizontal composition, seen in *Inscape* of 1963 (see colorplate 2), which is extended along the floor to maximize interaction with surrounding space.

Figure 49 (*left*). George Sugarman. *Yellow Top*. 1960. (Walter Art Center, Minneapolis, Minnesota.)

Figure 50 (*right*). George Sugarman. *Blue, Black and White*. 1961. Wood laminate, polychrome, 92″ high. (The Jewish Museum, New York.)

Weinrib had studied ceramics at Alfred University and taught at Black Mountain College during the fifties. When he first exhibited his scrap-metal constructions at the Howard Wise Gallery in 1961, he was considered to be another follower of Chamberlain, but soon established his own reputation with the inventiveness of his spatial engineering. Through the inversion of the normal floor-to-ceiling axis, Weinrib made pieces like the twelve-foot *Hoverer* (1962) or *Spatial Sculpture IV* of 1964 (Figure 51) sweep down from the ceiling or shoot out from a wall in seeming defiance of gravity. Using wood and then plastic in addition to scrap metal, Weinrib, like Sugarman, managed to create a continuous movement in space out of discontinuous forms by the careful manipulation of color.

In 1964 Weinrib and Sugarman were included in an exhibition at the Loeb Student Center of New York University which was titled "Concrete Expressionism," a group label intended to signify a common grounding in Abstract Expressionism and subsequent evolution to greater formal clarity. Also included in the exhibition, along with painters Al Held and Knox Martin, was sculptor Ronald Bladen, whose work, although sharing the basic principle of non-relational extension into space, was already moving in the new direction of the sixties.

By this time Pop Art had become the established style, and the advent of Primary Structures around 1963 was signalling that a dramatic shift in American sculpture was about to take place; Di Suvero was beginning to look like an "Old Master." Moreover, sculpture in this country had become increasingly geographical, as both Chicago and California were discovered by New York as having experienced art histories of unique character. The situation outside New York began to feed into the New York scene as artists began moving from center to center. The rather linear development of sculpture since the Second World War now became a structure of overlays and recapitulations, as continuities and new directions became more and more difficult to separate.

Figure 51. David Weinrib. *Spatial Sculpture IV.* 1964. Enameled steel, plastic, wood, 96″ high. (Los Angeles County Museum of Art.)

NOTES

1. At this time the Museum of Modern Art was still committed to European art, and the Whitney Museum of Art was not yet responding to the American avant-garde.

2. Irving Sandler, *The Triumph of American Painting* (New York: Praeger 1970), pp. 213–14. The Subjects of the Artist School failed financially and the loft was taken over the next year by some professors from New York University's School of Art Education and renamed Studio 35; the Friday night lectures and discussions continued until the spring of 1950.

3. From an interview with Pavia by Bruce Hooton, Archives of American Art (January 19, 1965).

4. For this and another detailed account of the Eighth Street Club see Sandler, *American Painting*, pp. 214–16, and Irving Sandler, "The Club," *Artforum* 4, no. 1 (September 1965), pp. 27–31.

5. Robert Goldwater, "Everyone Knew What Everyone Else Meant," *It Is*, no. 4 (Autumn 1959): 12.

6. Sandler, *American Painting*, p. 216.

7. Jack Tworkov, "Four Excerpts from a Journal," *It Is*, no. 4 (Autumn 1959): 12.

8. Interview with Pavia, Archives of American Art, p. 18.

9. Like so many New York artists of his generation, Pavia had attended the Art Students League and the Beaux-Arts in New York in 1930–33. During this time he became friends with Lassaw and also with Nakian, Hague, and Kohn; the latter three would figure importantly in the mid-fifties. Even in those days Pavia had organized impromptu discussions in the League's Tea Room, where he invited distinguished guests in wide-ranging fields to address the students. Pavia's father was an immigrant stoneworker who settled with his family in Connecticut where Pavia was born in 1912. In 1934 he went abroad to study sculpture, first to Italy and then to Paris; when he returned to the United States in 1937 he worked on WPA sculpture projects in Connecticut while frequently visiting Nakian and Hague in New York. Hague introduced Pavia to John Flannagan, and he often went to Connecticut to criticize Pavia's figurative marbles. After Flannagan died in 1942, Pavia lost his taste for stonecutting and began to experiment with simplified figures and colossal heads in plaster and wax. He had no shows, but was an integral part of the Eighth Street "Waldorf" scene as an exponent of plastic values in sculpture. When he quit The Club in 1955, Pavia organized *It Is*, a magazine for abstract art, often contributing and inviting polemics against Surrealist-type abstraction and all representational art. He also organized panel discussions for closed groups of advanced artists which were transcribed in the magazine in an attempt to recreate the original Club goals which had long since been relinquished for a more flamboyant, public profile.

10. Clement Greenberg, "The New Sculpture," *Partisan Review* 16 (June 1949): 637–42.

11. Clement Greenberg, "David Smith," *Art News* 44, no. 4 (Winter 1956–57): 30.

12. Clement Greenberg, "David Smith," *Art and Culture* (Boston: Beacon Press, 1961), p. 206. This is a slightly altered version of the piece which appeared in *Art News*.

13. Sam Hunter in the Introduction to the catalog of the "Irons in the Fire" exhibition (Houston: Contemporary Arts Museum, October 17–December 1, 1957), n.p.

14. Bourgeois attended "Studio 35" sessions (see footnote 2) and was one of the "advanced" artists asked to participate in the closed three-day panel discussions after which Studio 35 was dissolved.

15. Louise Bourgeois in a statement in *Design Quarterly*, no. 30 (1954): 18.

16. The idea of movable parts within a single unit rearranged by the spectator had precedent in such works by Giacometti as *Man Woman Child* (1931) but here the pieces are confined to specific tracks. However, Ferber's *Game II* (1950) utilizes the principle in the same manner as Bourgeois, and Nevelson's movable compartments would further define the concept of the spectator's involvement in the completion of the art work.

17. Bourgeois in *Design Quarterly*.

18. Quoted in Dorothy Gees Seckler, "The Artist Speaks: Louise Nevelson," *Art in America* 55, no. 1 (January 1967): 38.

19. Colette Roberts as quoted by Arnold B. Glimcher, ed., *Louise Nevelson* (New York: Praeger, 1972), p. 74.

20. Louise Nevelson in *Time* (February 3, 1958), p. 58.

21. As quoted in the catalog of the "Louise Nevelson" exhibition, text by John Gordon (New York: Whitney Museum of American Art, 1967), p. 9.

22. Jean Arp, "Louise Nevelson," *XXᵉ Siècle* 22, supp. 19 (June 1960).

23. As quoted by Glimcher, *Louise Nevelson*, p. 78.

24. As quoted in Harriet Janis and Rudi Blesh, *Collage* (Philadelphia: Chilton, 1967), p. 234.

25. Hilton Kramer, "Month in Review," *Arts* 33, no. 2 (January 1959): 50–51.

26. Clement Greenberg, " 'American-Type' Painting," *Partisan Review* 22, no. 2 (Spring 1955): pp. 179–96.

27. See Irving Sandler, "The Club," *Artforum* 4, no. 1 (September 1965): 31.

28. Clement Greenberg, "The Late Thirties in New York," *Art and Culture* (Boston: Beacon Press, 1961), p. 235.

29. John Canaday, "Good-By Forever," *The New York Times* (May 19, 1963).

30. Robert Goldwater, "Everyone Knew What Everyone Else Meant," *It Is* no. 4 (Autumn 1959): 35.

31. Greenberg, "Late Thirties," pp. 234–35.

32. Rosati was one of the founding members of the Artists Club.

33. Dore Ashton, *Modern American Sculpture* (New York: Abrams, 1969), p. 37.

34. Cited in Stanley Kunitz, "Sitting for Rosati the Sculptor," *Art News* 58, no. 1 (March 1959): 37.

35. Hilton Kramer, "The Sculpture of James Rosati," *Arts* 33, no. 4 (March 1959): 30.

36. Author's interview with the artist (February 5, 1969).

37. Philip Pearlstein, "The Private Myth," *Art News* 60, no. 5 (September 1961): 45.

38. See note 11.

39. Since 1953 Geist has been a respected sculpture critic; in 1968 he authored a major monograph on Brancusi.

40. Hilton Kramer, "Month in Review," *Arts* 33, no. 2 (January 1959): 49.

41. Hilton Kramer, "An Apology to Trajan," *Arts* 33, no. 7 (June 1959): 26–33.

42. Albert also worked in plaster. In the "6x6x6" exhibition at the Grace Borgenicht Gallery in 1952 he showed a plaster table setting in response to the gallery's request that each exhibiting artist do a "far out" thing. Peter Agostini's later plaster table settings may have depended in part on Albert's work of this type. In 1953 Albert perfected a metal shooting gun that shot molten metal directly into a plaster form, or onto an armature.

43. Quoted in Peter Agostini and Robert Mallary with Martin Friedman, *Art News* 63, no. 5 (September 1964): 58.

44. E. A. Navaretta, "Agostini Makes a Sculpture," *Art News* 61, no. 3 (May 1962): 30.

45. Max Kozloff in the catalog entry on Peter Agostini in "Recent American Sculpture" exhibition at the Jewish Museum, New York (October 15–November 29, 1964), p. 9.

46. Around 1964 Agostini turned to a new group of objects dealing with the effects of air—floating balloons, spinning tops, waving banners, and inflated tire tubes. With this banal imagery, Agostini's casts were soon assimilated into the Pop Art spectrum along with Oldenberg's soft sculpture and Segal's plaster tableaux. His work, however, although becoming more abstract, continued to maintain the interplay between form and materials determined by internal properties, and he never became involved with external attitudes and associations of objects imposed by the Pop artists.

47. Edward F. Fry in the Introduction to the Guggenheim International Exhibition (New York: Solomon R. Guggenheim Museum, 1967), p. 16.

48. Cited in Phyllis Tuchman, "An Interview with John Chamberlain," *Artforum* 10, no. 6 (February 1972): 39.

49. Donald Judd, "In the Galleries," *Arts* 38, no. 10 (September 1964): 71.

CHICAGO SCULPTURE

The counter-culture instinct that has persistently animated the Chicago self-image fermented in several young artists whose imagery in the late forties and early fifties characterizes the Chicago School. The desire to preserve regional individuality through enforced separatism and insularity was manifested in anti-traditional, anti-aesthetic, and especially anti-New York attitudes. Jean Dubuffet, the French progenitor of *l'art brut*, once remarked that Chicago is the place where Dada *should* have been born.

The situation for young artists in Chicago during the forties and fifties was in many ways similar to that for artists in New York. The Art Institute of Chicago was that city's counterpart to the Metropolitan Museum of Art, and the Chicago Arts Club was the equivalent of the Museum of Modern Art to the extent that it sponsored exhibitions of European Surrealists, German Expressionists, and such masters as Picasso, Klee, and Dubuffet. Though most private galleries were short-lived, there were important exceptions: Allan Frumkin Gallery, which opened in the early fifties and was an early and responsible supporter of avant-garde Chicago artists; Fairweather-Hardin; and Richard Feigen, which started showing Chicago artists in 1957.

The artists were, for the most part, products either of the Art Institute of Chicago or the Institute of Design (of the Illinois Institute of Technology). The ideologies of the schools were diametrically opposed: the Art Institute, while harboring some traditionalists, promoted Expressionism and a kind of Abstract-Surrealism; the Institute of Design, founded by Lázló Moholy-Nagy in 1937 under the name of the New Bauhaus, promoted a Bauhaus-type abstraction and Constructivism. As a result, the Surrealist-Constructivist dichotomy, familiar from the New York forties, was an issue of institutional magnitude.

The Swiss sculptor Hugo Weber (b. 1918), who taught at the Institute of Design from 1946 to 1955, was a leading figure among Chicago's abstract artists. Between 1939 and 1945 he had studied with Maillol, Arp, and Giacometti; a major show of his sculpture at the Art Institute of Chicago in 1951 brought him to the attention of younger Chicago sculptors. To the extent that his work appeared European (a Cubist-type sculpture imbued with the virtual action of late Futurism), it was resisted by the young avant-garde, who nonetheless respected him for having remained in Chicago in spite of critical success and sales in New York.

This was also true of Chicago-born Abbott Pattison (b. 1916), who taught at the Art Institute from 1946 to 1950, and was the sculptor most often exhibited in the Chicago area. Pattison's eclectic style, involving an "applied" Cubism, was popular among collectors. However, although his professionalism and allegiance to Chicago were widely respected by Chicago artists, he had no strong followers among

135

them. Pattison had a national reputation; in 1951 he was among the award winners in the Metropolitan Museum show that the New York artists had picketed, and in the first half of the fifties his sculpture was seen in group shows throughout the country as well as in New York at the Sculpture Center and the Nordness Gallery.

Underground art activity centered around provisional schools and galleries operated by artists. In the late forties the sculptor Ray Fink and the painter John Karney opened the Avant Art Gallery; Leon Golub, whose painting style has come to stand for Chicago art, had his first solo show there in 1950. The following year Karney and Fink were joined by Golub and the sculptor Cosmo Campoli in opening a school called Contemporary Art in a downtown garage loft. Group activity of this kind fostered consolidation among artists along more precise ideological lines than had been the case in the late forties. Much of the interaction was generated by informal meetings in Chicago's equivalents to the New York artists' Cedar Bar: Ricardo's Restaurant, Stuart Brent's "7 Stairs Bookstore," Werner's Bookstore.

The political climate in the New York art world that had fostered the 1951 picketing of the Metropolitan Museum had an analogy in Chicago where, in 1948, a protest exhibition was directed against the policies of the Art Institute of Chicago. In 1947, most of the prizes in the Institute Annual were captured by undergraduate students, to the chagrin of their teachers and local professionals who regularly entered the competition. In an effort to prevent a recurrence, the Institute rules of entry for 1948 excluded all undergraduate students. This catalyzed a massive petition drive, headed by Leon Golub, that resulted in several hundred signatures from students at both the Art Institute and the Institute of Design. On hearing that their petition had been denied, the students moved instantly to organize their own show. Ideological conflicts between the two schools were set aside: memberships in the Board were distributed between them; the first chairmanship was given to Roy Gussow from the Institute of Design; the following year it was reclaimed by the Art Institute students when Golub was installed. The selection of jurors was also distributed: the first jury consisted of Josef Albers, who favored Constructivism; Robert van Neuman, whose leanings were toward Expressionism; and Robert Jay Wolff, who was an ideal arbiter. Jurists in the succeeding years would include Robert Motherwell, Jackson Pollock, Clement Greenberg, Alfred Barr, Jr., and other respected artists and critics from the New York scene.

The organization and its exhibitions were titled "Momentum." Over the years, from 1948 to the mid-fifties, the Momentum Annuals caused considerable excitement on the Chicago art scene, especially since imported jurors tended to redefine Chicago art from show to show. The Chicago artists wanted impartial jurors, but they also wanted to know what New York thought of them. The sense of provincialism was strong and it was reinforced mercilessly by comments of New York artists and critics while they were there as Momentum jurists. In 1950, Clement Greenberg is purported to have said, "There are about fifty people in the United States who know what art is all about, and they are all in New York." [1] About the same time, Robert Motherwell announced to the Momentum exhibitors that all their work looked like reproductions in *Art News*. Tempers often flared during these exchanges and extremes of pro- and anti-New York sentiments polarized many artists. Jackson Pollock, a juror in 1951, came close to a fist-fight with Hugo Weber, who objected to Pollock's acceptance of a painting that was obviously in Pollock's own style.

In 1955 the Chicago Society of Contemporary Art sponsored a panel discussion with Ibram Lassaw, Hedda Stern, Roland Ginzel (a local abstract painter) and Cosmo Campoli. Campoli, by this time, had arrived at a personal means of expression and was incensed at the prevailing deferential respect for New York art. At a point during the evening when the sponsors brought out paintings by De

136

Kooning and Pollock for the sake of discussion, Campoli, gesticulating wildly, shouted: "It's all shit!" [2]

Campoli was the leading sculptor among the group of anti-New York artists whom the local painter-critic Franz Schulze labelled "The Monster Roster." George Cohen and Leon Golub were Campoli's counterparts in painting, but the Roster included several other painters: Nancy Spero, Ted Halkin, June Leaf and Seymour Rosofsky as well as sculptors Joseph Goto and Ray Fink. Other sculptors, notably Richard Hunt, H. C. Westermann, David Packard and Harry Bouras were latecomers who helped bring the Roster to its conclusion by the end of the fifties.

Campoli was born in South Bend, Indiana in 1922. In 1938, at the age of sixteen, he had come to Chicago for a summer course in sculpture at the Art Institute, where in 1945 he enrolled full-time and graduated in 1950. Over the next two years he traveled to France, Italy, and Spain on an Institute grant; on his return he began teaching at the Institute of Design. His European trip was the source of one of his most useful obsessive images: the chambers of the Altamira caves in Northern Spain, which are punctuated by calcareous stalagmites and stalactites. This experience had fused in his mind with an earlier preoccupation with the birth process, both as compelling imagery and as an analogy to the creative process of the sculptor. As a grotesque metaphor for the birth trauma, such works as his *Jonah and the Whale* of 1953 (Figure 1) communicate one of the most frequent and disquieting preoccupations of the Monster Roster artists: the fusion of birth and death, or the certainty of death in the fact of birth.

Figure 1. Cosmo Campoli. *Jonah and the Whale.* 1953. Lead, 10″ high. (Collection, Mr. and Mrs. Leon Golub, New York. Photo: Aaron Siskind.)

Figure 2. Cosmo Campoli. *Mother and Child.* 1949. Plaster, 9″ high.

Campoli had introduced birth imagery into Chicago art in 1949 (Figure 2) and opened up this genre of subject matter for other Monster Roster artists: in 1952 Golub utilized the theme in paintings based on his wife Nancy Spero's natural childbirth experience. During the late forties Campoli, Golub, and Spero had been close friends. Their interests at that time were in art that lay outside Western culture, especially primitive and Near Eastern, which they respected as tactile and imagistic. They often visited the Field Museum of Natural History which had a comprehensive collection of primitive art, kept up with *Cahiers d'Art* and *Minotaur* where much primitive art was reproduced, and had particular respect for the Mexican muralist José Orozco and the German expressionists Emile Nolde and Max Beckmann. Golub was particularly drawn to the totemic and ritualistic qualities of many primitive works; Spero's paintings reflected a fascination with schizophrenic and psychotic art. In 1950 she brought back from Europe an issue of *Art Aujourd'hui* devoted to paintings by the insane. This imagery entered as well into Golub's paintings in the formulation of the severe statements about humanity that all of the early Monster Roster artists made. Golub, and probably Campoli,

138

were also influenced by Victor Löwenfeld's *Kunst den Blinden,* in which the art of the blind represents an extreme emphasis on tactility in the creation of sculpture.

The "extremes" in Campoli's imagery were the opposite poles of the life process: the trauma of birth and the agony of death. In his attitude toward technique, tactility was expressed as the ultimate contact of the sculptor with the work—he has always resisted any technical process, such as welding, which interposed a mechanical device between sculptor and material. To this extent his approach reflected that of the carve-direct sculptors; but, in the tradition of modelers, he accepted casting as a process that preserved the surface as rendered by the sculptor's hand. In this way his insistence on the directness of experience, such as the feeling of pain, guilt, or terror, was complemented by a technique which depended as well on directness of expression.[3]

I like to think of the sculptor as the root, away from the glitter and glamour of swaying in the sunlight; or think of his hand, rooted in clay, giving sustenance to his being. His brain I think of as a sponge that absorbs from the atmosphere of everyday living, thoughts, dreams, etc., reworking, digesting and giving sustenance to his hand in the form of ideas to express in the clay his hand is embedded in. His hand, in essence, is the anchor that holds him to the earth from which all life springs.

Campoli did not share Golub's fascination for insanity as an extreme state of mental activity. But the emphasis on tactility was as important to Golub as it was to him, though in the differentiation of sculptor from painter, the tactile in Golub's paintings registered in a series of images titled *Burnt Man* and *Damaged Man.* The larger issue then, as Golub recalls, was how to get at feelings that were beneath the skin[4]—a parallel to the Surrealists' preoccupation with viscera and bones, or with David Hare's theme of "spaces of the mind." In Campoli's frequently-stated metaphor of the "tree of art," the sculptor is identified with the roots—that is, beneath the skin of the earth.

Campoli's metaphor may have been inspired by a lecture that Jean Dubuffet delivered at the Arts Club in Chicago at the time of his exhibition there in 1951. At that time Dubuffet was receiving considerable acclaim in the United States—as noted by Greenberg in 1948, he was "the one new painter of real importance to appear on the scene in Paris in the last decade [the forties]." [5] Dubuffet was an erudite, urbane painter who had turned against "fine" art, which he felt was cushioning artists from the essential confrontation with raw experience. He eschewed the superficial values of civilization and encouraged young artists to look at primitive art in all its contexts: the art of the "savage," the insane, and the child. In his lecture he stated:[6]

One of the principal characteristics of Western culture is the belief that the nature of man is very different from the nature of other beings in the world. Custom has it that man cannot be identified, or compared in the least with elements such as wind, trees, rivers . . . The Western man has, at least, a contempt for trees and rivers, and hates to be like them . . . On the contrary the so-called primitive man loves and admires trees and rivers. He has a great pleasure to be like them.

The surface texture of Campoli's sculpture registers the texture of earth, and unlike that of his painter-counterparts, is as much organic as psychological. He admired Henry Moore, Giacometti, Lipchitz and Noguchi, all of whom he regarded as "true" sculptors. In contrast to Golub, he remained disinterested in Dada   139

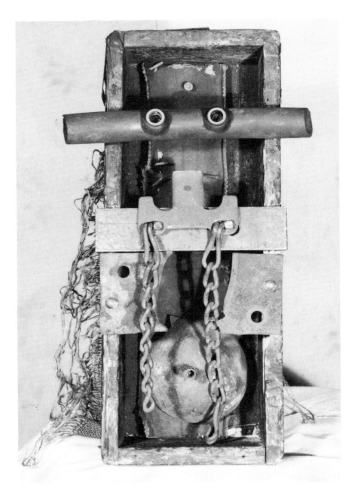

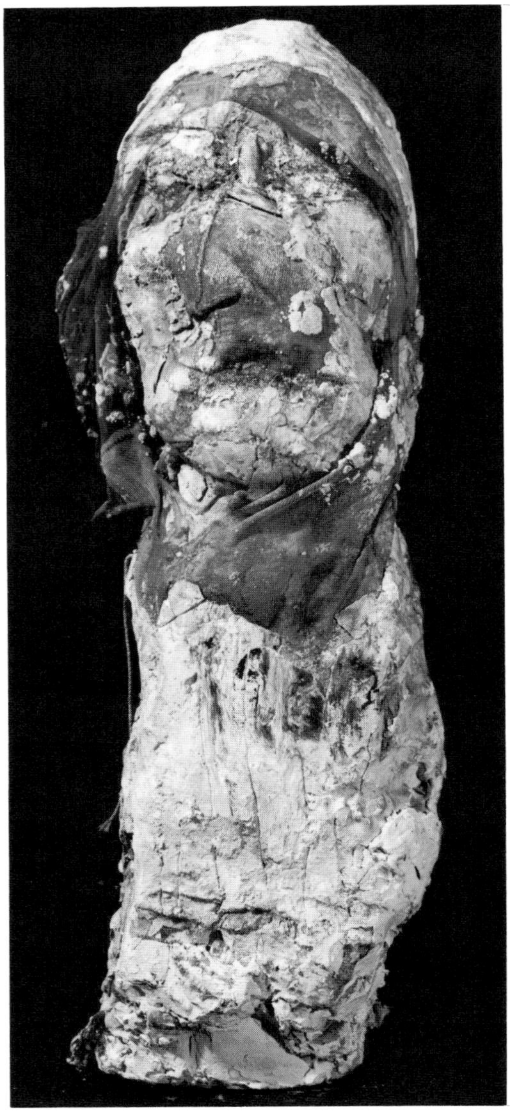

Figure 3 *(left)*. Leon Golub. *Clank Head.* 1953. Wood, rubber and iron, 20″ high.

Figure 4 *(right)*. Nancy Spero. *Mummified.* 1950. Plaster, nylon stocking, paint, paper, 15″ high.

imagery and the Dadaists' preference for assemblage. The occasional sculpture by Golub (Figure 3) and Spero (Figure 4) were errie, and macabre—in Golub's case even sardonic—and lay outside the parameters of Campoli's aesthetic.

Yet, after 1952, assemblage-type sculpture would dominate the Chicago scene. Dada and Surrealism had made strong inroads into Chicago art, even before its impact on New York sculpture. To a large extent, the acceptance of Surrealism was concomitant to the pervasive interest in Chicago in German Expressionist art, which, in turn, was reinforced by the exceptional presence there of the practice of psychoanalysis. Franz Alexander, a pupil of Freud, founded the first American Institute of Psychoanalysis in Chicago in 1932. Alexander and his many followers there explained all art since Cézanne in diagnostic terms, associating art imagery with varieties of psychosis, or departures from reality. There was considerable talk among artists of psychoanalysis. Students at the Art Institute were exposed as well to the psychological pictures of Ivan le Lorraine Albright which described psychotic states. And most of the students had contact during the forties and early fifties with the Art Institute teacher, Kathleen Blackshire, who was deeply interested in Dada, Surrealism, and psychology; her teaching stressed how individuality can be gained from self-analysis. In fact, most of the European Surrealists exhibited by Allan

Frumkin—Matta, Cornell, Ernst, Magritte—were looked upon by many as creatively insane people whose pictures were approximations of unconscious processes.

Surrealism had a more specific impact on the sculpture of Joseph Goto. Born in Hawaii in 1920, Goto came to the Art Institute as a student in 1947. Like Campoli, Goto worked toward a mode of sculpture that was analogous to forms in nature. Having been an industrial welder, he came easily to the technique of welded sculpture. During the early fifties, consistent with the national shift from the human figure to objects from nature, he constructed monstrous insect and plant-like works that accepted Dubuffet's call for the artist to return to a love of the raw, and even threatening, elements of nature. But around 1955, Goto's sculpture changed from a vertical to a horizontal orientation; the result was a series of "landscape" pieces done over the next two years that were remarkable for their linear reach (Figure 5). Less virulent in their probing of space, and less fantastic, they forecast the general inclination in much Chicago art away from the aggressiveness of the first wave of monster imagery.

Goto was an important influence on younger sculptors who took up the technique of welding. His most important follower was Richard Hunt. Born in Chicago in 1935, Hunt graduated from the Art Institute in 1957, and after 1960 sufficiently departed from Goto's influence to make his own mark. Like Goto, his pieces from the late fifties were based on plant forms, stretched and attenuated, sometimes with bristling or spikey elaborations. Suggestions of growth appear in the linearity of the shapes and sustain along more soft-spoken, or gracious lines, the theme of birth-and-life process that Campoli had stressed (Figure 6).

Raymond Fink went beyond Hunt and Goto in adapting the prevailing idiom of welded steel sculpture to the insular "Monster" style. Born in Long Beach, California, in 1922, Fink had studied at the Otis Art Institute in Los Angeles from 1938 to 1939. During the mid-forties he moved to Chicago and studied at the Art Institute until 1951, and from 1952 on was a seminal contributor to Momentum shows. His earlier work, like *Triptych* (1953), executed for U.S. Steel's "Iron, Man and Steel" show in 1953, involved delicate, Surrealist-tinged visceral shapes; by the mid-fifties he was utilizing more concrete and specific imagery. His welded metal sculpture often explored not only the birth phenomenon, but the totemic and ritualistic quality, with less vehemence, however, than earlier Monster Roster expressions. (See Figure 7.)

Figure 5. Joseph Goto. *Landscape.* 1955–56. Stainless steel, 8′ long. (Photo: Charles Reynolds.)

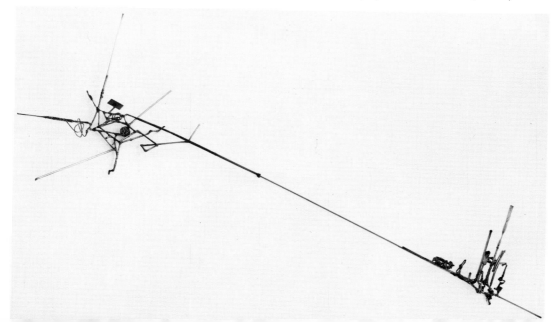

Figure 6 *(left)*. Richard Hunt. *Organic Construction #10.* 1961.
Welded steel, 23¼″ high. (Collection, Joel Starrels.)

Figure 7 *(right)*. Ray Fink. *Society Entrance.* 1956. Steel,
bronze, 22″ high.

H. C. Westermann was the last sculptor of major importance to emerge from
Chicago during the fifties. His meticulously crafted constructions utilizing wood,
metal, and found objects were characteristically sardonic and often assumed
anthropomorphic configurations. Drawing from many sources including Dada,
Surrealism, and the assemblages of Joseph Cornell, they demonstrated most
specifically the influence of psychoanalysis on Chicago artists.

Born in Los Angeles in 1922, Westermann had travelled with the circus,
sometimes performing as an acrobat, and he had served in the Marines in both the
Second World War and the Korean War. Westermann had studied off and on at
the Art Institute of Chicago from 1947 to 1954 and he was supporting himself there
as a janitor when his work began to gain attention. His earliest interest was in
painting but in 1956 he began to make sculptures and one of his pieces, *Confined
Murderer*, was exhibited in the 59th Annual Chicago and Vicinity Show that year.
Allan Frumkin and the Chicago collector Joseph Shapiro noticed his work in the No
Jury Show held at Chicago's Navy Pier in 1957 and Frumkin gave him his first
one-man exhibition in 1958. In a review of the show in *Art News*, critic Franz
Schulze immediately included Westermann in the Monster Roster.[7]

Some of Westermann's early pieces like *The Great Mother Womb* of 1957
(Figure 8) are more organically conceived and incorporate the onmipresent birth
reference that obsessed the Roster group. However, most of his works, like *Mad
House* (1957) and *Angry Young Machine* of 1959 (Figure 9) combine Dada-inspired
pictorial and word imagery with a comic sense of the absurd that seems to have
autobiographical associations with his circus years. Recurrent in his sculptures are
moveable parts that invite the exploration of interiors inhabited by found objects.

His preoccupation with what is within, replete with psychological connotations,

Figure 8 *(left)* H. C. Westermann. *The Great Mother Womb.* 1957. Wood and metal, 73" high. (Collection, Dr. & Mrs. Judd Marmor.)

Figure 9 *(right)*. H. C. Westermann. *Angry Young Machine.* 1959. Metal and wood, 96" high. (Allan Frumkin Gallery, Chicago, Photo: John D. Schiff.)

is stated through imagery less virulent than that of his Roster predecessors and in keeping with the trend toward geometric form that was beginning to manifest itself by the late fifties. Surveying Westermann's work in a show at the Los Angeles County Museum in 1968, Max Kozloff commented: "He is bottled up in a dialogue with himself, having resort . . . to that slang in which the voices of his divided self alone can speak. . . . Given the primordial drive which animates him . . . it is remarkable with what order and clarity he articulates his dreams." [8]

In 1959 curator Peter Selz, who had been associated with Chicago for many years as a teacher at the Institute of Design, staged the "New Images of Man" at the Museum of Modern Art in New York. Three Chicagoans: Campoli, Westermann and Golub, participated along with an international group which included Francis Bacon, Dubuffet, Giacometti, De Kooning, Pollock and Roszak. In the catalog introduction, Selz characterized the artists represented as inheritors of the   143 nineteenth-century Romantic tradition, manifesting "the passion, the emotion, the break with both idealistic form and realistic matter, the trend toward the demonic and cruel." [9] They were developing, he contended, a new iconography made possible by the liberating influence of such twentieth-century phenomena as Dada, Surrealism, and the formal proposals of Abstract Expressionism. Thus Selz dissociated this "New Image" trend with a revival of figurative imagery and hailed it as an unprecedented statement of anguish conditioned by the isolation and anxiety of a technologically dominated era.

The exhibition received a great deal of advance publicity and aroused a furor of controversy. The "monstrous" imagery, especially that of the Chicago contingent, offended the sensibilities of many who, by 1959, had begun to look upon even Pollock and De Kooning as artists of an extremely refined aesthetic. To many New York critics, Selz's show was intrepidly reckless and offensive. Aline Saarinen, in a pre-opening review in the *New York Times*, warned that the selections would send "emotions flaring" but conceded that those who had a "strong stomach, a stable psyche, and a perceptive and open eye" would find its existence justifiable.[10] John Canaday, the *New York Times* senior art critic was less profoundly shaken, but was motivated to review the show twice in a period of one week with his second installment revealingly entitled "Feeling Better." [11] With vituperation equal to that expressed against "New York-type art" by the Monster Roster a decade earlier, the New York art public was now protesting a sensibility the Chicago School had helped to legitimize.

The years from 1955 to 1959 were the halcyon years for the Monster Roster. In 1956 Allan Frumkin brought their work together in a large show at Beloit College in Wisconsin. In 1956 and 1957 the Annuals of the Art Institute of Chicago included Goto, Fink, Hunt, and the neo-Dada assemblages of Don Baum. But the cohesiveness of the movement was already eroding by the late fifties. Golub and Spero left for Italy in 1956, taking up residence in Paris. Campoli, though he continued to teach, influenced younger sculptors much less. Goto would soon depart for Rhode Island; Westermann moved to Connecticut in 1960; and several of the painters from the group moved to New York where the climate of acceptance was becoming more favorable, in spite of the reception given the "New Images of Man." After 1960 the Chicago art scene became uneventful, but, by the late sixties, the "Monster" spirit re-emerged as the "Hairy Who," a new group of young artists who were no less insular than their forebears, but whose work was nonetheless a late manifestation of New York Pop Art and an echo of Funk Art from California.

NOTES

1. Both Leon Golub and Cosmo Campoli recall this remark.

2. As recalled by Leon Golub.

3. Cosmo Campoli, "On Sculpture," *The Art League News* 3, no. 5 (January, 1956).

4. Conversation with Leon Golub.

5. Clement Greenberg, "Art Chronicle—Jean Dubuffet and 'Art Brut'", *Partisan Review* (1948): 295.

6. Transcription in the library of the Museum of Modern Art, New York.

7. Franz Schulze, "Review of H. C. Westermann Exhibition," *Art News* 57 (February 1959): 56.

8. Max Kozloff in *H. C. Westermann* (Los Angeles: Los Angeles County Museum of Art, 1968), p. 11.

9. Peter Selz in *New Images of Man* (New York: Museum of Modern Art, 1959), p. 12.

10. Aline K. Saarinen, "New Images of Man—Are They?" *New York Times* (September 27, 1959), Section 6, p. 18.

11. John Canaday, "Art: New Images of Man," *New York Times* (September 30, 1959), p. 40, and "Feeling Better," *New York Times* (October 4, 1959), Section II, p. 13.

144

CALIFORNIA SCULPTURE   V

The importance to many West Coast artists of maintaining the independence of their personal styles from any New York influence has both preserved the regional characteristics of West Coast art and punctuated the differences between the two major centers of activity—San Francisco and Los Angeles—centers that are often alleged to be more remote in spirit from each other than they are from New York. San Francisco is tied to tradition: "Everybody I know," says San Francisco artist William T. Wiley, "has a real nostalgia about something which happened a long time ago." [1] In contrast, Los Angeles is a city without a past; its history begins with the arrival of the Hollywood movie industry in the early twenties.[2] San Francisco has a steadfast Establishment, which seeks its culture in the opera and the symphony, largely excluding the visual arts from its patronage and consequently limiting the scope of museum and gallery activity. In Los Angeles, art and the city have grown up together; as a result, art has been able to secure both private and corporate patronage.

The art world in San Francisco is relatively low-keyed; the city functions as an incubator—a place where artists develop before facing the challenge of the more commercial environments of Los Angeles or New York. Art activity in San Francisco has centered not around the galleries and museums, but rather around the art schools, which have in effect taken over the role of major patrons in the Bay Area. The first significant art movement to come out of the West since Stanton MacDonald-Wright's Synchronism evolved in the late forties at the California School of Fine Arts which became the San Francisco Art Institute in 1961. The breakthrough was an instance of perfect timing: from 1945 to 1950 the school was endowed with an outstanding director, Douglas MacAgy, and during the same period was drawing an equally committed student body largely made up of veterans returning to school tuition-free through the impetus of the GI Bill. In 1949 MacAgy invited a group of painters, including Clyfford Still to join the faculty, along with Mark Rothko and Ad Reinhardt, who taught during the summer session. Still received very little attention there, although he managed to spark a concentrated group of mature and enthusiastic students into the Abstract Expressionist mode. His revelatory effect left San Francisco dominated by Abstract Expressionism throughout the fifties; as a painting movement, it tended to push sculpture into the background. In 1956 an *Art News* critic advised that "visitors to the Bay Area during the spring should not miss the most important group show of advanced painting done by local artists, the annual painting and sculpture exhibition of the San Francisco Art Association." [3] If sculpture received any attention at all, it was usually to lament its failure to equal the achievements of painting.

The two sculptors whose work transcended the general fare of second-generation New York and third-generation carve-direct styles were husband and wife,   145

Robert B. Howard and Adaline Kent. Howard (b. 1896) studied painting at the California School of Fine Arts from 1915 to 1917 and spent the next five years in France; he painted in Paris for two years and then toured the country. Howard was stirred by the great sculptural programs of the Romanesque cathedrals, and began carving in wood and magnesite upon his return to the United States in 1922. During a one-year stay in New York in 1926, Howard renewed his childhood acquaintance with Alexander Calder and was subsequently greatly inspired by Calder's mobiles. He began experimenting with fiberglass and resins in the early fifties (Figure 1), long before they became popular media. By the mid-fifties Howard was joining his molded fiberglass forms together to create polychrome sculpture with moving parts that showed a Calder influence.

Figure 1. Robert Howard. *Custodian.* 1952. Fiberglass, 63″ x 75″.

Figure 2. Adaline Kent. *Presence.* 1947. Magnesite, 44″ high. (San Francisco Museum of Art, San Francisco.)

Adaline Kent (1900–1957) received a degree from Vassar College and returned West to study sculpture with Ralph Stackpole at the California School of Fine Arts in 1923. She went to Paris in 1924 to intern with Emile-Antoine Bourdelle, remaining there for five years. During the thirties Kent worked within the carve-direct tradition, producing animal and human figures in granite, brass, and terra cotta. Around 1940, however, her sculpture became more abstract and more European, moving in the direction of the open forms of Henry Moore, the Cubism of Lipchitz, and finally the Surrealism of Picasso. Continuing the use of terra cotta for small figures, she began working with magnesite and hydrocal on a larger scale, articulating the surfaces with incised lines and polychrome designs (Figure 2). Complementing and eventually preempting the element of Surrealism in her mature work, however, was a strong archaizing tendency that stemmed from her sensitivity to shapes, textures, and colors in nature. She encountered various examples of primitive art during her travels in Europe, Greece, and Egypt and her frequent visits to Mexico; and she showed great interest as well in contemporary archaeological discoveries. The impact of these sources is apparent in her works of the fifties: vase-like pieces and primitive architectural forms that, with their blocky shapes and rough surfaces, reveal the natural properties of terra cotta. At the time of her death in an automobile accident in 1957, Adaline Kent was one of the few California artists to be recognized in New York.[4] In 1949 she had been singled out by Clement Greenberg as a sculptor of promise;[5] after her 1953 exhibition at the Betty Parsons Gallery, in fact, *Finder* (1953), a large two-part sculpture in magnesite, was praised as one of the best pieces of sculpture to be seen in New York, and ten years later she was hailed as the first Northern California sculptor to have created a strong body of work.[6]

147

At a time when the San Francisco painters were zealously cutting themselves off from outside influences, Robert Howard and Adaline Kent provided a link with the same European sculptural traditions that had inspired New York artists during the forties. Both had introduced abstraction and new materials into what had been a strictly figurative scene. Howard was especially important as a teacher; at the California School of Fine Arts during the fifties he promoted experimentation, supplied a vast amount of technical information, and further encouraged and supported his students by buying their work.

The modernism of Kent and Howard would feed directly into the process of sculpture in the San Francisco Bay Area. In Los Angeles, on the other hand, the "traditional" modernists had little effect on subsequent developments. This was partly because they were not teaching and partly because the schools had the most conservative offerings in the visual arts. During the forties and well into the fifties, the major art schools in the Los Angeles area offered limited sculpture courses. Pegot Waring, a respected, yet traditional stone carver, was teaching at the Otis Art Institute, and the University of Southern California was tied to figurative work; the Art Center School was strictly commercial; and there were no sculpture departments at all at UCLA and Chouinard. However, the craft movements, including ceramics, were receiving considerable attention and sponsorship throughout California. In 1956 sixteen art schools and institutions of higher learning in Los Angeles supported ceramics workshops and equipment. In fact, the first significant development in the history of Los Angeles sculpture began in 1954 as a crafts movement when Peter Voulkos, a celebrated potter from Montana, moved there.

The most prominent Los Angeles sculptor in the early fifties was Bernard Rosenthal (b. 1914), whose welded abstractions were very popular for architectural commissions. For two years during the war, Rosenthal was stationed in Paris where he met Brancusi. Upon his return to the United States in 1946 he settled in Malibu and began carving wood sculpture. After a period of making figurative sculpture in cast metal he started welding around 1950 but continued in the figurative vein with such works as *Three Musicians* (1951), which was included in the Metropolitan Museum's sculpture show that year. In 1952 Rosenthal was singled out as being at the forefront of architectural sculptors in California, for his "flair" and "audacity," and for the directness of his metal process. Much of his production during this period drew upon Giacometti and Gonzalez, and also David Smith, especially in the airiness of his imagery and technical aggressiveness (Figure 3).

Rosenthal received a great deal of publicity in 1954 when the Los Angeles City Council opposed his project for a fourteen-foot bronze sculpture for the façade of the Police Facilities Building with the then-familiar charge of "unamericanism." Attacking the semi-abstract figure group of a father, mother, son, and baby for demeaning the image of the family, the Council later tried to have the completed work melted down to make a plaque honoring dead soldiers.[8]

Two other sculptors whose names are often associated with Los Angeles in the fifties, Jack Zajac and Claire Falkenstein spent little time there; both are expatriates and their work was not a part of the larger process of Los Angeles sculpture.

Jack Zajac (b. 1929) left Los Angeles permanently for Rome in 1960 after working intermittently in Italy from 1954. He gained international recognition with a series of cast bronze sacrificial goats in tortuous postures (Figure 4) that were intended to dramatize graphically the agonizing moment before death. Utilizing a representational image that was not only loaded with iconological symbolism but directly inspired by the goats of North Africa as well as Picasso's *Man with Sheep* (1944), Zajac visualized what he called a sense of "urgency and alarm." At the same time he invested his traditionally modeled masses with a sensitivity to the

Figure 3 *(left)*. Bernard Rosenthal. *Oracle #1*. 1956.
Red brass, 32″ high.

Figure 4 *(right)*. Jack Zajac. *Easter Goat*. 1957. Bronze,
19⅛″ x 31¾″. (The Museum of Modern Art, New York.)

space-engaging concerns of open-form constructions. When he had his first solo
sculpture shows in 1959 at the Landau Gallery in Los Angeles and in 1960 at the
Downtown Gallery in New York, Zajac had been working three-dimensionally for
about five years. By 1953 he was recognized as an accomplished painter who had
developed in the Southern California figurative off-shoot of Abstract Expressionism.
During his years in Rome in the fifties, Zajac turned to figurative sculpture. At the
same time as his *Goat* series, Zajac executed a group of Christ figures in fiberglass,
among them *Descent from the Cross* (1958) and *Resurrection* (1959), which further
explored the theme of anguish and sacrifice without the formal virtuosity of the
Goat pieces. He also began working on a *Metamorphosis* theme which alluded to
the spiritual frenzy of Baroque religious statuary. The freshness and originality of his
response to traditional imagery linked him especially to Nakian, Trajan, and
Spaventa.

Claire Falkenstein (b. 1902) was associated with the national direct-metal vogue
of the fifties even though she had moved to France from California in 1950 when
she was already an established Los Angeles sculptor, teacher, and critic. She had
worked mainly in wood during the forties, but by the end of the decade was
experimenting with the idea of transparency through mixed media on plexiglass.
During her eight-year residence in Paris, she evolved a style of space drawing, using
techniques of brazing, soldering, and welding to conform to the international   149

Figure 5. Claire Falkenstein. *Sun #5*. 1954. Iron brazed with brass. (Collection, Michel Tapié, Paris.)

Abstract Expressionist mold. Falkenstein established another studio in Rome, and her work began to be exhibited in many major European capitals as well as in the United States and was widely sought after for architectural commissions. Fusing copper tubing, wire, and sometimes melted glass, she constructed irregular 3-D forms that had superficial affinities to Pollock's drip paintings and to Lassaw's constellations. At first her works were composed of close-knit filigrees that retained a semblance of mass and traces of visceral, Surrealist associations, as in her *Sun* and *Moon* themes of the mid-fifties (Figure 5). Without the adamant inner conviction of original action art, however, her sensibility became increasingly decorative, and by 1959, when she returned to New York, she was designing lighter, more open, amorphous pieces that were frankly imitative of bushes, thickets and vines.

Among the several sculptors whose works were occasionally seen in the Los Angeles area was David Tolerton (b. 1907) who was one of the older sculptors in this country to work in direct-metal. Based in Big Sur, he was associated more with the Northern than with the Southern California scene, as he had attended Stanford and the California School of Fine Arts in the twenties. In 1929 he had studied ancient ironwork in France, and during the thirties was a designer and fabricator of ornamental iron work in the Bay Area. His iron, and sometimes wood, sculpture started after a period of service in the Navy, in 1946. In 1955–56 he had major one-man exhibitions in Los Angeles, Santa Barbara, and at the DeYoung Museum in San Francisco. His style echoed that of David Smith, and to some extent that of Ferber, and was eclectic also in its resemblance to the iron work of the Europeans, from Gonzalez to Lardera (Figure 6).

Tolerton's show at the DeYoung Museum in 1956 was the biggest "official" sculpture event of the mid-fifties in the San Francisco Bay Area, and was typical in that most of the shows and museum awards were given to sculptors who worked on the surface of modernism rather than "underground." Direct-metal sculpture was in vogue and its best practitioners, Keith Monroe and Henri Marie-Rose, were seen

150

Colorplate 5. Claes Oldenburg. *Two Cheeseburgers with Everything (Dual Hamburgers).* 1962. Burlap soaked in plaster, painted with enamel, 7″ x 14¾″ x 8⅝″. (The Museum of Modern Art, New York).

Colorplate 6. Chryssa. *Five Variations on the Ampersand.* 1966. Neon light construction in tinted plexiglass vitrines.

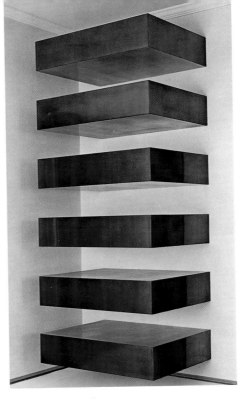

Colorplate 7. Donald Judd. *Untitled*. 1966.
Painted galvanized iron, 9" x 40" x 31".
(Collection, Joseph Helman, New York).

Colorplate 8. Lyman Kipp.
Flat Rate I. 1968. Painted
steel, 72" x 60" x 36".
(Photo: Richard Baldinger).

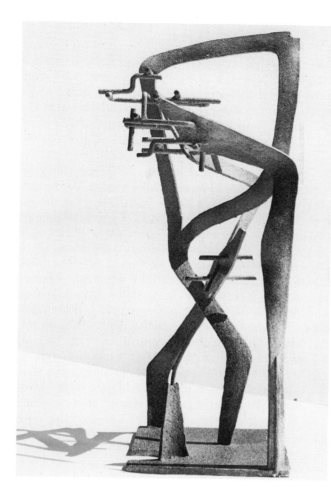

Figure 6. David Tolerton. *Theory of Communication.* 1955. Iron, 35″ high.

regularly in the Annuals of the San Francisco Museum of Art. Also highly acclaimed was Gurdin Woods, a teacher at the San Francisco Art Institute, and an accomplished sculptor in cast bronze. Woods built a foundry at the Institute in the early fifties and was important for the resurgence of bronze casting in the Bay Area. He was included in the São Paulo Biennial in 1955. Ruth Asawa's woven wire basket and fish-trap pieces were popular among collectors, but, as in the case of Monroe, Marie-Rose and Woods, she was not a factor in the larger process of modern sculpture even though she was highly regarded by her peers.

Jeremy Anderson (b. 1921) was one of the first sculptors to bridge the modernism of Kent and Howard and the new trends which would make themselves felt in the late fifties and early sixties. He enrolled at the California School of Fine Arts in 1946, studying sculpture with Howard and painting with Still, Rothko, and Californian David Park. After a few figurative pieces, mostly carved in wood, Anderson turned to non-objective sculpture in magnesite and plaster around 1948. These works were directly inspired by primitive sculpture, frequently recombining four or five specific archaic motifs; they also carry definite Surrealist overtones, utilizing visceral and skeletal paraphrases of Surrealism, and also Picasso's bone or anatomical drawings. In 1952 he produced several pseudo-architectural sculptures in plaster—openwork boxes of two or three levels topped with Giacometti-like "tablescapes." These were in continuity with his Giacometti-inspired cage forms of the late forties, made by coating wire armatures with plaster in the manner of Lassaw, his New York counterpart.

151

Anderson ascribes this Surrealist influence to an "underlying current" in San Francisco art. As a student he read the New York art magazines *View*, *VVV*, and Peggy Guggenheim's *Art of This Century*. The San Francisco Museum of Art had a number of Surrealist works in the Gordon Onslow Ford collection; in 1948 the museum installed an American Federation of Art traveling exhibition of "Abstract and Surrealist Art in America." Anderson also recalls that Still had discussed Surrealism in his slide lectures at the School.

In the early fifties, Anderson began carving in redwood, a material which was more durable than plaster and familiar from his early student work. At first he assembled separate carved parts horizontally on a single base; then, toward the mid-fifties, he intensified their totemic quality by orienting them vertically (Figure 7). All these works retained certain formal ties with the Surrealism of Giacometti and David Hare. Anderson had resisted the Dadaist tendency that was working underground in San Francisco as early as 1949 and would see the growth of so-called Funk Art during the fifties. His move toward a relative "Funkiness" was more in pursuit of the Surrealist "private myth" as introduced at the California School of Fine Arts by both Rothko and Still. By the late fifties Anderson was bringing together in his sculpture multiple illusions—as he had earlier combined multiple forms—and using specific literal images to control the intuitive ones. In the early sixties these images were based on limericks, such as *The Old Man of Calvacary* (1961) and *Shooting of Dan McGrew* of 1962 (Figure 8). Commenting on his work in 1963 Anderson noted: "The pursuit of images, ideas, obsessions, recorded by tangible materials, with the materials taking the shape that records these ventures best, is a partial explanation of what some sculpture is about." [9] Around that time

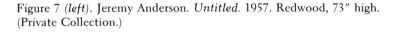

Figure 7 *(left)*. Jeremy Anderson. *Untitled*. 1957. Redwood, 73″ high. (Private Collection.)

Figure 8 *(right)*. Jeremy Anderson. *Shooting of Dan McGrew*. 1962. Wood, 6″ high. (Private Collection.)

he began transforming the appearance of the carved redwood by the use of brightly-colored enamel paints. He returned to polychrome as in *Early Morning Hours* of 1966 (Colorplate 3) when he felt that the grain of the wood was both old-fashioned and destructive of the form. In more recent works, such as *Celestial Bathtub* (1968) he has reverted to the use of plaster, along with wood, enameled in striking, cosmetic colors.

Seymour Locks (b. 1919) came out of the same transitional milieu as Anderson. Locks had already exhibited as a painter at the World's Fair of 1939. He studied painting at San José State College in the late thirties and spent four years in the army during the Second World War, where his talents were channeled into lettering and poster design. He became interested in sculpture while a graduate student at Stanford in 1947. Essentially self-trained, he started carving organic totem figures which resembled the contemporary work of Anderson and were influenced in tenor and form by what he refers to as the "provocative objects" of Giacometti.

Around 1948, Locks met Hassel Smith (b. 1915), who was at the center of a group of young artists at the California School of Fine Arts. Smith created many Dada objects in the late forties and early fifties, and exhibited junk collages with Richard Diebenkorn in 1950. Two years later Smith held a series of seminars on "Theories of Non-Objective Painting," focusing on the subject of "painting as a metaphor of expression." [10] These seminars doubled as weekly social gatherings, including a Dada party for which Locks made his first nail sculpture—blocks of wood overlaid with ordinary metal (Figure 9). His first concern was with making an

Figure 9. Seymour Locks. *Nefertiti.* 1952–53. (Detail.) Nails, miscellaneous materials on wood. (Photo: Jack Welpott.)

object that wasn't an object but an environment or "trip." From the time of his earliest wood sculpture, Locks was thinking in terms of total environments rather than individual pieces, and in creating the nail sculpture he found a fluid material with which he could establish both surface patterns and a shallow space having an extent in time for the viewer. In the mid-fifties Locks began to introduce foreign objects among the nails, increasing both formal and associative content, and developing a tone which was at once ominous and humorous. Changing his formal idiom in the sixties, Locks maintained his previous approach to sculpture, aimed at the direct involvement of the viewer through the creation of an extended experience. Beginning with the *Blue Table* of 1963, arrayed with nails, mop, umbrella, and mirror, Locks turned to assemblages of familiar objects upon furniture forms that were treated with putty or epoxy resins. Playing on multiple or relative associations, he brought the individual objects together to create what he called an "event." This kind of assemblage occupied a singular position in San Francisco sculpture throughout the fifties.

By 1953 in San Francisco an artistic depression had set in: Still and Rothko, Douglas MacAgy, and even the ex-GI's had left the California School of Fine Arts. Art went underground to reappear in coffee houses, bars, and small co-operative galleries. Locks had shown his paintings at the King Ubu Gallery on Fillmore Street, started by the painter-collage maker Jess Collins and the poet Robert Duncan. When the King Ubu closed in 1953, its location was taken over by the Six Gallery, a co-operative run by sculptor-painter Wally Hedrick, painters Deborah Remington, David Simpson, and Rayward Kind, and poets Jack Spicer and John Ryan, where, among many other events, Allen Ginsberg gave his first performance of *Howl*, and Stile's Place Bar opened in April 1954 with a "Dada" show of works by Wally Hedrick, Jess Collins, and Ben Langton. There followed frequent Dada nights and several performances of Hedrick's "liquid light" shows.

Among the group of artists who called their work "Funky" after the New Orleans blues term was the "Funk Daddy," Hedrick (b. 1927). He had been experimenting with light machines and light shows since 1947, and in the early fifties studied at the California School of Fine Arts with Howard. Howard introduced him to welding and Hedrick began to translate his mechanical ideas into metal sculpture. Inspired by Howard's articulated kinetic sculpture, Hedrick's 96-inch *Sunflower* (1952) poses a circular saw blade on a support of various rods and cogs turned by a crank. Hedrick was also attracted to the Russian Constructivists, and created several linear iron pieces such as the prophetic *Primary Structure 1* of 1953. His most original works, however, were those which transformed found objects into metal sculpture, retaining a strong sense of form while adding the element of wit and humor, as for example, *His Master Voice* of 1954 (Figure 10) or the *Xmas Tree* (ca. 1954), a grand assemblage incorporating record player, fan, fender, clocks, bells, springs, wheels, and sockets. Around 1956 he started using flattened beer cans in his constructions, aging them with acid if they were not sufficiently rusty when he found them; he later worked directly with unflattened cans, such as the giant *Ceiling Wings of Brew '52* of 1958 (Figure 11).

By the late fifties a number of younger San Francisco artists around Hedrick and the Six Gallery were involved in "Funky" art. These included Joan Brown, Manuel Neri, Fred Martin, and Jay De Feo. In 1957, the Fillmore Street group was joined by Wallace Berman, who came north from Los Angeles after his first and only gallery show of assemblages was closed by the police.[11] Berman moved to a barge at Larkspur, just north of San Francisco along with a follower, George Herms; and their place became a social center for the San Francisco artists. Berman had

154

Figure 10 *(top)*. Wally Hedrick. *His Master Voice.* 1954. Metal, 48″ high.

Figure 11 *(bottom)*. Wally Hedrick. *Ceiling Wings of Brew '52.* 1958. Welded beer cans, 7′ x 5′.

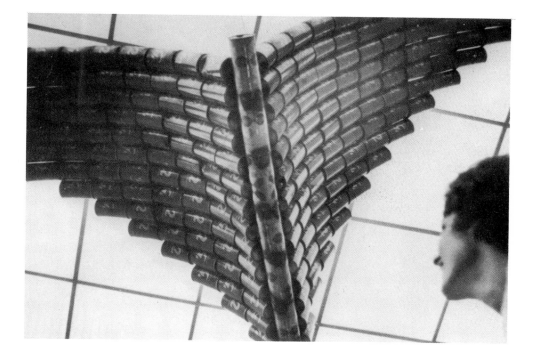

started making Surrealist, proto-Pop drawings in 1947, featuring such popular personalities as Harry the Hipster and Nat King Cole; and he turned to assemblage about two years later. By the time he came to San Francisco, according to Hedrick, he was "post-Beatnik," or "pre-Hippie." Berman's impact in San Francisco seems to have stemmed from his personality and his bridging of Beat poetry and underground art rather than his assemblages; for his main activity during his stay was the distribution of poetry, photo-montages, and drawings.

A more significant contribution to the assemblage group came rather from Bruce Conner (b. 1933), a native of Kansas who migrated to San Francisco a few months before Berman. Conner had been making collages for several years, but after his arrival in San Francisco, he began filling nylon stockings with small, discarded objects, ranging from jewelry and buttons to letters and photographs. Products of deliberation and chance with the option of being taken very seriously or not seriously at all, these sacklike assemblages bordered on the magical and grotesque. In 1959 Conner made his accumulations more sculptural by building up three-dimensional forms with black wax. Although an air of nostalgia persisted, the generally suggestive tone of the earlier work gave way to specific thematic content: *Nineteenth Century* (1959), *Bedroom Love Nest* (1959), and *Spider Lady* (1959). His works also became decidedly more biting and pessimistic. *Child* of 1959 (Figure 12), a mutilated doll in a stocking-swathed high chair, provoked reactions of shock and indignation when it was first shown at the DeYoung Museum in San Francisco.

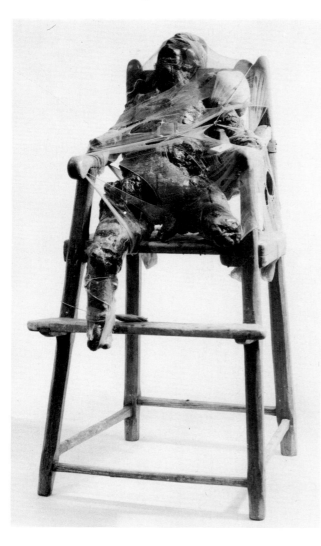

Figure 12. Bruce Conner. *Child.* 1959.
Wax, wood, nylon, 35″ high.
(Museum of Modern Art, New York.)

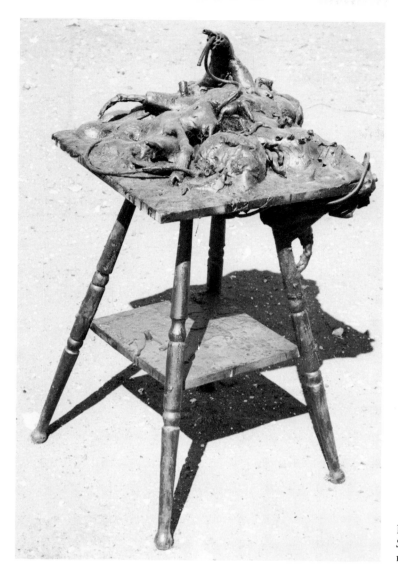

Figure 13. Bruce Conner. *The Last Supper.* 1960. Wax, wood, metal, etc., 36″ high.

Similar responses greeted his religious subjects, like *The Last Supper* of 1960 (Figure 13). During a visit to Mexico in 1961–62, Conner began to include native objects in his assemblages, anticipating, in effect, the Indian fad which later swept the Haight-Ashbury district. While in Mexico, Conner began to make films and won first prize in the 1962 Art Annual with his 16 millimeter *Bruce Conner's Movie.* In 1964 he received a Ford Foundation grant for filmmaking; and at that point, he explains, he ceased to be a sculptor, collagemaker, and craftsman in order to become a filmmaker who does sculpture, collage, and crafts. Since that time, however, he has stopped exhibiting his work in galleries and museums, which he dismisses as a "form of death in life," [12] cutting off the work of art from the artist. Such a gesture is consistent not only with the rest of Conner's activity, but also with the Funky attitude of underground art in San Francisco.

In 1960 Conner formed the Ratbastard Protective Association, the "first organized Funky art religion," which included in its eternal membership Joan Brown, Jay De Feo, Art Grant, Wally Hedrick, Fred Martin, and Manuel Neri. Their activities, like Dada nights at the Stile's Place Bar and poetry readings at the Six Gallery, were Happenings before there were Happenings, and as such were spontaneous and ephemeral.

Much of the Funk sculpture of the fifties has literally disintegrated because of the indiscriminate materials used. As Conner's antipathy toward museums graphically indicates, however, permanence was of little importance; the artists were looking for expedience of execution and directness of expression. The non-art attitude, with its preference for assemblage, domination of content over form, and undercurrent of wit and eroticism, is deeply imbedded among San Francisco artists.

Manuel Neri (b. 1930) was a product of the California School of Arts and Crafts in Oakland where he met the ceramist Peter Voulkos. Neri started working in clay in 1949, having been taken by its sensuous quality. He refers to clay, as "a fantastically sexy medium . . . you get your hands into and physically manipulate it." [13] After he returned from military service in the Korean War, Neri continued using clay for a while, but around 1956 he began to experiment in plaster. In a solo show at the San Francisco Museum of Art in 1957 he exhibited huge plaster figures that incorporated lumber and cardboard liberally painted in a De Kooning-like manner. At this time he was associated with Bay Area Abstract-Expressionist painters James Weeks and David Park. Weeks's way of manipulating paint and Park's figurative style would continue to dominate Neri's sculpture into the early sixties (Figure 14).

Figure 14. Manuel Neri. *Untitled.* 1963. Painted plaster, 68" high. (Private Collection.)

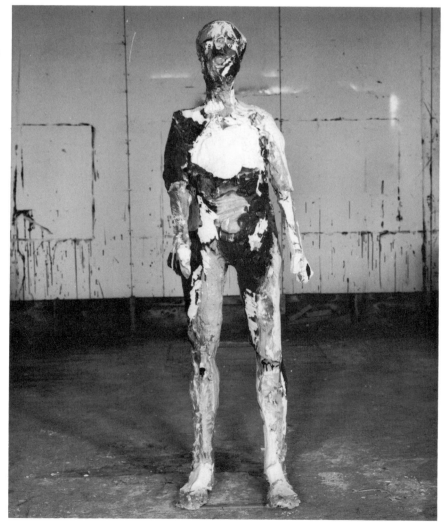

Figure 15 *(left)*. Alvin Light. *June, 1961.* 1961. Hardwoods, 115″ high. (Golden Gateway Collection.)

Figure 16 *(right)*. Arlo Acton. *Tumblers Last Tumble.* 1962. Hardwoods, 45″ high. (Collection, Mr. and Mrs. Arthur Formichelli, Berkeley, California.)

One sculptor who exhibited with Neri and others at the Spatsa Gallery, but who followed his own inclination toward a permanent classical style was Alvin Light (b. 1931). In the early fifties, Light studied at the California School of Fine Arts where he was greatly influenced by the Abstract Expressionist painter Frank Lobdell, and he returned to the school in 1956 to complete the BFA and newly-established MFA programs. In addition to his work with Lobdell he took sculpture courses with Robert Howard and Jeremy Anderson, but by 1958 he had developed his own distinctive approach to wood sculpture. Using both lumber and natural wood, Light glued pieces together and carved them away in a continuous operation to create structures which were both tectonic and organic as his *June, 1961* (Figure 15). The resulting forms have much in common with the interconnected organic shapes of Lobdell's paintings during the late fifties, such as *2 May 1955* or *April 1959.* Light's idiom altered little during the sixties, except for an increasing use of colored enamel, freely daubed on the wood and added to the glue, accentuating the changing character of the forms.

Arlo Acton (b. 1933) came to San Francisco in 1959 and entered the masters program at the California School of Fine Arts along with Light. Possibly influenced by Light, he too began working with wood, first carving and then making constructions. In the early sixties Acton started using found wooden shapes and objects, creating pieces by less carving than assembling, like *Tumblers Last Tumble* of 1962 (Figure 16), an assemblage of wooden forms capped with a protruding shoe   159

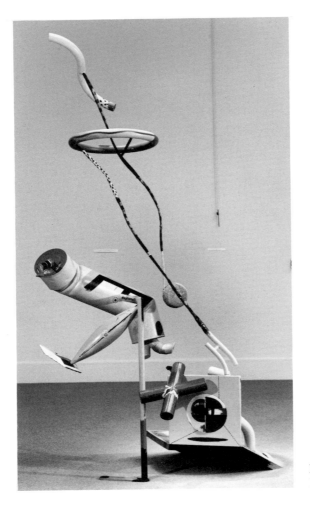

Figure 17. Robert Hudson. *Inside Out.* 1964. Painted metal, 104″ high.

tree. Around 1964 he became disenchanted with the limitations of wood, however, and began incorporating metal objects into the sculpture and working with moving parts intended to be activated by the viewer. In 1966 he devised an altogether new format: combinations of highly polished metal spheres which rock or spin on formica bases. Acton had included army surplus parts in earlier assemblages, and for the new pieces, he found that he could use rejected rocket fuel tanks to avoid the costly process of spinning the spheres on a metal lathe. Acton's spheres are "found" objects transformed from their original drab state as an economical substitute for custom-made originals, and have none of the connotations usually associated with found object usage. The shiny surfaces and clean geometric shapes of these pieces appear to be a departure from his wood sculpture, revealing, instead, the influence of the Bauhaus-oriented design training he received as an undergraduate at Washington State University. Consistent with his earlier constructions, however, is a general concern for surface effects, the comic-erotic appearance of the gangly rods projecting from the spheres and producing a jerky, systematic movement, and the attempt to involve the viewer with the workings of the pieces.

Acton places himself in a period of transition between Abstract Expressionism and a "new sense," [14] which is not limited to the negative anti-"serious art" reaction of the Funky underground, but exhibits a synthesis of Abstract Expressionism and formal assemblage. A non-art aesthetic, opposed to what Acton calls "art on a pedestal," prevails in the new sense, but revived interest in techniques and materials has brought greater emphasis to bear on form and craftsmanship.

Figure 18. Robert Hudson. *Skeptical Space*. 1965. Painted metal, 45″ x 30″ x 30″.

A whole group of artists, mostly graduates of the California School of Fine Arts, retained strong ties with both the Abstract Expressionism of the early fifties and the so-called Eccentric Abstraction of the second half of the decade. Many of the sculptors, including Robert Hudson, William Geis, and William Wiley, began their careers as painters, and their work retains strong ties with painting, almost to the point of negating sculptural form.

Robert Hudson (b. 1938), who received a BFA at the San Francisco Art Institute in 1962 and an MFA there in 1963, moved from painting to leather sculpture and constructions, and finally arrived at welding as the "easiest way to put things together." His first metal sculpture came out of the tradition of David Smith, Roszak (whose retrospective appeared at the San Francisco Museum in the spring of 1957), and Wilfrid Zogbaum, and developed into a kind of comic abstraction once described as a cross between Stankiewicz and Dr. Seuss.[15] The sculptural effects that arose from the maze of gangling shapes and found objects were completely overpowered by the brightly-colored motifs painted on the metal. Running the gamut from geometric patterns to surreal or psychedelic designs, the surface decoration in pieces such as *Inside Out* of 1964 (Figure 17) or *Skeptical Space* of 1965 (Figure 18) produces a mock epic effect where the metal itself is practically reduced to the role of armature. Although he continued to minimize formal preoccupations in his sculpture, Hudson's work of the mid-sixties became increasingly geometric and spatially involved. Sharper contours and angles appear in *Skylight* of 1964; the painted steel *Space Window* of 1966 replaces found objects with prefabricated parts, and *Discoflex* (1967) is strikingly simplified in form and surface design compared with the elaborate structures of the early sixties.

161

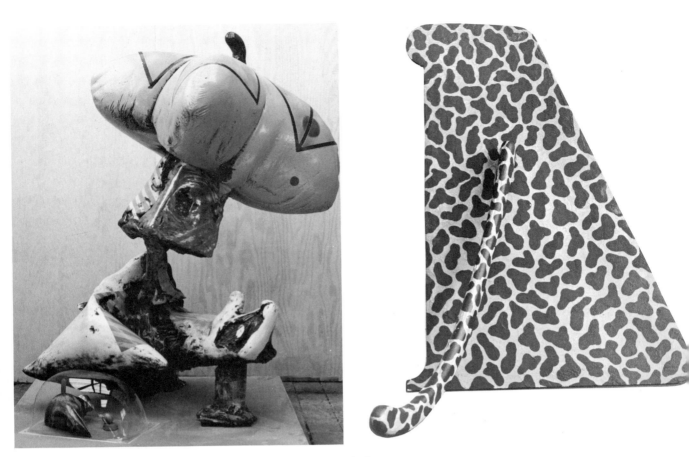

Figure 19 *(left)*. William Geis. *Chic'y of Insult un.* 1966. Painted plaster.

Figure 20 *(right)*. William Wiley. *Enigma Bone.* 1964. Mixed media, 48″ x 24″ x 54″.

Closely related in attitude to Hudson are two of his fellow-students at the Art Institute, William Geis (b. 1940) and William Wiley (b. 1937). Geis has been labeled "one of the Bay Area's finest monster makers" [16] for his organic polychrome sculptures which erupt in masses of plaster within metal, wood, and plastic-containing shapes (Figure 19). Geis is the mystic to Hudson's magician, relying heavily on automatism and emphasizing self-liberation and discovery as the goals toward which his sculpture is directed. Much of Geis's imagery goes back to Still and Lobdell, who was his teacher at the Art Institute. This imagery is merged with the jarring forms and colors of psychedelic art, however, to create sculpture which is as improbable as Hudson's early works and vaguely menacing.

Wiley's work is the most explicit and verbal of the Hudson-Wiley-Geis group, coming out of the didactic tradition of Marcel Duchamp, Jasper Johns, and Robert Rauschenberg that colored so much of San Francisco assemblage. Wiley holds to no definition of sculpture or non-sculpture; he first exhibited as a painter, collaborated with Hudson and Ronald Davis on a Happening called *Schultz Eats Rats* in 1961, designed sets and costumes for Davis's San Francisco Mime Troupe production of Alfred Jarry's *King Ubu* in 1963, and then began making object sculpture in a wide variety of materials. Wiley plays on multi-level associations and the power of artistic transformation to generate a sense of the enigmatic that echoes De Chirico and Magritte. His visual and verbal puns are often sexual, but far more humorous than erotic—such as *Enigma Bone* of 1964 (Figure 20), a leopard-spotted hockey stick

Figure 21. Don Potts. *Untitled.* 1965. Wood and fur, 30″ x 30″.

projecting from a similarly patterned background. Like most dialogue art, Wiley's sculpture is highly introspective; it raises frequent questions about the nature of art itself and makes explicit references to the mechanics of art and art history, as in his famous copy of Helen Gardner's *Art Through the Ages*, served up in a canvas bag sealed with beeswax (1966).

Wiley's predisposition toward "art about art" is shared by two other San Francisco artists who are generally considered his protégés: William Allen and Bruce Nauman. Allen knew Wiley and Hudson in high school and joined them at the Art Institute as a painting student. Early in the sixties he began making constructions, notably out of lead toothpaste tubes. Around 1964 he took up a modified assemblage approach in the form of collections of objects neatly presented in shallow glass cases. In contrast to most other assemblage, and in particular to the boxes of Joseph Cornell and George Herms, however, Allen did not deal with found objects, but with collected, and even "renovated" ones running from decorated lima beans to test tubes full of lint. These are presented illustratively rather than expressively. Moreover, in order to convey a particular way of looking at various phenomena, such as *Architects' Nature Trees*, he fashioned a kit containing handmade stereopticon slides of ultra-green, antiseptic trees for the architects who envision nature in terms of the pieces of sponge they use in their models. Bruce Nauman was similarly involved with "idea pieces," as Allen calls them.[17]

Operating on the outer fringes of the Hudson-Wiley-Geis circle was Don Potts (b. 1936), who began making sculpture in the early sixties. Potts worked with black encaustic in 1964, modeling wall plaques and then massive free-standing sculpture with a distinctive hide-like surface. The following year he became involved with laminated wood and made a series of large, meticulously-crafted pieces in wood and fur, all of which are graphically sexual, generating a kind of bawdy humor but at the same time achieving a sensual beauty of a high order (Figure 21). An analogous combination of delicate sensuality and forcefulness governs the project Potts worked on for more than two years—a full-scale dragster chassis, nominally functional, but created principally as an illusion of speed and power (Figure 22). Potts has been guided mainly by his own ingenuity. Operating outside the conventions of both auto mechanics and sculpture, he has fashioned the chassis from such diverse materials as racing bike wheels, wheelchair spokes, go-cart brakes, surplus valves from F-111 bombers, and a two-cycle aircraft engine with a maximum speed of ten miles per hour. He intends to fabricate a series of bodies in fiberglass and aluminum and to exhibit the finished car in hot rod shows as well as strictly art environments.

163

Figure 22. Don Potts. *My First Car (The Master Chassis)*. 1970. Mixed media. (Photo: M. D. Hamer.)

Although the "Funky" attitude toward art would continue to prevail in Bay Area sculpture, important changes occurred in the mid-sixties, brought about partly by the migration of New York Pop Art to California, but also by the move of Peter Voulkos from Los Angeles to Berkeley in 1958 and his subsequent influence on many young Bay Area sculptors.

Voulkos (b. 1924) had begun making pottery at Montana State University in the late forties, did graduate work at the California College of Arts and Crafts in Oakland from 1950 to 1952, and then taught ceramics at the Archie Bray Foundation in Montana and Black Mountain College in North Carolina. It was in Los Angeles, however, that he began visiting museums and galleries and where he came in contact with the New York Abstract Expressionists. Greatly impressed with their work, he became dissatisfied with the decorative nature of his ceramics and sought a more expressive use of the clay medium. Remaining within the limits of his craft, Voulkos dispensed with symmetry and began to enrich the surface colors and textures of his pots in the manner of the Abstract Expressionist paintings. In 1954 he was hired to set up a ceramics department at Otis Art Institute.

Voulkos's reputation drew many students to Otis, and when the ceramics effort there burgeoned into sculpture, it was a collaborative effort. John Mason (b. 1927), who had been studying ceramics at Chouinard, teamed with him; they were then joined by Kenneth Price, Billy Al Bengston, and Malcolm McLain; later, Michael Frimkess and Henry Takemoto. The group worked fourteen hours a day, seven days a week, turning out as many as one hundred pots a day.[18] They had little awareness of a "Southern California clay movement," according to Mason, but were simply looking for something that was "not a copy of past work and fun to do." [19]

Voulkos's first sculptures consisted of slabs of clay piled into asymmetrical blocks over an armature of thrown cylinders. Committed to an Abstract Expressionist aesthetic, he was nonetheless greatly inspired by the slab-like configurations of the Cubist sculptor Fritz Wotruba, carrying into his own work Wotruba's handling

164

of mass and void.[20] By the late fifties his scale moved out of the range of pottery with massive structures like *Rondena* (1958) and *Little Big Horn* of 1959 (Figure 23). Abandoning the craft concept of "truth to the medium," he used epoxy glue to join separate units together, replaced glazes with brushed enamel, and began to use color as a means of altering and denying the form of the clay itself.

John Mason's first ceramic sculpture consisted of Abstract Expressionist reliefs emphasizing the responsiveness of the clay with rich, agitated surfaces. Only three years younger than Voulkos, Mason had first come to Otis in 1949 on the GI Bill. He switched to Chouinard in 1951, after he became interested in pottery, but remained dissatisfied with the uniformly technical approach that was applied to ceramics. He had seen the ceramic sculpture of Picasso at the Frank Perls Gallery and that of Miró at the Los Angeles County Museum and was struck by their imaginative manipulation of material. Like Voulkos, however, he was attracted to the vigorous handling of their medium by the action painters rather than to the decorative effects of the European artists (Figure 24). After the reliefs, Mason began making large, free-standing sculpture in 1957, building up the clay in pieces, modeling the surface with his hands, and then adding splashes of color. As he became more involved with color, however, Mason found that the broken surfaces were disruptive. He began to solidify his forms, arriving in the early sixties at simple x- and cross-shapes which were further reduced to hard-edge rectangular solids colored with glazes.

Diverging from the scale, ruggedness, and expressiveness of both Voulkos's and Mason's ceramic sculpture is the work of Kenneth Price (b. 1935). After attending the University of Southern California Price went to Alfred University in New York State, the oldest ceramics school in the country. Unlike the intuitive approach of Voulkos and Mason, Price received a thoroughly technical instruction dealing with clay as a material to be used for scientific and engineering as well as for creative purposes.[21] When he returned to Los Angeles in 1959, Price began fashioning little

Figure 23. Peter Voulkos. *Little Big Horn*. 1959. Colored fired clay. About 60″ high. (Oakland Art Museum, Oakland, California.)

Figure 24. John Mason. *Gray Wall.* 1960. Clay, 7' x 14'.

hinged boxes with glass fronts in which he displayed his ceramic cups, along with illustrative collage materials. The cups gave way to non-functional, ceramic forms; these in turn developed into independent sculpture in organic, pod-like shapes with slender protuberances visible through circular openings. The forms recall the biomorphic sculpture of Brancusi and Arp (and have been traced back to Price's college lab drawings of primitive organisms), but go beyond them with their own Surrealistic, fetishistic quality. Since 1962 Price has been working with serial images spray-painted in a variety of brilliant car colors, beginning with smoothly delineated egg-shapes, punctuated with mysterious apertures and decorated with bands and patches of contrasting color. Price has also become interested in less regular forms more uniformly colored, such as the dented *S. L. Blue* (1966) or the bulbous *S. D. Green* of 1966 (Colorplate 4).

Peter Voulkos was hired at Otis as a master potter, but the school was less receptive to his unprecedented work as a ceramic sculptor, and in 1958 he was dismissed. He left Los Angeles and joined the faculty at the University of California, Berkeley, where another group of students formed around him, among them Michael Frimkess from Los Angeles, Ron Nagle, Stephen De Staebler and James Melchert.

Figure 25. Stephen De Stabler. *A Man.* 1964. Fired clay, 20" x 71".

Figure 26. James Melchert. *Still Life with Rapt Heart*. 1965. Painted clay, 15″ x 15″ x 8″. (Collection, Gerald Hoptner, Davis, California.)

De Staebler (b. 1933) is the only one of this group to continue in the expressionist vein of Voulkos and Mason, while Frimkess, Nagle, and Melchert remain much closer to the San Francisco assemblage and Funk sculptors. After receiving a degree from Princeton University, De Staebler undertook an M.A. under Voulkos at Berkeley, graduating in 1961. Throughout the early sixties his ceramic sculpture received awards in Bay Area exhibitions. Around 1964 De Staebler's sculpture shifted from the landscape sensibility that was implicit in Voulkos's work to one involving human forms embedded in the landscape, like *A Man* of 1964 (Figure 25) which is associated with the Genesis myth of creation from clay. Resisting the influence of New York Pop imagery, as he had also resisted Funkiness, De Staebler remained a fundamental humanist; his sculpture went through what he felt to be the "artificial stimulation" of Pop culture. In 1965 he wrote: "If something is shiny enough, or shocking enough, it's supposed to con us into that cockle-warming feeling that we're alive and swinging. I want to put a human being someplace less whimsical than in this year's car." [22]

James Melchert (b. 1930) first met Voulkos at the 1958 summer session of Montana State University; he then came to Berkeley as a graduate student in design. Melchert had graduated from Princeton in 1952, taught English in Japan for four years, and then switched to art at the University of Chicago. After finishing his master's degree at Berkeley in 1961, he was hired to head the ceramics department at the San Francisco Art Institute. There he began making object sculpture out of clay, such as *Door F* and *Legpot* (1962); he then evolved toward more contrived images, drawing heavily on literary symbolism and on Pop iconography. The series of masks, ghost heads, and ceramic assemblages from the mid-sixties can be compared to the seventeenth-century still life genre, *momenti mori* in modern guise, such as the *Still Life with Rapt Heart* of 1965 (Figure 26) and *Silvery Heart* (1965). In the more recent *game* series, consisting of ceramic objects distributed on large checkered game boards, Melchert uses the Wittgensteinian game format to involve

167

Figure 27. Robert Arneson. *Typewriter.* 1965. Ceramic, 10″ x 12″. (University Art Museum, University of California, Berkeley, California. Photo: Ron Chamberlain.)

the viewer in dealing with relationships among the objects, or evidence, that he has assembled. Some pieces are cast from real objects; others bear short comic-strip like captions. As a result, the inherent properties of the clay become almost incidental.

Melchert's use of the ceramic medium is at the opposite pole from the attitude of Voulkos and Mason. It is common, however, to a number of Bay Area sculptors who were associated with the newly-established ceramics department at the University of California, Davis. This group, which grew up around Department Chairman Robert Arneson,[23] has represented for Northern California sculptors the same liberation from craft conventions, as had Voulkos's circle in the south.

Arneson (b. 1930) studied ceramics at Mills College with Antonio Prieto, a much-respected ceramist in Northern California. In 1962 he went to Davis to set up a ceramics department, and began making ceramic sculpture as well as pottery there. Like Melchert, Arneson uses Pop imagery, but confines himself to single objects, creating ceramic six-packs, telephones, and typewriters, miniature toilets, like *Throne* (1967), and numerous models of his house in Davis. Vestiges of hand-modeling and a shiny teacup-finish preserve their ceramic appearance sufficiently to play on the translation of materials in the manner of Claes Oldenburg's soft sculpture. At the same time, Arneson injects his own Surrealist shock value in the form of comic asides, as in his *Typewriter* of 1965 (Figure 27), where the usual keyboard is replaced with a matrix of brightly-enameled fingertips.

By the time that Davis was a focus of activity in ceramics, Berkeley had become the center of another ambitious sculptural enterprise. The same year that Peter Voulkos came to Berkeley, Harold Paris (b. 1925), a New York sculptor who had just returned from four years in Europe, was hired to teach bronze casting. There were no foundry facilities in the area, however, and Paris set up temporary headquarters in the ceramics workshop. Voulkos, meanwhile, had found that he was no longer committed to ceramics and teaching, as he had been in Los Angeles, and was searching for a new medium. When Donald Haskins, who had operated a foundry in Minnesota, was brought to Berkeley to start a foundry in 1960, Voulkos, Paris, and Haskins collaborated. They built their own equipment in a space rented from the Engineering Alloy Foundry in Berkeley. Haskins contributed his knowledge of foundry operation, Paris his experience in bronze casting, and Voulkos his reputation. In 1961 they were joined by Julius Schmidt, a skilled iron sculptor from the Cranbrook Academy of Art, Michigan and soon the Garbanzo Works, as the foundry was called, had involved some thirty or forty sculptors, or sculpture students.[24]

Although the operation produced no radical innovations of technique, as the ceramics effort had done, the totally collaborative project contributed greatly to individual developments. For Voulkos, the new material enabled him to work on a larger scale than that permitted by clay. At the same time he was able to retain the immediacy of hand modeling through the sensitivity of the wax casting process. In his earlier pieces, slabs of bronze were joined on a movable wooden base, either piled together like the ceramic sculpture, as in *Bad Day at Shattuck* of 1962–64 (Figure 28), or strung out in a rhythmic sequence, as in *Vargas* (1961–64). After several years of this mode, which was basically a continuation of his ceramic sculpture, Voulkos turned to a more controlled appearance with regular shapes and smooth surfaces, consisting of undulating tubes of bronze or aluminum set within a rectangular framework—seen in *Hiro* (1964–65) and *Big A* of 1964–65 (Figure 29).

Harold Paris meanwhile had been working with explosive organic forms—unpleasant images with tortured surfaces—while in France. At Berkeley, however, he altered his style, replacing violent expressionism with a measure of control and poise—seen as in his *Blue Hour I* of 1963 (Figure 30). Along with McIntyre, Paris began to cast from real objects, creating a kind of found object in bronze, which included a series of chairs rescued from second-hand stores and immortalized as *The Big Chair, Clementine,* and *Throne Figure* (1961). While he was working in the ceramics shop at Berkeley, Paris also became interested in clay sculpture and executed a series of three ceramic walls; later he constructed complete rooms

Figure 28. Peter Voulkos, *Bad Day at Shattuck.* 1962–64. Cast bronze. About 48″ x 60″.

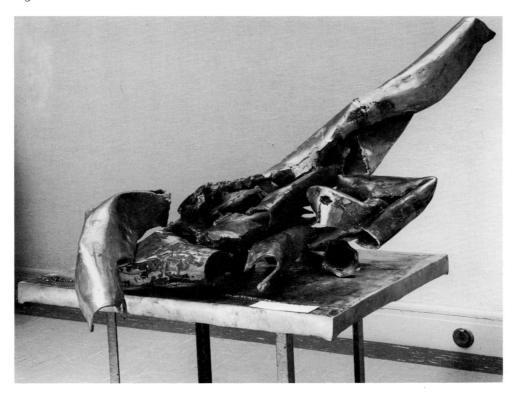

Figure 29. Peter Voulkos. *Big A*. 1964–65. Bronze, aluminum oxide, 111″ high. (Fresno City. Photo: Joanne Leonard.)

Figure 30. Harold Paris. *Blue Hour I*. 1963. Bronze, 102″ x 90″ x 36″.

Figure 31. Harold Paris. *Room I.* 1965. Mixed media, 43′ x 22′ x 12′.

involving shapes cast in rubber, like *Room I* of 1965 (Figure 31). These pieces follow the Abstract Expressionist mode of Voulkos and John Mason, who was a visiting professor at Berkeley in 1960, but retain the organic, erotic forms of Paris's bronzes from the fifties.

Following the success of the Garbanzo Works, Haskins and Voulkos set up their own foundry in Berkeley. Paris worked in the pot shop, and Tio Giambruni was hired to start another foundry at Davis. Before he began casting, Giambruni had been working in magnesite, creating horizontal forms somewhat in the manner of Picasso's bone figures. He was dissatisfied with the impermanence of the material, however, and like Voulkos, was looking for a new medium when the foundry activity began. His earliest works in bronze exhibit a debt to the expressionist imagery of Roszak, whose retrospective Giambruni had also seen in San Francisco in 1956. Around 1963 he switched to smaller closed forms with a definite frontal orientation, and in several instances applied pencil drawings to the flat surfaces. Seeking a more direct-casting method, he began to work with aluminum rather than bronze, and in this material created his most distinctive sculpture—great tubes of individually cast circular units that resemble steam conduits or sewer pipes and that wind along the floor to envelop the viewer in their self-contained environment.

A few New York sculptors settled in San Francisco, but the trend of movement between the two centers has been from West to East, bringing artists such as Ronald Bladen, Mark di Suvero, Peter Forakis, and Robert Morris from the San Francisco Art Institute to the New York scene. By contrast, with the appearance of good commercial galleries in Los Angeles in the late fifties, New York as well as European artists became frequent visitors. The Dwan Gallery, in particular, operating from 1959 to 1965, was responsible for the visits of Yves Klein, Larry Rivers, Niki de St.-Phalle, Claes Oldenburg, Jean Tinguely, Ray Parker, Arman, Ad Reinhardt, Martial Raysse, and Robert Rauschenberg, while Pop artists Andy Warhol and Roy Lichtenstein had shows in Los Angeles before the big Pop Art breakthrough in New York.[25]

The effort to identify a native Los Angeles art scene was made first by Edward Kienholz, Walter Hopps, and then Irving Blum with the Ferus Gallery. Had Kienholz never created the tableaux for which he is now famous, wrote Maurice Tuchman in 1966, he would still be known as a "builder and owner of vanguard galleries."[26] Kienholz (b. 1927) came to Los Angeles in 1953 from Las Vegas, and three years later, started the Now Gallery in the lobby of the Turnabout Theatre, which exhibited the works of painters, sculptors, and "allied artists," including filmmakers, who were not represented in the commercial galleries.[27] In 1957, the gallery was merged with Walter Hopps's Syndell Gallery to create the Ferus Gallery, which gained in stature through the presentation of the "spiritual descendants" of the California School of Fine Arts—Still, Hassel Smith, Richard Diebenkorn, Sonia Gechtoff, and Julius Wasserstein.[28] In 1959, with the accession of Irving Blum, the native Ferus group emerged. The artists represented at that time were mostly "tough-minded, younger locals, who knew what was going on in New York and San Francisco, and who negated almost everything then going on in Los Angeles."[29]

Kienholz, meanwhile, had left the gallery and had begun making assemblages. He had come to Los Angeles as an Abstract Expressionist painter; soon after his arrival he did a series of paintings with wooden projections, and then three-dimensional constructions with material culled from neighborhood thrift shops. The junk assemblage was not as popular in Los Angeles as it was in San Francisco, and Wally Berman, whose 1957 show Kienholz arranged at the Ferus Gallery, was probably the only other assemblagist of note working there at that time. Kienholz was regarded as somewhat of an eccentric and worked by himself. He denies the influence of any other artist except for Julius Wasserstein, whose paintings were shown at the Ferus. Attracted by the ugliness he saw in them, explains Kienholz, he consciously sought to eliminate aesthetic appeal from his own work. The ghoulish figure of *John Doe* (1959) was his first free-standing piece, followed by *Jane Doe*, and a number of polemic works, bringing various documentary items together, usually in a box-like format, such as *Psycho-Vendetta Case* (1960), referring to the execution of Sacco and Vanzetti, or *History As a Planter*, which calls into question the lessons actually learned from past events.

In 1961 Kienholz expanded the theatrical nature of the object pieces into life-size tableaux. Intensifying the characteristics of the earlier assemblages, the tableaux offered more pointed social commentary, deeper psychological drama, and greater involvement of the viewer as a result of the mode of presentation. A clamor developed around Kienholz's 1966 retrospective at the Los Angeles County Museum because of his *Back Seat Dodge '38* of 1964 (Figure 32), which depicted a pair of lovemaking teenagers strewn across the back seat of a truncated car.[30]

Less controversial was *The Beanery* of 1964–65 (Figure 33), which recreates on a two-thirds lifesize scale, the bar of the venerable restaurant located just off Sunset Strip. A newspaper outside the door is dated August 28, 1964; inside, Barney and his customers are grouped around the bar, all but Barney sporting clocks in place of

Figure 32 *(top)*. Edward Kienholz. *Back Seat Dodge '38*. 1964. Mixed media tableau, 20′ x 12′ x 5′6″.

Figure 33 *(bottom)*. Edward Kienholz. *The Beanery*. 1964–65. Mixed media tableau, 22′ x 7′ x 6′.

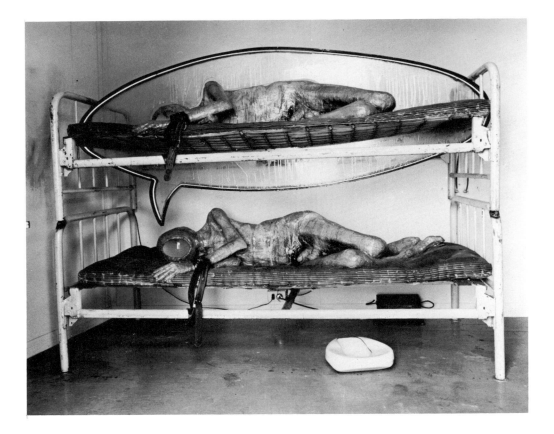

Figures 34, 35. Edward Kienholz. *The State Hospital.* 1964–66. Mixed media tableau, 8' x 12' x 10'.

heads. These have uniformly ceased to function at 2:10, while the clock behind the bar has started running backwards. A jukebox stands in the corner, presenting jibes at the art world with titles like "It's Delightful, It's Delovely, It's DeKooning." "The whole thing," explains Kienholz, "symbolizes going from real time—the August 28 headline—to Surrealist time inside the bar where people waste time, lose time, escape time, ignore time." [31] The same preoccupation which appeared in *History As a Planter* recurs throughout the tableaux: the specific moment is captured in *The Birthday* (1964), the era in *Back Seat Dodge '38* and *Roxy's* (1961), and the perpetuity of time in *The Wait* (1964). This theme, which is both real and surreal, serves to strengthen the moral pronouncements that are everywhere present, singling out the bordello in *Roxy's*, abortion in *The Illegal Operation*, or public institutions in *The State Hospital* of 1964–66 (Figures 34, 35). "I am a romantic;" declared Kienholz, "I preach." [32]

Kienholz's tableaux have been distinguished from Pop Art, notably the re-creations of Segal and Oldenburg, because of his apparent disregard for style or form-consciousness.[33] Elsewhere the distinction is made between collector's art and Kienholz's "studio art," the "inconvenient work of art." [34] At the same time, however, the tableaux stand apart from underground assemblage in their attention to craftsmanship and the subtle transformation of the objects to make up a flawless presentation. In this respect Kienholz is a typically Los Angeles artist.

The combined effects of Kienholz and Pop Art are seen in the work of Tony Berlant (b. 1941), one of the youngest Los Angeles sculptors. Berlant became acquainted with Kienholz in 1951, and participated in Claes Oldenburg's Happenings in 1962. Oldenburg was making his giant shirts at that time, and the following year Berlant, a student at UCLA, started working with constructions of painted female figures decked out in real clothing. In 1964 he turned to collages made out of metal scraps cut out of toys, cans, cookie tins, serving trays, and all that Los Angeles junk shops had to offer. Combining this technique with the earlier female images, Berlant made his first *house* series in 1965. Looking like large Monopoly pieces, the houses consisted of wooden frames which were completely covered with metal scraps, forming human figures on one or more sides. Later houses had window-like openings on all four sides that reveal within single found objects, toy animals, plastic guns, and bowling balls. In 1967 Berlant began to make large-scale houses out of plywood covered with aluminum. Maintaining the ritualistic quality of the miniature houses, which he calls "fetish objects," Berlant used the columnar temple form for the large ones, variously modernized in *The Marriage of New York and Athens* of 1966 (Figure 36) and split apart in *The Cracked White House*. Berlant considers the house a "comfortable format" which is rich in associations, contributing to a non-art effect, and the product of considerable labor.

Similar concerns are manifest in the leather sculpture of Stephan Von Heune (b. 1932). Trained as a painter, he began making sculpture out of bread, wood, and leather in 1964, and since then has been working with leather over wood to create complex anatomical forms, such as the *Hermaphroditic Horseback Rider* of 1966 (Figure 37). Combining his sculpture with a long-term interest in machines, Von Heune also constructed from 1965 to 1967 a whimsical music machine— the *Kaleidoscopic Dog*, which was operated by means of vacuum-controlled pressure.

Apart from the work of Kienholz, Berlant, and Von Heune, which has much in common with the eccentric art of Northern California, the predominant trend in recent Los Angeles sculpture has been toward a refinement of form, exclusive of non-visual content, and great attention paid to surface effects. Here the influence of Pop Art, with its appreciation of commercial appearances and processes cannot be underestimated; but even before there was a Pop Art movement, Los Angeles was a

175

Figure 36. Tony Berlant. *The Marriage of New York and Athens*. 1966. Aluminum over plywood, 124″ high.

Figure 37. Stephan Von Huene. *The Hermaphroditic Horseback Rider*. 1966. Wood and leather, 78″ x 26″ x 29″. (Collection, John Gibbon.)

Pop Art city, and the Funk Art of the San Francisco Bay Area was rooted in the soil of the nostalgic past that has always nourished its culture.

NOTES

1. William T. Wiley in an interview with Joe Raffaele, December 1966, cited in Maurice Tuchman, *American Sculpture of the Sixties* (Los Angeles: Los Angeles County Museum of Art 1967), p. 52.

2. See Kurt Von Meier, "Los Angeles: The Failure and Future of Art," *Art International* 11, no. 5 (May 20, 1967): 54–57.

3. Herschel B. Chipp, "Art News from San Francisco," *Art News* 55, no. 1 (March 1956): 12.

4. Kent had exhibited in solo shows at the Betty Parsons Gallery in 1949 and 1953.

5. Clement Greenberg, "The New Sculpture," *Partisan Review* 16 (June 1949): 637–42.

6. John Coplans, "Sculpture in California," *Artforum* 2, no. 2 (August 1963): 4.

7. Richard Peterson in *Craft Horizon* 9, no. 10 (1956): 32.

8. See Jules Langsner, "Art News from Los Angeles," *Art News* 53, no. 5 (September 1954): 44, 54, and no. 1 (March 1955): 14. In 1951 the City Council had turned the annual exhibition held in the Greek Theater into a trial of modern art, where a witness from a group called "Sanity-in-Art" testified that modern art was a cryptic form of espionage, and that paintings were being used to transmit information about weak spots in United States fortifications. Their action was reversed the following year, but not before Huntington Hartford declared that abstractionists were ineligible for fellowships from his foundation on the grounds that abstract art was "out of touch with reality." See Jules Langsner, "Art News from Los Angeles," *Art News* 50, no. 8 (December 1951): 52ff., and Arthur Millier, "Los Angeles Events," *Arts Digest* 26 (January 15, 1952): 12.

9. Catalog of the exhibition at the Dilexi Gallery, San Francisco, 1963.

10. See mimeographed announcement in the archives of the California School of Fine Arts.

11. John Coplans, "Circle of Styles on the West Coast," *Art in America* 52 (June 1964): 36.

12. *Time* (January 5, 1968).

13. From a personal interview (June 3, 1970).

14. *San Francisco Chronicle* (August 13, 1965).

15. Fidel A. Danieli, "Robert Hudson," *Artforum* 6, no. 3 (November 1967): 32.

16. *San Francisco Chronicle* (October 18, 1967).

17. Nauman's work will be taken up in Chapter IX.

18. John Coplans, "Abstract Expressionist Ceramics," *Artforum* 5, no. 3 (November 1966): 34.

19. Quoted from a personal interview (June 15, 1968).

20. John Coplans, "Voulkos: Redemption through Ceramics," *Art News* 24, no. 4 (Summer 1965): 65.

21. Henry T. Hopkins, "Kenneth Price," *Artforum* 2, no. 2 (August 1963): 41.

22. From a letter to the author (March 25, 1965).

23. The group also included David Gilhooly, Stephen Kaltenbach, Richard Shaw, Peter VandenBerge, Chris Unterseher, and Gerald Waldburg.

24. Richard O'Hanlon, a long-time stone carver; Tio Giambruni, who was teaching at Arts and Crafts; and among the students, Bruce Beasley, Reed McIntyre, David Lynn, and Bill Underhill, as well as James Melchert and Stephen de Staebler.

25. Gerald John Nordland, "A Succession of Visitors," *Artforum* 2, no. 12 (Summer 1964): 64.

26. Maurice Tuchman, "A Decade of Edward Kienholz," *Artforum* 4, no. 8 (April 1966): 41.

27. Gerald John Nordland in *Frontier* 8, no. 2 (December 1956): 24.

28. Gerald John Nordland in *Frontier* 8, no. 7 (May 1957): 25.

29. Henry T. Hopkins in the introduction to the catalog of the "West Coast Now" exhibition (Portland, Oregon: Portland Art Museum, February 9–March 6, 1968).

30. *San Francisco Chronicle* (April 3, 1966), p. 23. After much debate, the tableau was allowed to remain in the show, but the door of the car was closed to all but the "sophisticated

adults" who took a one-hour tour of the entire exhibit to catch a fifteen-second glimpse of the interior of the car.

31. Tuchman, "Edward Kienholz," p. 44.

32. *San Francisco Chronicle* (April 3, 1966), p. 23.

33. Sidney Tillim, "The Underground Pre-Raphaelitism of Edward Kienholz," *Artforum* 4, no. 8 (April 1966): 40.

34. John Coplans, "Assemblage: The Savage Eye of Edward Kienholz," *Studio International* 170, no. 869 (September 1965): 112.

POP ART AND
POP SCULPTURE

VI

The Pop Art movement received immediate critical attention as well as official sanction from its beginnings in the early sixties. The tangent of the decade was previewed in 1960 when the Martha Jackson Gallery presented "New Media–New Forms" with the works of Jasper Johns, Robert Rauschenberg, Yves Klein, Claes Oldenburg, Jim Dine, Allan Kaprow, Chryssa, Robert Indiana and Red Grooms.[1] In 1962 the Sidney Janis Gallery organized "The New Realists" which featured Oldenburg, Dine, and Indiana, along with Roy Lichtenstein, James Rosenquist, George Segal, Andy Warhol, and Tom Wesselmann. On the West Coast, Walter Hopps exhibited "New Paintings of Common Objects" at the Pasadena Art Museum. The following year, the English critic Lawrence Alloway showed "Six Painters and the Object" at the Guggenheim, and "Popular Art" was offered by the Nelson Gallery in Kansas City.

By 1962 the American Pop Art movement was delineated around Lichtenstein, Oldenburg, Rosenquist, Warhol, and Wesselmann; Johns and Rauschenberg were identified as founding fathers, and artists like Indiana, Marisol, Dine, and Segal, as peripheral figures. However, the precise nature of the work which was being exhibited, reviewed, and patronized as Pop Art remained unclear, partly because critics had difficulty in distinguishing it from its British counterpart. The label, Pop Art, along with its correlative "Pop Culture," was first used by Alloway in the mid-fifties to describe a specific British phenomenon. In London, between the winter of 1954–55 and 1957, the term acquired currency in conversations and discussions about the "latent" art of popular culture—advertising, mass media, fashion, automobiles. Alloway has pointed out that the term did not originate in reference to a group of artists in England, not even to works of art that draw upon popular culture, but rather to mass media.[2] But as he himself later recognized in presenting the 1963 exhibition at the Guggenheim, this attempt to "oppose a broad view of culture to the prevailing exclusive one"[3] developed instead, and especially in New York, into an adaptation of the imagery, forms, and materials of popular culture to the category of fine art. Unprepared for such an adaptation, the public was stunned by the array of comic strips, soup cans, and advertising iconography; and the critics who might have seen beyond them were busy creating an historical overview, albeit from their critical perspective.

In a symposium on Pop Art sponsored by the Museum of Modern Art in December of 1962, critics Hilton Kramer and Stanley Kunitz bore down hard. Kramer accepted the movement only as a kind of "emancipation proclamation for the art critic" while relegating the works themselves to "a school of painting which has radically deprived art of significant visual events."[4] He blamed it all on Marcel Duchamp, whom he characterized as "the most overrated figure in modern art." Kunitz blamed it on the "art promoters" and predicted the movement would fade

179

into insignificance as little more than a "nine days' wonder." [5] The verdict of the remainder of the panel, and most criticism in the following years were more objective. Discussing "Dada Then and Now" in early 1963, Barbara Rose maintained that the return to imagery, in the form of "the recognizable object as we encounter it in everyday experience," was a common denominator among Pop artists, and she further characterized them as "icon painters" for their choice of subject matter.[6] Around the same time, Sidney Tillim attempted to deal with the attitude that the imagery reflected, which he saw as the pursuit of the "American Dream." [7] Robert Rosenblum, in a later article reflecting on the situation of the early sixties, pointed out that imagery was far from the whole story; for iconography, as he called it, had never proven sufficient grounds for the identification of an entire movement.[8] Rosenblum wished to establish a concurrence of subject and style; yet as it was pointed out much later, the imagery of Pop Art was so striking, so unexpected, so "outrageous," that formal concerns received little attention. In 1963, G. R. Swenson took the "What Is Pop Art" question directly to the artists in a series of eight interviews published in *Art News*. Lichtenstein, perhaps the most articulate of the Pop group, answered, "The use of commercial art as subject matter in painting," and Warhol made the now-famous statement that he would like to be a machine.[9]

In retrospect, it is apparent that the effort among critics to define a group art form was already under way before any one artist had established his personal style. The phenomenon of the "movement," complete with manifestoes and members, has never been a part of the American art scene, and Pop Art was no exception. The artists involved developed independently, although they shared a common point in time that situated them in the wake of Abstract Expressionism, in the middle of a Neo-Dada inspired resurgence of "junk culture." The "Art of Assemblage" exhibition—an exhaustive survey organized by curator William Seitz at the Museum of Modern Art in the autumn of 1961—culminated the first phase of the junk aesthetic that had drawn its materials from urban detritus and the junkyard. Appearing fresh in the exhibition—and also derived from what Seitz called our "collage environment"—were assemblages that drew upon commercial signs and advertisements. These stood out by virtue of the acceptance of commercial raw materials and the rejection of the sentiment, mystery, and nostalgia that had marked the rise of detritus in the fifties' work of such sculptors as Nevelson, Stankiewicz, Di Suvero, Conner, and Kienholz. In 1962 Jim Dine admitted that he had stopped using found objects because "there was too much of other people's mystery in them." [10] This attitude prevailed among a large group of younger artists who directed their efforts away from the associative and the picturesque character of the art of the fifties toward a new, non-associative abstraction focused chiefly on anonymous objects or commercial motifs.

The shock value of the popular image has been all but exhausted, if not in the repetition of one-hundred soup cans, then in the repetition of the one-hundred-soup-can format. Innovations can be sorted out from traditional, even conservative features, and individual styles are seen to transcend the group. At the core of the Pop Art phenomenon is the conjoining of two aspects of urban culture—popular imagery and junk materials. The first finds precedence in the "American Scene" painting of Stuart Davis and Gerald Murphy during the 1920's. Beginning with his *Washington Crossing the Delaware* of 1953, Larry Rivers reintroduced this imagery in the context of Abstract Expressionism. As Rauschenberg was soon to use the objects themselves, Rivers used representations of cigarette packs, cigar boxes, cars, or menus to impose an objective order on the Abstract Expressionist canvas. His detached, reportorial attitude, evident in his 1954 sculpture *Double Portrait of John Meyers* (Figure 1), still remains within the conventional limits of two- and

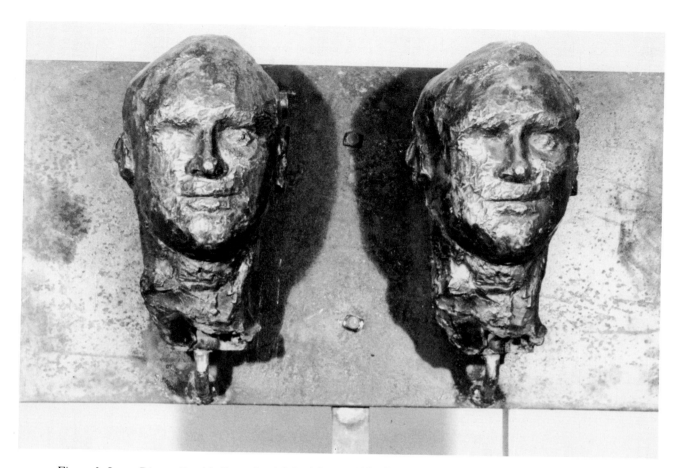

Figure 1. Larry Rivers. *Double Portrait of John Meyers.* 1954. Bronze, 72″ high. (Photo: Peter Moore.)

three-dimensional media, but certainly presages the objective repetition of common imagery undertaken by Johns and Rauschenberg within the next few years.

More significant than the representation of the common image in painting and sculpture, however, is the adaptation of urban materials—an outgrowth of successive developments from Dadaism, Surrealism, and Abstract Expressionism to assemblage, environments, and Happenings. From urban materials the Pop artists turned to urban technology, and through the use of commercial matter and industrial processes, they not only exploded the limits of culture, but obliterated the time worn distinctions between painting and sculpture by equating both with the common object. Allan Kaprow, writing on "The Legacy of Jackson Pollock" in 1958, had commented prophetically: "The young artist of today need no longer say, 'I am a painter' or 'a poet' or 'a dancer'. He is simply an 'artist'. . . . But out of nothing he will devise the extraordinary and then maybe nothingness as well. . . . these, I am sure, will be the alchemics of the 1960's." [11] In the Pop genre, Kaprow's "artist," no longer a painter or a sculptor, is an object-maker. He exploits the techniques and materials of the commercial manufacturer to produce his own salable commodities, which, when stripped of their utilitarian functions and extracted from their everyday contexts, reflect back on their technological milieu.

To speak of Pop Art sculpture, then (that is, to label as sculpture those objects associated with Pop Art which are not paintings), is to create a category which does not necessarily exist for the artist. The only Pop artist who has come to deal with   181 sculptural form within the Pop idiom is Claes Oldenburg, whose first "sculptures" were mere props for Happenings and environments. The figure sculpture of George Segal, Escobar Marisol and Ernest Trova remains on the fringes of Pop Art as does the light-sculpture of Chryssa and Stephen Antonakos. Conversely, the Pop Art objects of Warhol and Lichtenstein stand on the outer limits of sculpture.

As was the case with Dadaism and Surrealism, much of the impetus behind Pop Art came from sources outside painting and sculpture. The transition from the prevailing attitudes of Abstract Expressionism was largely mediated by Rauschenberg and Johns, but these two men in turn were strongly influenced by composer John Cage. Steeped in Zen Buddhism as well as in Dadaism and Surrealism, Cage denied preexisting limitations on the nature of art and sought to eliminate the separation he felt between art and life. As Cage explains, "Everything we do is music. Wherever we are, what we hear is mostly noise. When we ignore it, it disturbs us. When we listen to it, we find it exciting." [12] Seeking to eliminate the marks of his own authorship, an attitude antithetical to Abstract Expressionism yet common among Pop artists, Cage began to compose aleatory music. In the early fifties, Cage staged the first of his mixed-media programs at Black Mountain College. This "concerted action," the score for which was arrived at by chance, featured Cage reading one of his lectures, two poets reciting, Merce Cunningham dancing around the audience, David Tudor playing the piano, Robert Rauschenberg (whose all-white paintings were hung from the rafters) playing scratchy records on a windup phonograph, and movies and still photographs being projected onto the walls.[13]

By 1960 Kaprow, who had studied with Cage, was staging Happenings in New York alongside those of Oldenburg and Dine. Cage's appreciation of the aesthetic possibilities of the banal and repetitious led him to compose a silent sonata for the piano, titled 4'33", which was performed by Tudor in 1952 before an incredulous audience in upstate New York. "What they thought was silence, because they didn't know how to listen," Cage explained, "was full of accidental sounds." [14]

Analogous to Cage's use of silence were Rauschenberg's white paintings, neutral canvases used as a background for reflected shapes and shadows and hung at Cage's proto-Happening at Black Mountain College in 1952. Born in 1925 in Port Arthur, Texas, Rauschenberg had studied at Black Mountain with Albers during 1948–49; he then spent a year at the Art Students League with Vaclav Vytlacil and Morris Kantor. In 1953, the year that Stankiewicz had his first exhibition of junk sculpture, Rauschenberg, too, began to scour Fulton Street for materials, creating found-object sculpture which was shown along with his dirt and grass pictures at the Stable Gallery. Two years later Rauschenberg merged Abstract Expressionist painting and junk assemblage into what he called the "combine painting." In *Satellite* of 1955 (Figure 2), for example, a stuffed bird was perched on a canvas which had on its surface comic strips from the *Journal American*, a paper doily, and an advertisement for toothpaste. The precedents for Rauschenberg's collage treatment of the canvas reverted back to the early experiments in that medium by Picasso and Braque; Schwitters included part of a comic strip in his 1947 collage *For Kate*; De Kooning incorporated a female mouth from a Camel cigarette ad in his *Study for Woman* (1950), and an offset newspaper clipping image into his *Gotham News* of 1955 (Figure 3), thus bringing popular imagery right into Abstract Expressionism. Rauschenberg's addition of the found object to the painting, or his technique of brushing paint onto a real object like *Bed* of 1955 (Figure 4), completely alters the frame of reference for painting. Bypassing the Cubists' issue of reality and illusions and the Dada question of, "What Is Art?" Rauschenberg affirms that just as the canvas is an object, so is a stuffed bird, or a bed, or a combine

Figure 2. Robert Rauschenberg. *Satellite*. 1955. Mixed media, combine Painting, 80″ x 42½″. (Collection, Mrs. Claire Zeisler, New York. Photo: Rudolph Burckhardt.)

Figure 3. Willem de Kooning. *Gotham News.* 1955. Oil on canvas, 69″ x 79″. (Albright-Knox Art Gallery, Buffalo, New York.)

painting. "Paint itself is an object, and canvas also," he explained in a 1961 interview. "In my opinion, the void which must be filled does not exist." [15]

Rauschenberg's reaction to the sacrosanct integrity of the Abstract Expressionist canvas became explicit as he relied more and more on the interposition of the object to detach his work from himself and project it into the everyday environment. The influence of Cage was still apparent; in *Broadcast* (1959), Rauschenberg included radios that were to be tuned by the viewer to produce a collage of sound, specifically recalling Cage's 1951 *Imaginary Landscape #4*, a four-minute "composition" of twelve radios regulated in tuning and volume by twenty-four performers on the stage of Columbia University.

Cage's concerts and mixed-media programs, like the Happenings which they spawned, offered a new dimension to the visual artist: the performance. As Alloway noted, Happenings, along with experimental movies and dance, have become "exercises in time by artists trained to the space arts." [16] The time factor, which is properly a performance, is implicit in the process, but not the product of action painting. With Rauschenberg's *Broadcast*, as in *Revolvers* (1967), that performance becomes a part of the product itself, which is now an object separate from the act of its own creation.

Out of this direct, empirical approach, channeled into Happenings and environments, comes the sculpture of Oldenburg and Marisol. From the other aspect of Cage's work, however—the contemplative, cerebral core of preparation behind the performance—developed a parallel stream of activity beginning with Jasper Johns and spreading to Lichtenstein and Warhol.

Johns was born in 1930 in Augusta, Georgia. After a short period at the University of South Carolina, he came to New York in 1949, was drafted into the

184

Figure 4 *(left)*. Robert Rauschenberg. *Bed.* 1955. Mixed media, combine painting, 74″ x 31″. (Collection, Mr. and Mrs. Leo Castelli. Photo: Rudolph Burckhardt.)

Figure 5 *(right)*. Jasper Johns. *Target with Four Faces.* 1955. Encaustic and collage on canvas with plaster casts, 30″ x 26″. (The Museum of Modern Art, New York. Photo: Rudolph Burckhardt.)

army, and spent two years in Japan. Returning to New York in 1952, he began to paint seriously. In 1955 he teamed up with Rauschenberg; with studios in the same building, they collaborated as window decorators under the collective alias of Matson Jones, and shared work for the next five years. With his *Flags* and *Targets* dating from 1955, Johns presented an alternative to Abstract Expressionism that retained the textural surface of the earlier style but submitted it to a larger compositional organization coinciding with the form of the image he used. Even among the earliest of these works, however, Johns introduced foreign objects, as in his *Target with Four Faces* of 1955 (Figure 5), in which four painted plaster casts from life are lined up across the canvas, in much the same way that Rauschenberg was to arrange an equal number of Coke bottles in *Curfew* (1958). Where Rauschenberg depended on the found object, however, Johns was making his own—four subtly differentiated casts which record successive mouth positions. Johns thus sets up an ambiguous situation which probes the nature of illusion in the manner initiated by Picasso's *Still Life with Chair Caning* (1911–12), the first collage in which materials were affixed to the surface of the picture. The plaster faces are clearly imitations of human forms, yet, denied their familiar context, they become objects which are "real" in their own right.

185

Figure 9. Robert Indiana. *Love*. 1966. Polychrome aluminum, 72″ high.

numbers and words stenciled on them. Indiana (who adopted his last name from the state of his birth) came to New York in 1954 from Chicago, where he had a show with Claes Oldenburg while the two were students at the Art Institute of Chicago. His interest in lettering began when he found some old brass stencils lying around his studio on Coenties Slip at the tip of Manhattan. Well aware of Johns's trademark, he turned to constructions to find his own idiom. Planks of wood, iron, and wheels, scavenged around the waterfront, were decorated with words and symbols, as in *Star* (1960), *Moon* (1960) and *Soul* (1960). These pieces exhibit little of the sense of accident associated with Dada or junk assemblage. For Indiana, however, the constructions retained a strong sense of dock history. As totem figures, they share the elusive quality of Johns's cast sculptures, the fake authenticity of an object which is potentially functional but denied that function by art. Indiana knowingly pursued this paradox when he began his sign paintings in 1961, challenging the poet T. Henry Smith's observation: "There have been many American/SIGN/painters . . . there never were any American/sign/PAINTERS." Indiana's refinement of form and technique culminated in the aluminum letter sculpture, *LOVE* (Figure 9), which was issued in an edition of six by Multiples, Incorporated in 1966.

This development from a synthesis of junk assemblage and popular imagery is characteristic of early ventures in Pop-oriented sculpture and object-making. The figure sculpture of Marisol and Ernest Trova derives directly from assemblage.

Escobar Marisol, who was born in Paris in 1930 of Venezuelan parentage, moved to New York in 1950 and studied for a year at the Art Students League with Yasuo Kuniyoshi; between 1951 to 1954 she took classes at the Hans Hofmann

188

Figure 10 *(left)*. William King. *Sick Man*. 1956. Wood, 73½" high.

Figure 11 *(right)*. Marisol. *The Family*. 1962. Painted wood and other materials, 82⅝" high. (The Museum of Modern Art, New York.)

School, where her interest shifted to sculpture. Marisol's early work, exhibited in her first uptown solo show at the Leo Castelli Gallery in 1957–58, included small clay figures in high relief, terra-cotta tiles, free-standing figures, and wood carvings. Her painted, wooden figures, shown in 1961, retain a strong link with folk art through the influence of Marisol's mentor, William King. Among King's sculptural portraits and vignettes in wood, plaster, and bronze made in the mid-fifties, there is a plaster *Marisol* from 1955.

King was probably the first to deal with the anonymous genre-types, like the *Sick Man* of 1956 (Figure 10), *The Painter* (1954), or *The Italian Man* (1958), which were variously developed by Marisol, Trova, and Segal. Marisol reinterpreted King's sculpture in construction form, fashioning her mannequin-like figures out of separate pieces of wood and plaster. Faces, hands, and feet are cast from life, recalling Jasper Johns's target constructions[19] but adding a distinctly autobiographical mark with the frequent appearance of Marisol's self-portraits in her work. Unlike hard-core Pop, Marisol approaches contemporary society through human psychology rather than machine technology; she depends on carpentry far more than on commercial techniques. The psychological characterization of her subjects—the vaguely menacing *Family* of 1962 (Figure 11), the totemic *Blacks* (1961–62), the

189

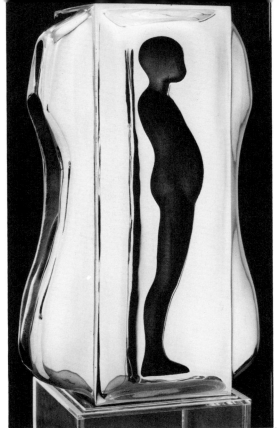

Figure 12 *(top)*. Ernest Trova. *Study: Falling Man (4 Sided Intaglio)*. 1967. Silver bronze, 14½″ high. (Photo: Ferdinand Boesch.)

Figure 13 *(bottom)*. Ernest Trova. *Venice Landscape*. 1965–66. Bronze, 90″ x 168″ x 72″. (Phoenix Art Musuem, Phoenix, Arizona. Photo: Ferdinand Boesch.)

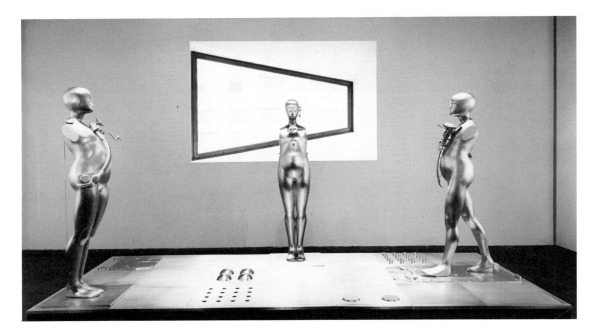

toylike *Generals* (1962–63), or the galloping cowboy hero *John Wayne* (1963)— establishes her contemporaneity, and is perhaps most adequately described as the New Realism.

More oriented to the image of man in the context of science and technology is the sculpture of Ernest Trova. Working in his native St. Louis, where he was born in 1927, and away from the New York mainstream, Trova developed a metaphor for

190

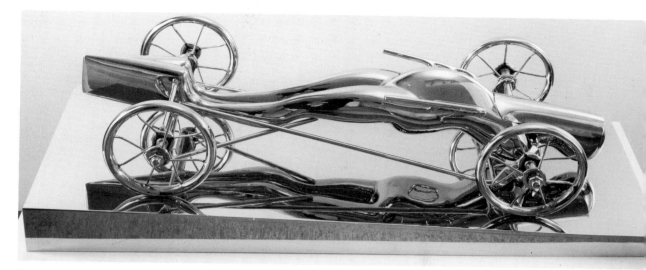

Figure 14. Ernest Trova. *Study: Falling Man (Carman)*. 1968. Nickel-plated bronze, 8″ x 12¼″ x 31½″. (Collection, Dr. Joseph Attie, Great Neck, New York. Photo: Ferdinand Boesch.)

the union of man and machine (termed "mechanomorphism" by Lawrence Alloway)[20] in the *Study: Falling Man* series. This series began with paintings in 1961 and assumed sculptural form in 1964 (Figure 12). On seeing De Kooning's *Woman* series in 1953, Trova was inspired to work with the male figure in a similar way, venturing into the image of popular culture heroes with *Ray Charles Brown* (alluding to the blues singers Ray Charles and Ray Brown) and *Study for a Portrait of Ray Charles* (1953–54). During this period Trova, like Rauschenberg and Johns, was supporting himself through window displays and commercial design. In 1959, he, too, began to work with junk assemblage, creating monumental male figures like *Father* (1960) and *Study for a Portrait of Hitler* (1960–61). Early in the sixties, however, Trova turned specifically to the use of old medical and dental equipment —artificial limbs, trusses, operating instruments—as symbols of the scientific devices used to compensate for man's physical defects; these also showed him to be dependent upon the machinery of medicine. Later these devices were appended to the uniform figure of the *Falling Man* series, as in *Venice Landscape* of 1965–66 (Figure 13), a twentieth-century amalgam of the Renaissance schemas of Leonardo and Dürer, the machine images of De Chirico and Oskar Schlemmer,[21] the Bauhaus and the Bufferin commercial. In this study the man has no face, no arms, no sex organs; he, like the instruments he bears in their stead, is functionless. His fall represents a state of being rather than a physical position: "I think that man is an imperfect creature," [22] he says. Here, the "extensions of man" signify the darker side of Marshall McLuhan's *Understanding Media*, which was published the year Trova made his first cast versions of the *Falling Man*. Commissioned to prepare an exhibition for the St. Louis Bicentennial, Trova was given all the resources of a local department store, including men, materials, and a warehouse for studio space. Here he investigated industrial techniques, arriving at the process of casting and chrome-plating that produced the streamlined *Falling Man*. The interchangeability of man and machine becomes explicit with the racing car series, including *Super Car Kit #1* (1964), and *Carman* of 1968 (Figure 14), where the *Falling Man* torso becomes the body of a car, thus attaining new mobility as a machine, but relinquishing all human mobility. This process of metamorphosis (the reverse of Oldenburg's anthropomorphic soft sculpture) conveys a mixture of intellectual optimism and emotional pessimism that relates back to the Dada appreciation of the machine age, demonstrated chiefly in the work of Picabia and Duchamp, who labeled his *Bride Stripped Bare* "An Agricultural Machine" in his project notes.

191

Trova's groups of *Falling Men*, subtitled *Landscapes*, as *Venice Landscape* (see Figure 13), accentuate the absence of human qualities, the object state of the non-communicating figures. This expansion to an environmental scale, seen also in the figure groups of Marisol, is an outgrowth of the sculptural environments that began with Bourgeois and Nevelson. Instead of emphasizing the human nature of inanimate objects, however, the human forms themselves are presented as objects, and the observer is brought into contact with them just as he is confronted by manufactured objects in his home, or objectified human situations in advertising and other forms of mass media.

George Segal is the chief proponent of this objectified environment. Segal was born in New York in 1924. After a period at the Pratt Institute of Design in 1947, he studied Art Education at New York University and in 1963 received an MFA from Rutgers University. Living and working near Rutgers, Segal was involved with a group of young artists, which included Allan Kaprow and the assemblagist Lucas Samaras, collectively identified as the "New Brunswick School." Out of their common concern for contemporary experience, the directness of art and its interaction with the environment, came Kaprow's "Happenings," the first of which was staged on Segal's chicken farm in 1959.

In the late fifties, Segal began to transfer his large, expressionistic figure paintings to three-dimensional forms of plaster-soaked burlap on chicken wire. These were set against a painted landscape, introducing a limited real space into his work. In 1960 he developed the environmental format, where the setting as well as the figures was virtual rather than illusionistic, and in the following year he made his first cast from life.

Created in response to a gift of Johnson & Johnson bandages from George Brecht, *Man Sitting at the Table* of 1961 (Figure 15) is a self-portrait, and was conceived as a "Dada joke," a "ready-made person at a ready-made table." [23] The pieces which followed assumed the dimensions of a theatrical presentation, with

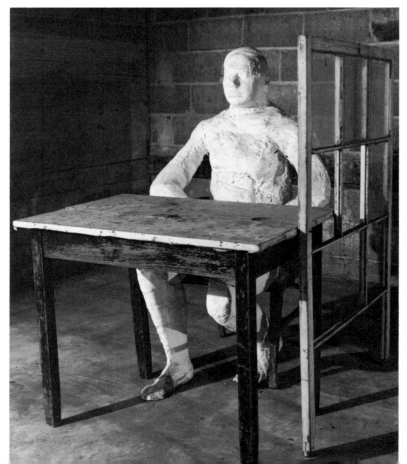

Figure 15 *(left)*. George Segal. *The Man Sitting at the Table*. 1961. Plaster, wood, glass, 53″ x 48″ x 48″. (Städtisches Museum Mönchengladbach.)

Figure 16 *(opposite, top)*. George Segal. *Woman Shaving Her Leg*. 1963. Plaster, porcelain, shaver, metal, 63″ x 65″ x 30″. (Photo: David Van Riper.)

Figure 17 *(opposite, bottom)*. George Segal. *Dinner Table*. 1962. Plaster, wood, metal, 72″ x 120″ x 120″. (Collection, Schweber Electronics, Westbury, Connecticut. Photo: David Van Riper.)

Segal creating a situation, arranging a setting, and choosing participants from among his family and friends. Works like *Lovers on a Bed* (1962), *Woman Shaving Her Leg* of 1963 (Figure 16), and *The Dinner Table* of 1962 (Figure 17) present common situations in a natural, yet permanent fashion, exemplifying Kaprow's prescription for the Happening that, "The composition of all materials, actions, images, and their times and spaces should be undertaken in as artless, and again, practical a way as possible." [24]

Figure 18. Paul Cézanne. *The Card Players.* Oil on canvas, 32⅛″ x 25⅝″. (The Metropolitan Museum of Art, New York.)

As art, these figures are symbolic interruptions of life processes, comparable to the lava-encased bodies of the Pompeii volcano victims; as objects, casts from life, they are literal interruptions of the artistic process of making a three-dimensional image from a mold. In both instances, a reduction to object status occurs as a result of the interruption. This process is further exaggerated in Segal's later works, like *The Shower Curtain* (1966) and *The Movie House* (1966–67), where the action is subordinated to the situation, and where that situation is no longer presented in its entirety but rather as a fragment of the whole environment. At the same time, the situations themselves become less personal and more related to Pop Art preoccupations with mass culture, as in *The Billboard* (1966), or *The Laundromat* (1966–67).

By his own admission, Segal's work is "saturated" with art history, ranging from the allusion to Egyptian Old Kingdom sculpture in the *Man Sitting at the Table* and Masaccio's painting of the death of St. Peter in *The Execution* (1967) to Cézanne's *The Card Players* (Figure 18) in *The Diner* of 1964–66 (Figure 19) (recreating Segal, Kaprow, and their wives, with fellow artists Lucas Samaras and Jill Johnston), to Hopper's *Nighthawks* of 1942 (Figure 20) in *The Diner*. The predominance of paintings among these historical precedents may be taken as an indication of Segal's adherence to the fundamentally pictorial approach of collage and construction, seen in his positioning of figures and objects in relation to an implied picture plane.[25] However, even this planar organization does not constitute a rigid formal composition. Instead, it serves as a means of establishing a psychological orientation, the direct confrontation of a life event. Segal's sculpture, like the Happening as characterized by Kaprow, is not formless but devoid of "form theory."[26] This is another Dada legacy that sought not to deny art but to deny preconceived notions of what art had to be, as a category separate from life.

194

Figure 19 *(top)*. George Segal. *The Diner*. 1964–66. Plaster, wood, chrome, formica, masonite, 102″ x 108″ x 87″. (Walker Art Center, Minneapolis, Minnesota.)

Figure 20 *(bottom)*. Edward Hopper. *Nighthawks*. 1942. Oil on canvas, 30″ x 60″. (The Art Institute of Chicago.)

Claes Oldenburg is the one artist who has most intensively developed the implications of softness or formlessness as form. Coming out of Happenings and environments into the thick of Pop Art activity, Oldenburg is an artist with seemingly unrestricted appreciation of every aspect of contemporary art and of the whole of contemporary society. Autobiography and self-analysis, parody and social analysis, technology and technique are all encompassed within the limits of his innovative sculptural form.

Born in Sweden in 1929, Oldenburg settled in Chicago with his family in 1936. After graduating from Yale in 1950 and working as a journalist, he enrolled in 1952 in the Art Institute of Chicago, where he was a fellow student of H. C. Westermann as well as of Robert Indiana. In 1956 Oldenburg came to New York as a classical figure painter, but the change of environment soon altered his perception of art. "The streets, in particular, fascinated me" he recalls. "Ordinary packages became sculpture in my eye, and I saw street refuse as elaborate accidental compositions." [27] Three years after his arrival he had his first one-man show at Judson Memorial Church, featuring abstract sculpture made from wood, string, and paper. In the work that followed, "city nature," as he calls it, became his major theme, reflecting the intensity of his reaction to the city culture of New York which had affected so many artists during the fifties. Oldenburg also encountered around this time the *art brut* of Jean Dubuffet and the novels of Céline. These further prompted him to explore the use of city materials in his work.[28] Through Dubuffet, moreover, he was exposed to the possibilities of primitive art, the subconscious, and banal imagery.

Oldenburg began the *Ray Gun* series in 1959 with a phallic, gun-shaped object made out of newsprint on a wire frame. Ray Gun spelled backwards, Nug Yar, was for Oldenburg *New York*; the Ray Gun, he explains in his Studio Notes from 1962–64, is a talisman, a phallic symbol, an image of "ambition and vision." [29]

Oldenburg collaborated with Jim Dine to set up an environment called *Ray Gun Street* at Judson Memorial in 1960. His studio became the Ray Gun Manufacturing Company, where he presented his second environment, *The Store*, in 1961. In January, 1962, the studio also became the Ray Gun Theater, where he staged a number of Happenings, including *Store Days, Nekropolis, Injun,* and *World's Fair*.

Oldenburg had exhibited his burlap and wood sculpture in 1960 at the Reuben Gallery, which, under the influence of Allan Kaprow, ardently promoted Happenings and Pop Art activity. This street sculpture was created within Oldenburg's self-imposed limitations of color and materials. With *The Store*, his emphasis shifted from monochromatic form to a polychromy that favored the strongest of pure primary and secondary colors. By this time, Oldenburg was familiar with the imagery of Dine, Lichtenstein, and Warhol, and he, too, turned his attention to popular culture: food—*7-Up* (1961); *Dual Hamburgers* of 1962 (see colorplate 5); clothing—*Red Tights* (1961); appliances—*Sewing Machine* (1961). He had been enlisting the aid of his wife in sewing props and costumes out of canvas and burlap for the Happenings. Much of this, he explained, had to be thrown away for lack of storage space, until finally, in 1962, a sculptor friend, David Hayes, suggested "a more conservative attitude" toward the props—that they be looked upon as sculptures. The adoption of this suggestion was the beginning of Oldenburg's "soft sculpture" made of sewn canvas or vinyl, stuffed with kapok.

From consumer products of *The Store*, Oldenburg turned to everyday items of *The Home*. His interest in *The Home* came with his move to Venice, California in 1963, where he created his famous *Bedroom Ensemble* (1963), later exhibited at the Sidney Janis Gallery. This tableau was followed by individual pieces, like the *Soft Typewriter* of 1963 (Figure 21), *Ironing Board with Shirt and Iron* (1964), and soft

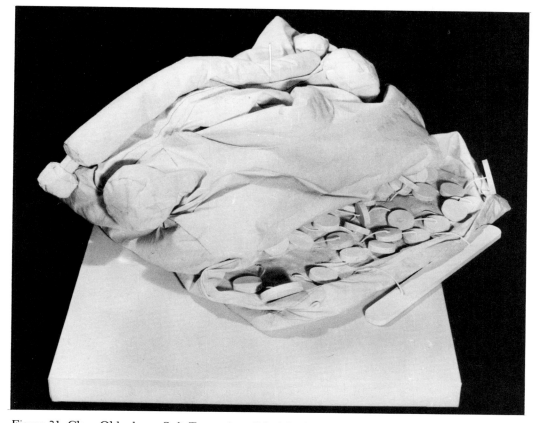

Figure 21. Claes Oldenburg. *Soft Typewriter. (Model "Ghost" Typewriter.)* 1963. Cloth, kapok, wood, 27½″ x 26″ x 9″. (Collection, Mr. Karl Ströher, Darmstadt, Germany.)

versions of all the apparatus—washstand, toilet, bathtub, and scale—from his New York studio bathroom (1965–66).

Reflecting on the formal implications of soft sculpture in his Studio Notes, Oldenburg points to the emphasis of mass, the de-emphasis of color, and the physical re-creation of the fluidity of a paint surface,[30] that quality he had tried to approximate with his earlier plaster objects. Yet, traditional values of form, in terms of hard sculpture, have little relevance to the sculpture which rejects the very premise of solid or unchanging form. Thus, Oldenburg's soft sculpture is largely denied the art context of sculpture and must, as a result, be seen primarily in the life context of things. At the same time, however, their physical state dissociates them from their normal functions and permits them to be reconsidered in previously unconnected contexts.

"Softening," for Oldenburg, is a perception of mechanical nature as body. Reversing the procedure of the Dadaists, he counters the mechanization of man with the humanization of the machine, creating what he has described as "an object in the shape of the artist," [31] and no doubt reflecting his own girth in the expanse of so many pieces like the *Giant Ice Cream Cone* (1962), or *Giant Blue Shirt with Brown Tie* (1963). Describing the *Soft Typewriter* Oldenburg comments, "Sanding the wooden typewriter keys I felt like a manicurist."

Oldenburg creates parody by juxtaposing the commonplace with his fantastic vision of it. Phallic Dormeyer mixers and limp baseball bats (1966) become metaphors of human sexuality. Attitudes are likewise made concrete and incorporated into their sources: giant billboard-scale food and clothing reflect advertising stereotypes, and efficiency becomes the shiny vinyl surface of a sink or bathtub.   197

Figure 22. Claes Oldenburg. *Colossal Monument, Baked Potato, Grand Army Plaza, N.Y.C.* 1965. Crayon, ink, 17½″ x 21″. (Photo: Geoffrey Clements.)

Seizing upon his conceptual liberties as an artist, he assumes a variety of roles—manufacturer, cook, decorator, scientist, or mechanic—to create himself the products which are otherwise in the domain of the other professions (professions which are, according to the Studio Notes, taken more seriously than art in the United States).[32] He re-created five versions of the *Soft Airflow* (1965–66), based on the Chrysler Airflow—"the first American, mass-produced cars designed aerodynamically for minimum wind resistance."[33] Oldenburg then ventured into "city planning" with a series of proposed projects for monuments, including in 1965 a *Baked Potato* (Figure 22) for Brooklyn's Grand Army Plaza, and a monolithic cement war monument in 1968 to serve as an obstruction at the intersection of Canal and Broadway in New York. Here again, relieved of the functional obligations of the professional, he re-channels the product into a new function, as an artifact of society. In this respect, the crucial point in his development comes with the change from Ray Gun Street to the Ray Gun Manufacturing Company, to a direct confrontation not with the sub-culture of city detritus but with the full-fledged culture of middle-class life.

In the making of his soft sculpture, Oldenburg proceeds from sketches to models in cardboard and muslin to the finished product; he becomes an expert in the structural make-up which he is finally to negate. The recourse to professional techniques and materials is even more characteristic of the Pop Art objects of Warhol and Lichtenstein.

Warhol, whose background remains purposefully obscure, emerged as the
198   exemplar of Pop Art with his soup can paintings. At "The Supermarket," an

exhibition of Pop Art objects brought together at the Bianchini Gallery in 1964, Warhol contributed shopping bags decorated with the Campbell's soup can, pyramids of Campbell's soup cans, and the notorious Campbell's tomato juice and Brillo boxes (Figure 23) which came to be regarded as the ultimate in banality. As John Rublowsky has pointed out, in turning to commercial art, advertising, and various industrial processes, the Pop artists were able to benefit from the researches of their sources, such as the tried and true soup can label or Brillo box design.[34] As a result, the end product of the commercial artist or designer (Warhol was himself a commercial artist before his emergence as painter, sculptor, and filmmaker) becomes a useful mechanism for the Pop artist.

For Lichtenstein, the comic strip has provided one such vocabulary of form in which might be called a visual vernacular. Just as Oldenburg captures and objectifies attitudes with soft sculpture, so Lichtenstein objectifies style with his comic-strip format. He painted Cubist-inspired Americana during most of the fifties, then adopted an Abstract Expressionist idiom around 1957. "New Media–New Forms" introduced him to the work of Dine and Oldenburg in 1960 and the same year, teaching at Rutgers, he came in contact with Allan Kaprow and the rest of the New Brunswick School. Through Kaprow's Happenings his attention was turned to the possibilities of merchandising and industry, no doubt already familiar to him through his previous work as an industrial designer. From his earliest imagery, lifted from such popular magazines as *True Romance* and comic books, Lichtenstein has

Figure 23. Andy Warhol. *Brillo.* 1964. Silkscreen on wood, 17″ x 17″ x 14″. (Photo: Rudolph Burckhardt.)

Figure 24 *(left)*. Roy Lichtenstein. *Head with Red Shadows. (Ceramic Head.)* 1965. Glazed ceramic, 15″ high. (Collection, Mr. and Mrs. Horace Solomon, New York. Photo: Eric Pollitzer.)

Figure 25 *(right)*. Roy Lichtenstein. *Blonde.* 1965. Glazed ceramic, 15″ high. (Wallraf-Richartz Museum, Cologne, Germany. Photo: Eric Pollitzer.)

treated advertisements, common objects, classical ruins, landscapes, and old master paintings, all represented as configurations of Ben-Day dots. The blown-up comic strip painting, which Lichtenstein compares to Rosenquist's billboard paintings and to Warhol's repeated silkscreen prints, becomes an object itself, rather than a picture of that object because, as with Jasper Johns's flags and targets, there is no separation of image and canvas.[35] Ben-Day dots, moreover, accord an anonymity to the object-painting which is, like Rosenquist's use of sign-painting techniques and Warhol's silkscreen, the antithesis of the Abstract Expressionist gestural approach (as Lichtenstein himself emphasizes with his Ben-Day brush-stroke paintings and lithographs of 1965–66). "I want my painting to look as if it has been programmed," he insists. "I want to hide the record of my hand." [36]

Lichtenstein first ventured into three-dimensional object-making with two ceramic heads, *Ceramic Head* of 1965 (Figure 24) and *Blonde* of 1965 (Figure 25), and ceramic cups and saucers (1965–66), where the two-dimensional symbols of comic strips, complete with artificial shadows and highlights, were presented on the object itself. This juxtaposition of image and object shatters any pretense of representation and isolates the comic-strip style as a convention. Lichtenstein's preoccupation with style ultimately led him to "Modern Art"—a series of Ben-Day paintings and aluminum sculptures designed in the manner of 1930's architectural decoration.[37] Lichtenstein was attracted to the decorative style of the thirties as another "discredited area," like the comics.[38] In *Modern Sculpture with Horse*

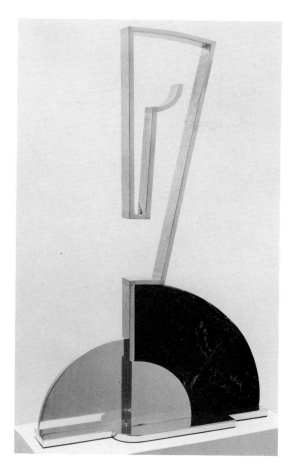

Figure 26. Roy Lichtenstein. *Modern Sculpture with Horse Motif*. 1967. Marble, aluminum, 28¾″ high. (Photo: Rudolph Burckhardt.)

Motif of 1967 (Figure 26), or *Modern Sculpture with Black Shaft* (1967), however, the slick, self-consciously modern style is objectified. Like the objects of Oldenburg, or Warhol, *Modern Sculpture* is functionless in its literal sense: it is not modern, hardly sculptural, and it decorates nothing. In its deliberately anachronistic state, however, *Modern Sculpture* bears witness to the taste of the earlier period consolidated through the critical eye of the present.

Chryssa in many ways typifies the class of artists who incorporated the machine aesthetic into the larger scheme of Pop Art. Once asked: "What about Pop Art? Do you like any of it?" Chryssa replied: "Well, there's only so much you can put on a hot dog." [39] Chryssa's *Times Square Sky* (1962) which led to her monumental *The Gates to Times Square* of 1966 (Figure 27) was her first piece to incorporate neon into the total structure of an image that dealt with both the idea of sign and environment. She describes *Times Square* as the "square of the times" [40]—the inversion reflects the consistency of Chryssa's sculpture with the traditional sculptural "blocks": all of her pieces start from the block. In a personal interview she speaks of signs as having tremendous energy and depth; of her wish to get inside them; to study them from all angles; to turn them inside out, while remaining alert to the basic problem of sculpture: how to have motion within a static form (see colorplate 6).[41]

More than any other of the sculptors who began to adopt a technique or images from the mass communication industry in the early sixties, Chryssa, along with Antonakos, increasingly worked toward the aesthetic. Chryssa has said that all she wants to do is to make beautiful sculptures; she compares the neon sign

201

manufacturers to Turner in their way of handling light—the tinting, shading and contrasting of colors.[42] Antonakos, too, adopted neon sculpture as a means of achieving the most pure and vivid experience of color, just as Don Flavin, working with fluorescent tubes, wished to define the purest geometry of architectural spaces by the geometric placement of pure light.

Lichtenstein himself has commented on certain similarities between Pop Art and the machinist style of the thirties: the rejection of handicraft, the rejection of nature, and the shift to a machine aesthetic. The Pop Art phenomenon generally suggests a revival of the Bauhaus ideal of the noble marriage of art and industry. Where the Bauhaus effort, seemingly overwhelmed by the industrial means at its disposal, lapsed into artistic sterility, Pop Art reapplied those means to more fruitful ends. In essence Pop Art was the exaggerated terminal stage of the need to enter art into the social process without reference to natural processes or the appearance of nature. The bold appropriation of images, techniques, and materials which are not anonymous castoffs, but the very working parts and processes of contemporary society has had no small effect on the art of the sixties. The "nothingness" which Allan Kaprow projected and Warhol realized has found its logical extension in Minimal Art; repetition has led to serial sculpture and painting; mass production, to multiples. If nothing else, Pop Art cleared the introspective air of Abstract Expressionism, and with this definitive break, released the attention which had been fixated on painting to be re-focused on three-dimensional art.

Figure 27. Chryssa. *Gates to Times Square.* 1966. Steel, neon, plexiglass. About 10′ x 10′.

NOTES

1. The show, which also included sculptors John Chamberlain, Ron Bladen, and Tom Doyle, as well as established figures like Cornell, Stankiewicz and Nevelson, was such a success that it was repeated as "New Media–New Forms II."

2. Lawrence Alloway, "The Development of British Pop," in Lucy R. Lippard, et al. *Pop Art* (New York: Praeger, 1966): pp. 27ff.

3. Lawrence Alloway, "Roy Lichtenstein," *Studio International* 175, no. 896 (January 1968): 29.

4. Hilton Kramer, "A Symposium on Pop Art," *Arts Magazine* 37, no. 7 (April 1963): 38.

5. *Ibid*, p. 41.

6. Barbara Rose, "Dada Then and Now," *Art International* 7, no. 1 (January 25, 1963): 25–27.

7. Sidney Tillim, "Month in Review," *Arts* 36, no. 5 (February 1962): 34–35.

8. Robert Rosenblum, "Pop and Non-Pop: An Essay in Distinction," *Canadian Art* 23 (January 1966): 50.

9. G.R. Swenson, "What Is Pop Art," *Art News* 62, no. 7 (November 1963): 25.

10. *Time* Magazine (February 2, 1962), p. 44.

11. Allan Kaprow, "The Legacy of Jackson Pollock," *Art News* 57, no. 6 (October 1958): 57.

12. Quoted in John Kobler, "Experiments in sound. John Cage: 'Everything we do is music'," *Saturday Evening Post* 241, no. 21 (October 19, 1968): 46.

13. Calvin Tomkins, *The Bride and The Bachelors* (New York: Viking Press, 1965), p. 117.

14. Kobler, "Experiments in sound," p. 92.

15. Interview with Robert Rauschenberg in William C. Seitz, *The Art of Assemblage* (New York: Museum of Modern Art, 1961), p. 25.

16. Lawrence Alloway, "Robert Rauschenberg," *Vogue* Magazine (October 15, 1965), p. 154.

17. Walter Hopps, "An Interview with Jasper Johns," *Artforum* 3, no. 6 (March 1965): 34–36.

18. Max Kozloff, *Jasper Johns* (New York: Abrams, 1972), p. 24.

19. Lawrence Campbell, "Marisol's magic mixtures," *Art News* 63, no. 1 (March 1964): 39.

20. Lawrence Alloway, catalog of the Trova exhibition at the Hayden Gallery, Massachusetts Institute of Technology, Cambridge, Mass. (February 20–March 19, 1967), p. 11.

21. Jan van der Marck, "Ernest Trova-Idols for the Computer Age," *Art in America* 54, no. 6 (November–December 1966): 64.

22. Lawrence Alloway, catalog of the Trova exhibition, p. 12.

23. Ellen H. Johnson, "The Sculpture of George Segal," *Art International* 8, no. 2 (March 1964): 48.

24. Allan Kaprow, "The Happenings Are Dead–Long Live the Happenings," *Artforum* 4, no. 7 (March 1966): 37.

25. Sidney Tillim, *Arts Magazine* 37, no. 6 (March 1963): 62.

26. Allan Kaprow, "Happenings," p. 37.

27. John Rublowsky, *Pop Art* (New York: Basic Books, 1965), p. 62.

28. Interview with Claes Oldenburg in "Lichtenstein, Oldenburg, Warhol: A Discussion," Bruce Glaser moderator, *Artforum* 4, no. 6 (February 1966): 21.

29. Claes Oldenburg, "Extracts from the Studio Notes (1962–64)," *Artforum* 4, no. 5 (January 1966): 33.

30. *Ibid.*

31. Barbara Rose, "Claes Oldenburg's Soft Machines," *Artforum* 5, no. 10 (June 1967): 32.

32. Claes Oldenburg, "Extracts from the Studio Notes."

33. Harris Rosenstein, "Climbing Mt. Oldenburg," *Art News* 64, no. 10 (February 1966): 58.

34. John Rublowsky, *Pop Art*, p. 6.

35. In an interview with Roy Lichtenstein by Jeanne Segal, "The Artist and the New Media," WBAI, taped 1968.

36. John Coplans, "Talking with Roy Lichtenstein," *Artforum* 5, no. 9 (May 1967): 34.

37. Lawrence Alloway, "Roy Lichtenstein," p. 29.

38. *Ibid.*
39. Unpublished interview by Ann Geracimos, 1968.
40. *Ibid.*
41. *Ibid.*
42. *Ibid.*

MINIMAL ART AND PRIMARY STRUCTURES

VII

Pop Art was interpreted by many as evidence of a concerted effort to lower art from the level of "fine art" to that of the ordinary object. Correspondingly, the activity of the artist was seen as no more special than the work of the sign painter, the merchant displaying his produce, or the waiter furnishing a restaurant table. Yet, the "Hard-Edge" of Pop Art imagery, the advocacy of commercial materials and techniques, and the cool, detached manner of the Pop artists, though superficially appearing to be an effort toward depersonalizing art and artist, soon came to be viewed not only as a new criterion of "fine art" but as historically essential to the reconstitution of certain formal attitudes of the fifties that had been subordinated to the generalities of Abstract Expressionism.

Young artists, looking back from the lessons of Pop Art, saw in the basic geometry of the paintings of Barnett Newman, Ad Reinhardt, and Ellsworth Kelly a corollary to Pop Art's attention to the ordinary, or basic, object. Many of the sculptors who would figure among the Primary Structuralists of the mid-sixties had been involved with Pop Art, but as they moved away, they took their lead from the non-relational, holistic format of painting that had been previewed as early as 1951 in the object-like monochromatic canvases of Newman, followed by the one-color panel paintings of Kelly, and the all-red and all-blue paintings of Reinhardt. Recognition of the viability of this stream, which had paralleled Abstract Expressionism, came into focus by the end of the fifties when Reinhardt issued his "Twelve Rules for a New Academy," [1] a statement that was effective in reasserting emphasis on geometric form. Newman's Bennington College exhibition was triumphantly repeated in New York; Kelly, Reinhardt, Alexander Liberman and Agnes Martin were all showing paintings labeled "Hard-Edge" at the Betty Parsons Gallery from 1958 to 1961.[2] This group was not involved with Pop Art. Rather it represented a decisive split with Abstract Expressionism in the fifties from which emerged a new group of younger painters centered around Frank Stella and indebted to Jasper Johns.

Stella made his debut at the Museum of Modern Art in 1959 with his "black paintings" of 1958–59 (Figure 1) which definitely established the flatness and opticality essential to both "modernist" painting and sculpture. As Mark Rothko had done in the early fifties, Stella used deep stretchers to emphasize the reality of the canvas as an object; where Rothko painted the edges, however, Stella left them bare to enforce frontality. His imagery remained strictly on the surface of the canvas, held there by the tendency for "all over" patterns—when organized evenly and non-hierarchically across a surface—to distribute space laterally rather than in depth. By 1963, the shapes of Stella's canvases, especially the "copper" paintings of 1961 and the cut-out "purple" paintings of 1963 (Figure 2), had fully responded to the needs of the surface imagery to determine the shape of its boundaries. Joined in this process by Paul Feeley and others, including Larry Poons, who produced a

205

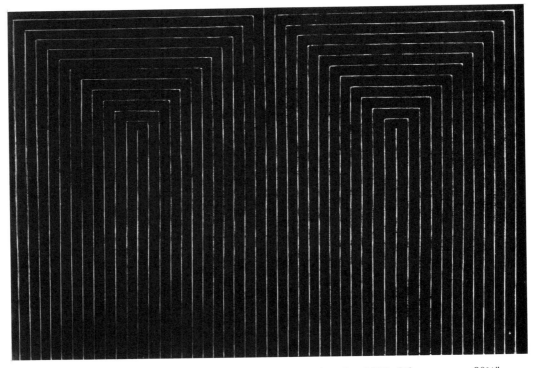

Figure 1 *(top)*. Frank Stella. *The Marriage of Reason and Squalor*. 1959. Oil on canvas, 90¾"
x 132¾". (The Museum of Modern Art, New York.)

Figure 2 *(bottom)*. Frank Stella. *Ileana Sonnabend*. 1963. Oil on canvas, 89" x 127".
(Photo: Rudolph Burckhardt.)

segmented, or constructed, painting in 1962 (Figure 3), the shaped canvas soon
appeared as a standard format for such painters as Neil Williams, Ed Ruda, and Leo
Valledor. The emphasis on the canvas as shape was recognized by many sculptors as

206

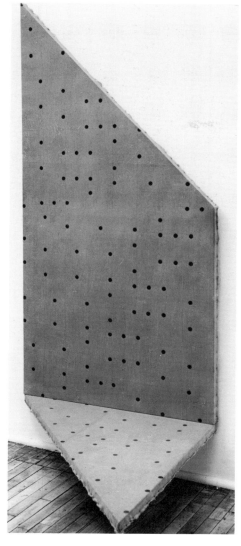

Figure 4. Anne Truitt. *Shrove*. 1962. Painted wood, 60½″ high. (Collection, Mr. and Mrs. Charles Pratt, New York. Photo: Charles Pratt.)

Figure 3. Larry Poons. *Slice and Reel*. 1962. Acrylic and fabric dye on canvas, 80″ x 40″ x 40″. (Photo: Rudolph Burckhardt.)

a reinforcement of the growing awareness that sculpture as shape, as non-referential object in real space, was the best way to rid sculpture of illusionism and enforce its authenticity as real object.[3]

By the early sixties a full-fledged "third stream" tendency, fusing painting and sculpture, was discernible among the array of shaped canvases, polychrome reliefs, and free-standing painted sculpture which combined the two-dimensional surface articulation of painting with the three-dimensional structure of sculpture. Typical of this group, as well as anticipating Minimalism in sculpture, was Anne Truitt (b. 1921). Her first show, early in 1963 at the Andre Emmerich Gallery in New York, later prompted Clement Greenberg to comment: "The surprise of the box-like pieces [Figure 4] . . . was much like that which Minimal Art aims at. Despite their being covered with rectilinear zones of color, I was stopped by their dead-pan 'primariness', . . . Far-outness here was stated rather than merely announced and signalled. At the same time it was hard to tell whether the success of Truitt's best works was primarily sculptural or pictorial, but part of their success consisted precisely in making that question irrelevant."[4]

207

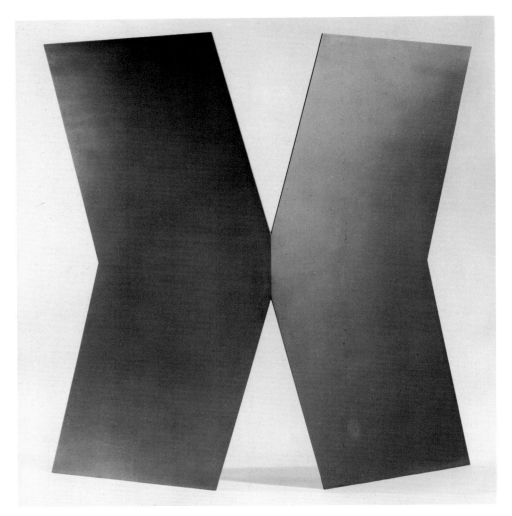

Figure 5. Ellsworth Kelly. *Gate.* 1959. Painted aluminum, 67″ high. (Collection, Hall James Peterson, Petersham, Massachusetts. Photo: Geoffrey Clements.)

The question of differentiating between the pictorial and sculptural also greeted Ellsworth Kelly's "Hard-Edge," flat sculpture, beginning with his *Pony* and *Gate* of 1959 (Figure 5). Although Kelly (b. 1923) was developing throughout the fifties as a painter of non-relational "Hard-Edge" images, he had begun experimenting in 1956 with painted aluminum sheets when he constructed a frieze of multicolored bands over the lobby entrance of the Philadelphia Transportation Building. This event was linked to a studio experiment in 1956, when, in an effort to make color stand for itself, rather than just describe the surface of an image, Kelly had cut out a white X-form from a painting and placed it against another canvas. The visual effect was that of a white sculpture standing in front of a painted ground not unlike Stella's realization that a shape should define its own boundaries rather than depend upon the framing edge of a rectangular canvas. Kelly's sculpture consists of well-defined individual figures, which in most cases are lifted from his canvases; *Gate*, for example, repeats the X-configuration seen in several paintings from 1956 to 1959 (Figure 6). Shape and color are thus isolated to the point where they no longer relate to the outline of the canvas but to their own shape in space. The sculptures are presented as simply as possible: the matte surface of the paint eliminates reflections and intensifies the optical sensation; flat planes, as in *Blue Disc* (1963), are bolted to the floor, while rocking pieces like *Pony* or *Red-Blue Rocker* of 1963 (Figure 7) function as mutually supporting sheets. In this way, the

Figure 6 *(top)*. Ellsworth Kelly. *South Ferry.*
1956. Oil on canvas (2 panels), 44″ x 38″.
(Waddington Gallery, London. Photo:
Geoffrey Clements.)

Figure 7 *(bottom)*. Ellsworth Kelly.
Red-Blue Rocker. 1963.
Painted aluminum, 185″ x 101″ x 155″.
(Stedelijk Museum, Amsterdam.)

traditional relationship of shape to canvas to stretcher—surface to support—is eliminated along with the traditional "figure-ground" confrontation that one finds in paintings that "contain" shapes.[5]

In Kelly's sculptures there are distinct functional analogues with Rauschenberg's combine paintings (see Chapter 6, Figure 2). The process coexists with the product; support, the mechanism of that process, is not only non-relational but "readymade." Kelly's work, however, shares few of the *a priori* preoccupations of Rauschenberg and Johns; his forms are pure abstractions from nature in the tradition of Miró, Arp, Matisse, and Calder. Nonetheless, the seminal importance of Johns and Rauschenberg to the larger issue of the new sculpture cannot be overlooked, for if Hard-Edge painting provided a vocabulary for the modernists of the sixties, Johns's target and flag paintings and Rauschenberg's combines supplied, both physically and conceptually, the vital syntax, the reinforcement of image and structure. Implications of this syntax, moreover, as they were shared by the music of John Cage, the dance compositions of Merce Cunningham, and the various writings of Robbe-Grillet, Wittgenstein, and McLuhan provided the basis for expansive evolution beyond the dialectic which Clement Greenberg calls "modernist reduction."

Only after the upsurge of Pop Art was a progression discernible from Duchamp through Rauschenberg and Johns to sculptors like Robert Morris, Walter de Maria and Carl Andre. Just as many of the Pop artists had trained for careers in commercial art, most of the new sculptors were painters who had ventured into three-dimensional art with few preconceptions of what sculpture had to be—other than an alternative to the limitations of two-dimensional painting. These artists, in effect, isolated Pop Art from its popular imagery. The banality, repetition, readymade forms, industrial materials, and commercial or non-art processes that remained became Minimal, Reductive or Rejective art—more specifically for sculpture: Primary Structures.

Robert Morris's Minimal or Reductive sculpture, first exhibited at the Green Gallery in 1964, constituted only one of his interests at that time; he was also making distinctly Pop objects (shown at the Green Gallery in 1963 and 1964) and producing dance Happenings. Morris, who was born in Kansas City in 1931, studied at the California School of Fine Arts in 1951 and at Hunter College in 1961–62. In his debt to Marcel Duchamp, Morris appears to parallel rather than to follow Jasper Johns. Echoing the appearance of Johns's object sculptures through the use of grey Sculp–metal and stenciled letters, Morris's objects nonetheless allude most often to Duchamp's trademarks: Morris's cracked plate glass, for example, refers to *The Large Glass*; his notes affixed to an untitled masonite wall piece refer to *The Green Box*; and his two, measured cracks, to *The Standard Stoppages*.[6] Like Duchamp, moreover, Morris presented physical objects not as the culmination of conceptual processes but rather as evidence of their continuation, as in the *Box with the Sound of Its Own Making* (1961); the *I-Box* of 1963 (Figures 8a,b) with a photograph of the artist naked inside; the *Metered Bulb* of 1963 (Figure 9), which records the electricity expended in its operation; and the mirror cubes of 1965 (Figure 10) which expend their own geometric imagery in reflecting the gallery floor, walls, and ceiling.

Barbara Rose, reviewing Morris's exhibition at the Green Gallery in 1963, observed that his works were concerned with the relation of the façade or exterior, which is impersonal, to the interior, which is often unknowable, or useless if known. "Most specifically it considers *process* a more definitive expression of the nature of a thing than means or ends."[7] Even in these early works Morris demands the participation of the viewer; we must open doors to learn their secrets as in the *I-Box*. Everything is given, Rose observes, nothing is revealed; or everything is revealed and

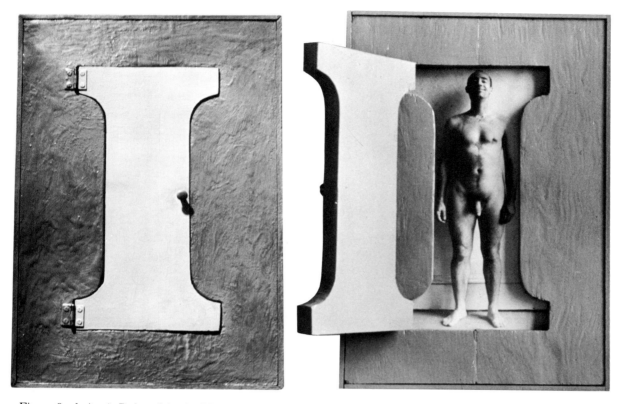

Figure 8a, b *(top)*. Robert Morris. *I-Box*. 1963. Mixed media (closed), (open). (Collection, Hanford Yang. Photo: Bruck Jones.)

Figure 9 *(bottom)*. Robert Morris. *Metered Bulb.* 1963. Mixed media. (Collection, Jasper Johns.)

Figure 10. Robert Morris. *Untitled*. 1965. Plexiglass mirrors on wood, 21″ x 21″ x 21″ each.
(Galleria Sperone, Turin, Italy. Photo: Rudolph Burckhardt.)

we remain with a sense of complete impersonality. An electroencephalogram of Morris is appended to the piece, recording the artist's thought process. Though all the information is there, it essentially tells us nothing.

Morris's second one-man show at the Green Gallery was staged in two parts during the winter of 1964–65. The first part included quasi-Pop objects and lead reliefs decorated with the imprints of common objects, again in the manner of Duchamp; the second, a group of seven plywood constructions (Figure 11) which were promptly christened "Minimal Art." [8] The constructions, uniformly painted a Merkin Pilgrim Grey, performed specific spatial functions. *Corner Beam* spanned a corner; *Cloud*, suspended from the ceiling at eye level, established the enclosed space of the gallery; and an untitled triangle, fitted to a corner, altered the rectangular space of the room.

Discussing Morris's early constructions, Donald Judd had remarked at the time in his characteristically terse manner, "Morris's pieces exist after all, as meager as they are. Things that exist, exist, and everything is on their side. They're here, which is pretty puzzling. Nothing can be said of things that don't exist." [9] Morris himself has offered considerably more descriptive—and prescriptive—commentary on his work in the manifesto-like form of his "Notes on Sculpture" published in 1966 and 1967. [10] Seemingly repudiating his own early object sculptures and lead reliefs,

Morris asserted the rigid autonomy of sculpture as a medium distinct from painting. According to Morris, the relief, which dealt with surface-like painting fell outside the domain of sculpture; hanging sculpture (such as *Cloud*) was likewise proscribed because it denied the force of gravity, and color was eliminated as an "optical, immaterial, and non-containable" property of painting. Sculpture, he proposed, should focus on "unitary forms," such as the simpler polyhedrons that by means of "Gestalt sensations," resist perceptual fragmentation and allow the viewer to apprehend them conceptually at once. In his own work, Morris played heavily on Gestalt relations of part to whole with geometric solids, like the bisected ring or quartered cube, physically divided into sections but bound together by their conceptual unity.

Morris acknowledged the debt of the new sculpture to Pop Art: "[Warhol's] Brillo boxes sit deeper in the psyches of some Primary Structuralists than they care to admit," [11] in that their common referents lie in industry rather than in past art. In a pronouncement entitled "Anti Form" Morris connected the prevailing sculpture aesthetic with the industrial criterion of "well-built." [12] The predominance of planar and linear forms, symmetry and rigidity, is determined not by artistic selection but by the functional requirements of industry. Morris goes on to say, "It is part of the work's refusal to continue estheticizing form by dealing with it as a prescribed end." [13]

Figure 11. Robert Morris. *Exhibition View at Green Gallery,* including *Cloud* and *Corner Beam.* 1964–65. Plywood, 24″ x 144″ x 12″. (Collection, David Bourdon. Photo: Rudolph Burckhardt.)

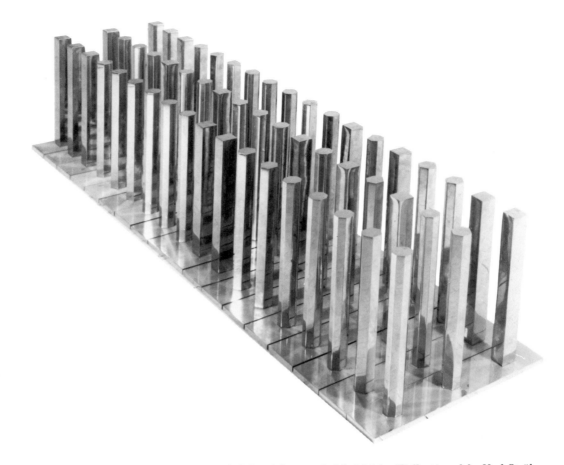

Figure 12. Walter de Maria. *4-6-8.* 1966. Solid stainless steel, 16¼″ high. (Collection, Mr. Karl Ströher, Darmstadt, Germany.)

The dual aspects of Morris's reductive form and conceptual content are further developed in the sculpture of Walter de Maria and Carl Andre. The influence of Morris is evident in De Maria's (b. 1935) early columns, arches, and constructions, exhibited at the Johnson Gallery in 1965. More original, however, are De Maria's object sculptures, which focus in particular on the visual and verbal concretization of abstract ideas—literally Pop Art without the Pop image. *Cross* (1965) is a channeled aluminum cross with a ball resting in the center: *4-6-8* of 1966 (Figure 12) consists of eighteen sets of three stainless steel bars of four, six and eight sides each; and *Face* includes a steel shaft, cut off at an angle of forty-five degrees to provide a mirror-like surface for the reflection of the observer.

In a similar vein, Carl Andre's sculpture gives visible form to physical conditions, just as verbal abstractions are exploited in his "calligrammatic" poetry. Andre, who was born in 1935 in Quincy, Massachusetts, started out as a painter and attributes much of his plastic sensibility to Stella, who was his classmate at Andover Academy and a close friend in New York. Through Stella, Andre arrived at what he would call "anaxial symmetry," the kind of symmetry "in which one part can replace any other part." [14] Later he associated this idea with Brancusi's *Endless Column* (Figure 13) which, though delimited in height, could be continued upward endlessly by incremental additions.

Andre's *Cedar Piece* of 1964 (Figure 14), described by Sam Hunter as "a mirror reflection structure, with echoing inverted pyramidal forms," [15] has been related by Hunter and others to Stella's geometric black-striped paintings of 1959–61 (see Figure 1). Just as in Stella's paintings the line between the painted stripes

Figure 13 *(top)*. Constantin Brancusi. *Endless Column.*
1918. Oak, 80″ high. (Collection, Mary Sisler,
Palm Beach, Florida. Photo: Robert E. Mates.)

Figure 14 *(bottom)*. Carl Andre. *Cedar Piece.* 1964. Cedar,
72″ high. (Collection, Hollis Framton, New York.)

constituted the "space" of the image, the "cut" or separation of Andre's increments
became the "space"; the alignment of the increments as in *Reef* and *Lever* of 1966
becomes only distance—an indeterminate distance as also implicit in the "endless-
ness" of Brancusi's *Endless Column.* 215

Figure 15 *(top)*. Carl Andre. *Installation view of firebrick configurations at the Tibor de Nagy Gallery*, New York City. 1966.

Figure 16 *(bottom)*. Carl Andre. *Lever*. 1966. Firebrick, 4″ x 360″ x 4″.

From this conception of "mass and anti-mass" came stacks of readymade components: wooden beams, iron bars, and magnets assembled in cubes and pyramids on the gallery floor. At his first one-man show at the Tibor de Nagy Gallery in 1965, Andre exhibited three styrofoam constructions—blocks of styrofoam stacked and subsequently dismantled. His second show there in 1966 included eight configurations, each one made up of 120 white firebricks placed on a parquet floor (Figure 15). In an intended interplay of positive and negative space, these constructions carved out the negative environment of the gallery.

In the "Primary Structures" show at the Jewish Museum in 1966, Andre exhibited *Lever* (Figure 16), a construction of 139 firebricks placed end to end from wall to doorway. Whereas Andre previously had been concerned with works built up from the ground, he now began to build along the ground. "All I'm doing," he explains, "is putting Brancusi's *Endless Column* on the ground instead of in the sky. Most sculpture is priapic with the male organ in the air. In my work Priapus is down on the floor. The engaged position is to run along the earth."[16]

Three years later, at the Dwan Gallery, Andre used plates of magnesium, lead, and copper to form three metal "rugs" of contrasting appearances, one of them *144 Pieces of Lead* (Figure 17). Like the styrofoam and firebrick blocks, the metal plates are essentially neutral—raw materials in standardized units, neither natural nor particularly industrial. Assembled in as impermanent a manner as possible, they exemplify a given condition by a process of magnification: the volumes of giant styrofoam constructions, the length of 139 firebricks, the weight of 144 pieces of lead. Andre succinctly explains the history of sculpture in poetic form:[17]

> The course of development
> Sculpture as form
> Sculpture as structure
> Sculpture as place.

Figure 17. Carl Andre. *144 Pieces of Lead.* 1969. Lead, 144″ x 144″.

Andre's "rugs" indeed fulfill the requirement of sculpture as place in that the only dimension of these pieces is "surface," just as the only dimension of a line of 139 firebricks is "distance" expressed in "length." Lacking an effective three-dimensionality, these works can be neither form nor structure.

Despite its physical divergence from the work of Morris, Andre's sculpture is perhaps most consistent with Morris's theoretical position. The tendency, however, has been to interpret Morris's critical writings as the definitive blueprint for anything remotely Minimal.

Morris's work has been linked most often with that of sculptor Donald Judd despite the vast disparity in their styles. As Lucy Lippard and others have pointed out, the structural approach of Judd departs radically from the cerebral, Duchampian orientation of Morris.[18] Judd's sculpture is direct and factual, more perceptual

Figure 18. Donald Judd. *Installation at the Green Gallery*, New York City. 1964. (Photo: Rudolph Burckhardt.)

Figure 19. Donald Judd. *Untitled.* 1965. Perforated steel, 8″ x 120″ x 66″. (Photo: Rudolph Burckhardt.)

than conceptual. A former painter, Judd began making wall reliefs and wooden constructions in 1963 because, like most painter-sculptors, he wanted to escape the inherent illusionism of painting. At the same time, however, he felt that oil paints and canvas were restricted by their art connotations and lacked the possibilities of commercial materials: "Actual space is intrinsically more powerful and specific than paint on a flat surface. Obviously, anything in three dimensions can be any shape, regular or irregular, and can have any relation to the wall, floor, ceiling, room, rooms, or exterior, or none at all. Any material can be used, as is, or painted." [19]

Judd's first three-dimensional works, exhibited at the Green Gallery in 1964 (Figure 18), included curved wall reliefs of painted wood and ribbed metal, as well as boxy constructions articulated with plastic sheets and sections of metal pipe. Unlike Morris, Judd never relinquished color or texture as a means of enlivening form. Where Morris has described the interplay of shape—or Gestalt—with the experienced variables of space and light,[20] Judd rejects the *a priori* system for the concrete presentation of visual effects.

While continuing to make large floor pieces, some in plexiglass and others in perforated steel (Figure 19), Judd began to develop around 1965 the wall relief work in terms of the serial imagery implicit in the repeated forms of his early work. Now, series of cubes, rectangular bars, or semicircular discs are aligned horizontally or vertically on the wall, usually connected to a base or beam (see colorplate 7). Within the basic format, however, each piece creates a specific perceptual experience: the repeated members may support the block, hang from it, rest upon it, 219

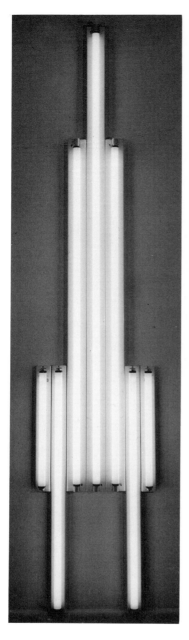

Figure 20 *(left)*. Dan Flavin. *Monument 7 for V. Tatlin*. 1964–65. Cool white fluorescent light, 120″ x 23″ x 4″. (Photo: Rudolph Burckhardt.)

Figure 21 *(right)*. Dan Flavin. *The Diagonal of May 25, 1963*. 1963. Daylight fluorescent light, 96″ x 3¾″. (Photo: Rudolph Burckhardt.)

or be attached directly to the wall. They are uniform or varied in size, as are the intervals between them. More than one kind of metal—aluminum, brass, copper, or iron—may be used, and these are either exposed or coated with sensuously-colored lacquers. Like Morris's large sculptures, Judd's pieces are all fabricated according to his specifications. But whereas Morris could send plans of pieces of sculpture rather than shipping the original,[21] Judd would insist that, "Even if you plan the thing completely ahead of time, you still don't know what it looks like until it's right there." [22]

In the case of Dan Flavin's sculpture (Figure 20) the elements of the work are subordinate to the installation; the neon fixtures and tubes that he uses are of no sculptural consequence in themselves. In 1963 Flavin (b. 1933) took a step beyond what he called the "vertical bar play" of Barnett Newman and the "dry multi-striped consecutive bare primed canvas-pencil-paint frontal expanse play" of Frank Stella.[23] He affixed on his studio wall an ordinary eight-foot strip of fluorescent light (Figure 21). Placed at a forty-five degree angle, the strip called to mind Brancusi's *Endless Column* which, like Andre, Flavin read as a regular, formal consequence of adding similar elements in a single direction. To Flavin the diagonal strip, though a reduction of Brancusi's idea in being more overt in formal simplicity, seemed to excel its limitation of length and apparent lack of expressiveness through the emission of light:[24]

Now the entire interior spatial container and its parts—wall, floor and ceiling, could support this strip of light but would not restrict its act of light except to enfold it. Regard the light and you are fascinated—inhibited from grasping its limits at each end. While the tube itself has an actual length of eight feet, its shadow, cast by the supporting pan, has none, but only an illusion dissolving at its ends. This waning shadow cannot really be measured without resisting its visual effect and breaking the poetry.

Realizing this, I knew that the actual space of a room could be broken down and played with by planting illusions of real light (electric light) at crucial junctures in the room's composition. For example, if you press an eight-foot fluorescent lamp into the vertical climb of a corner, you can destroy that corner by glare and doubled shadow. A piece of wall can be visually disintegrated from the whole into a separate triangle by plunging a diagonal of light from edge to edge on the wall; that is, side to floor, for instance.

Of all the names invented to encompass works ranging from the plywood constructions of Robert Morris and sheet-metal wall sculpture of Donald Judd to the neon tubes of Dan Flavin and the metal "rugs" of Carl Andre, the most appropriate seems to have been proposed by Lawrence Alloway in 1966 to describe what was actually a painting exhibition at the Guggenheim: "systemic." Alloway outlined three characteristics of systemic painting in the catalog essay: that they were not impersonal but were conceptually identified with the artist; that their richness was not dependent on formal complexity; and that they were conceived in a series.[25] The "system," then, can be seen to provide an outlet for the ultimate modernist reduction; with the elimination of internal relationships, the emphasis shifts to external ones. As with Rauschenberg's combine paintings and Johns's object sculpture, the "work of art" can become part of a larger, environmental frame of reference.

Judd's and Flavin's systemic yet empirical approach to sculpture is shared by Tony Smith, whose black monumental sculpture and uniform boxes are conceived in terms of cubic modules modified in the course of construction. Prior to two exhibitions held simultaneously at the Wadsworth Atheneum and the Philadelphia Institute of Contemporary Art in 1966, only two of Smith's sculptures had been seen publicly: *The Elevens Are Up* (1963) (Figure 22) in the "Black, White, and Grey" show at the Wadsworth Atheneum in 1964 and *Free Ride* in the "Primary Structures" exhibition. Holding his first one-man show in 1967 when he was 55 years old, Smith nonetheless became the retroactive "patriarchal figure" among the sculptors of the sixties.[26] Born in 1912 and trained in the Art Students League and the New Bauhaus in Chicago, Smith enjoyed a twenty-year career as architect and painter before turning to sculpture in 1960. As early as 1938 Smith learned of the modular principle of Frank Lloyd Wright through *Architectural Forum* (he served

Figure 22 *(top)*. Tony Smith. *The Elevens Are Up.* 1963. Wooden mockup, 8′ x 8′ x 8′.

Figure 23 *(bottom)*. Tony Smith. *Marriage.* 1965. Wooden mockup, 10′ x 10′ x 12′.

Figure 24. Tony Smith. *Cigarette*. 1961. Wooden mockup, 180″ x 312″ x 215″. (Photo: John A. Ferrari.)

as Wright's apprentice for the next two years), and some twenty years later, while teaching a design course at Pratt Institute, he began to make cubic constructions out of steel plate and developed them onto a sculptural scale. From the basic tetrahedron, Smith generates non-relational forms of considerable complexity. Unlike Morris and Judd, he ignores symmetry in favor of "structural regularity," a theory postulated by architects Phillip Johnson and Henry Russell Hitchcock in the early thirties.[27] Both structure and scale, moreover, relate his sculpture to architecture; his idiom is monolithic rather than minimal. "In my studio," he writes, "they [his sculptures] remind me of Stonehenge."[28] *The Elevens Are Up*, for example, consists of two walls, measuring eight feet x eight feet x two feet, set apart to form a four-foot corridor (and an all-over eight-foot cube). *Marriage* of 1961–65 (Figure 23) and *Cigarette* of 1961 (Figure 24) both create modified portals that allow free passage. While the work of Judd and Morris appears to be keyed to the gallery, or at least to a controlled indoor environment, Smith himself believes that his work is best presented when it is outdoors, surrounded by trees and shrubs, where each piece can be seen separately.

A number of artists, including Tony Smith, have sought to develop a reductive format in terms of structure rather than object; Smith, Ronald Bladen, Robert Grosvenor and Lyman Kipp all dealt with the problem on a monumental scale.

223

Figure 25. Lyman Kipp. *Stack II*. 1962. Bronze (unique cast), 23″ high.
(Photo: Oliver Baker.)

Kipp (b. 1929) has been an important figure in the formulation of the Primary
Structure aesthetic. During the first half of the fifties he was a student at Pratt
Institute in New York and Cranbrook Academy near Detroit. His work of the
mid-fifties included experiments in the general style of open-work, welded sculpture
(especially that of Herbert Ferber) and later, constructions which showed the
influence of Gabriel Kohn who was a fellow student at Cranbrook. In 1958 he was
heading toward a Minimalist style, showing at Betty Parsons Gallery that year a
series of boxy, mesa-like constructions made by plaster casting in cardboard boxes
and recasting in bronze. By 1962 Kipp was casting very simple block shapes arranged
around a vertical shaft (Figure 25).

Kipp's contribution to the 1964 Whitney Museum Annual was a plywood box
painted grey-green on the outside and blue on the inside. Disturbed by the drabness
of the piece, he began to reinforce shape through color, first by using only black or
white, and then by using clear, strong colors to enunciate the separation or
positioning of the elements of his structures. His first large outdoor pieces were
exhibited at Betty Parsons in 1965. These were wooden structures called *Dolmens*,
which were eight feet high and shaped like letters (Figure 26). Continuing this vein
he created monumental environmental structures (see colorplate 8) that recalled the
primary color arrangements of the De Stijl Constructivists.

For Kipp and Tony Smith the Primary Structures phase of American sculpture
was just a continuation of the direction in which their work was leading from the
fifties. Though Smith has acknowledged an interest in topology, and Kipp in the

Figure 26. Lyman Kipp. *Dolmen*. 1965. Painted wood, 96″ high. (Photo: Rudolph Burckhardt.)

formal interplay of solid and negative space, neither became involved in the scientistic aspects of the "systems aesthetic"—at least not to the extent that several others did. Nor did their efforts involve the theoretical excursions of Morris, Judd, and Andre. Judd has applied the Set Theory of modern mathematics to his "specific objects." Sol LeWitt, who entered the Minimal scene in 1965 with closet-like boxes and segmented plywood constructions, was preoccupied with serial forms, as, for example, his *47 3-Part Variations on 3 Different Kinds of Cubes* of 1968 (Figure 27) which is based on the permutations and combinations of predetermined modules.

Figure 27. Sol Lewitt. *Series 3,2,3: 47 3-Part Variations on 3 Different Kinds of Cubes*. 1968. Baked enamel/aluminum, 45″ x 105″ x 15″. (Photo: Walter Russell.)

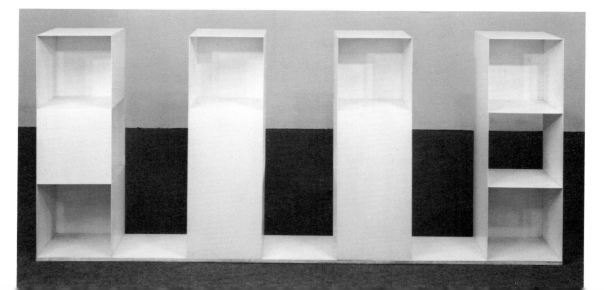

Figure 28. Kenneth Snelson. *Needle Tower.* 1968. Anodized aluminum, stainless steel cable, 720″ high.

Kenneth Snelson, once a student of Buckminster Fuller, has used geodesic principles to construct networks of aluminum cylinders and steel wires, like the thirty-foot *Needle Tower* of 1968 (Figure 28). Kipp and Tony Smith remained sculptors in the more traditional sense, and as such, their sculpture stands in a more logical relationship to that of the late fifties work of Gabriel Kohn and the *Cubis* David Smith constructed after 1962.

By 1966 a large group of geographically widespread sculptors were involved with one or more of the stylistic characteristics of Primary Structures—the title of the major exhibition that year at the Jewish Museum. The most conspicuous of these sculptors, especially in New York shows, were Ronald Bladen, Robert Murray, Robert Grosvenor and later Beverly Pepper, who worked mainly in Italy. Each was concerned above all with an energetic interaction of sculpture and space, a concern that acknowledged deeper roots in Abstract-Expressionist sculpture of the late fifties and early sixties—the progression of Di Suvero, Ginnever, Sugarman, and Weinrib.

Bladen (b. 1918) had studied as a painter at the California School of Fine Arts. On coming to New York he came under the influence of the painter Al Held, whose bold, graphic imagery, rendered in strong colors, directed Bladen away from the brushiness of San Francisco-style Abstract Expressionism. In 1963, following his transition from paintings to wood reliefs, Bladen undertook his first free-standing sculpture, a cantilevered construction which extended eighteen feet across the floor in three sections painted red, black, and yellow. Two years later, eliminating both complexity and the ordering of color, Bladen created an all-white construction of two rectangular planes mounted vertically and tipped forward at top and bottom. Another construction from 1965, a twenty-foot-high outdoor piece, posed two uprights on a beam which was supported by three pontoons. A third construction of 1965 titled 3 *Elements* (Figure 29) consisted of three identical units of aluminum and wood, rectangular solids slanted at a sixty-five degree angle to the floor. Included in the "Primary Structures" exhibition, this piece shared the reductive, formal tendencies of the other works; at the same time, however, it retained the distinguishing features of dynamic or even precarious balance that are found in

Figure 29. Ronald Bladen. 3 *Elements.* 1965. Painted aluminum, 108″ x 48″ x 120″ x 21″.

Figure 30 *(top)*. Ronald Bladen. *Black Triangle.* 1966. Painted wood, 112″ x 120″ x 117″.

Figure 31 *(bottom)*. Ronald Bladen. *The X.* 1967. Wooden mockup, 22′ x 26′ x 14′.

Figure 32. Robert Murray. *Mesa.* 1968. Painted aluminum, 144″ high. (Collection, Mr. and Mrs. David Mirvish, Toronto.)

Bladen's earlier constructions and related them to the work of Sugarman, Weinrib, and Di Suvero. A similar situation prevails with the *Black Triangle* of 1966 (Figure 30) which is set on its tip not on its base, completely dominating the gallery space for which it was constructed. *The X* of 1967 (Figure 31) was also commissioned for a particular setting—the "Scale as Content" exhibition at the Corcoran Gallery of Art, where Bladen again filled the architectural space with a dynamically expansive form.[29]

Robert Murray (b. 1936), who like Bladen came from Vancouver, began as a painter; since 1959, however, he has been concerned with large-scale sculpture. Murray feels that his work, rather than dealing with structures, suggests volumes without actually boxing in the form (Figure 32). He would like his pieces to activate more space than they fill. One of the first to have his works industrially fabricated, Murray preferred the directness and clean finish characteristic of fabricated form, covered with one overall color.

Both Bladen's and Murray's adoption of the industrial aesthetic came as a by-product of their determination to retreat from organic imagery. Bladen's matte-black surfaces, for example, like Tony Smith's, serve chiefly to focus on the imposing structure of his work and avoid reference to the surfaces. Robert Grosvenor, in contrast, uses vivid color and glossy finishes to impart a definite slickness and grace to his sculpture. The apparent suspension of forms in Bladen's work, moreover, becomes actual with Grosvenor's cantilevered constructions like his *Transoxiana* of 1965 (Figure 33) or *Still No Title* of 1966, which cut through the space of the room in their sweep from ceiling to floor.

Although she has lived in Rome since 1951, Beverly Pepper has shown in New York and received many public commissions throughout the United States from the mid-sixties on. After beginning as a painter, Pepper worked briefly in wood and cast bronze before turning to welded metal sculpture in 1961. The pieces she had perfected by 1965 in stainless and Corten steel were irregular, box-like constructions with jagged edges and textured surfaces, and bold color accenting an interior plane. 229

Figure 33 *(top)*. Robert Grosvenor. *Transoxiana*. 1965. Wood, polyester, steel, 126″ high.

Figure 34 *(bottom)*. Beverly Pepper. *Ventaglio*. 1967. Stainless steel, with blue enamel. 240″ high.

The work was indebted not only to Abstract Expressionism but to David Smith, whom Pepper had met when she was working in Voltri, and at the same time showed a tendency toward reductive form. By 1968 Pepper was involved with many of the issues of Primary Structures art. She was concentrating on precise, open, geometric imagery in stainless steel with mirror polish surfaces that, like Morris's mirror cubes, engaged the surroundings. Conceived for exterior spaces, the sculptures fostered a dialogue between the voids that framed the real environment and the solids that reflected it. Color was still used to articulate interior surfaces, and Pepper employed serial concepts to explore the problem of intricately balanced segments within a single piece as in *Ventaglio* of 1967 (Figure 34).

Grosvenor (b. 1934) studied architecture in France for three years and was an Abstract Expressionist painter before he turned to sculpture in 1962. He was one of the original members—along with sculptors Mark di Suvero, Peter Forakis, Bernie Kirstenbaum, Anthony Magar, Forrest Myers, and painters Ed Ruda, Tamara Melcher, and Leo Valledor—of the Park Place Group, an artists' cooperative founded by Paula Cooper at 79 Park Place in New York in the fall of 1963. Grosvenor's technical preoccupations are in fact characteristic of the Park Place Group, which programmatically sought to link its creative processes with scientific and mathematical principles. Dealing with topology in particular, the artist-members focused their attention on spatial ambiguities, often in the form of optical and structural illusions.

The Park Place Group disavowed any relationship with the Minimal tendency and was in turn dismissed as dilutants and "mannerist" imitators.[30] The mark of Abstract Expressionist gesturalism, carried into the group by Di Suvero, remained indelibly on members' work. And even though they shared the basic involvement with mathematics and science which characterizes the "systems aesthetic," the geometry of this sculpture, often thrusting and eccentric, was in marked contrast to the strict and contained objectivism of such sculptors as Judd. "We use an extremely flexible geometry," says Ruda, "because the space it implies can stretch, shrink, warp, twist, change position or become weightless."[31]

To a large degree this geometric form can be seen in the works of Peter Forakis (b. 1927) and Forrest Myers (b. 1941), both of whom were first identified with the California "eccentric" scene. Both were Westerners and both studied at the California School of Fine Arts from 1954 to 1957. In 1958, Forakis taught at the School and worked as a painter; he turned to sculpture only in 1960. Much of his work of the mid-sixties was based on the tetrahedron. As a member of the Park Place Group, he constructed free geometric shapes from a plane surface using one aluminum sheet to establish his forms as seen, for example, in *The Eight* (1965), a relief frieze with background panels of red, white, and black plexiglass and eight aluminum triglyphs. Forakis often exhibited works with complex interactions of closed and open, cut-out areas generated by permutations on the perimeter of an eccentric cube, like *Port and Starboard List* of 1966 (Figure 35).

Forrest Myers was among the youngest of the Park Place Group. In 1965 he was working with cones and conic sections of steel, painted in fluorescent hues and interconnected by narrow rods and curved wires; sometimes he used polished plastic prisms that attracted light and amplified any color present throughout the material. Myers described himself as influenced by Calder and Buckminster Fuller, an influence which can be seen in such works as *Aluminum Sculpture* (1967–68), an open, geometric diamond-shaped work. Most impressive was his contribution to the New York City Park Department's exhibition of environmental sculpture, distributed throughout Manhattan. Myers's piece was made by four searchlights which cut a geometrical pattern into the night sky (Figure 36).

231

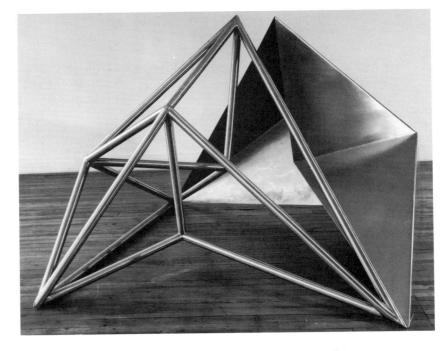

Figure 35 *(top)*. Peter Forakis. *Port and Starboard List*. 1966. Stainless steel, 60″ high. (Collection, Mr. and Mrs. Albert List. Photo: Geoffrey Clements.)

Figure 36 *(bottom)*. Forrest Myers. *Light Sculpture*. 1967. Four searchlights. (Photo: Fred W. McDerrah.)

Figure 37. David von Schlegell. *Untitled*. 1967. Aluminum, 84″ x 444″ x 60″. (Collection, J. Patrick Lannon Foundation, Palm Beach, Florida.)

Often associated with the sculpture style of the Park Place Group is David von Schlegell (b. 1920) who had been a painter since his days at the Art Students League. He switched to sculpture in 1961. Working principally in Maine and associating with Boston galleries, he did not show his sculpture in New York until 1965. Most of his pieces from the second half of the sixties were fabricated of aluminum, and utilized industrial techniques he had acquired as an aircraft construction engineer in the early 1940's (Figure 37). Von Schlegell sees his sculpture as having evolved from his painting, but without the "excess of emotion" he feels had dominated Abstract Expressionism. He parallels his development with that of Richard Smith and other painters whose shaped canvases bridged painting and sculpture. At the same time, like Grosvenor, he resisted the extreme Minimalism of Judd as well as the scientism of the "systems" aesthetic.

If in the geometric eccentricity of much of the work by Forakis and Myers there was an ingredient of San Francisco Funk Art, the Primary Structure output of the Los Angeles sculptors reflected a cool slickness that characterizes much of the art produced there in the late fifties and early sixties. Sufficient background existed in Southern California for a Minimalist tendency without the direct assistance of New York sculptors. The predominant trend in Los Angeles sculpture during the early sixties was toward refinement of form; nonetheless the influence of New York movements was directly connected to Los Angeles, as travel by artists between the two cities steadily increased. The "streamlining" of sculpture in Los Angeles started less with what artists saw in galleries or in art magazines than with what was part of everyday Los Angeles experience:[32] the fetish finish of sleek auto bodies, surfboards, neon lights, and plastic signs. Among the Ferus group—especially Billy Al Bengston, Kenneth Price, Ed Moses, Robert Irwin and later, Larry Bell—there was a strong interest in motorcycles and racing cars.

Figure 38. Larry Bell. *Death Hollow.*
1963. Glass, mirrors, 24½″ x 25″ x 12″.
(Photo: Frank J. Thomas.)

Bengston had been a professional cycle racer; around 1957 he became involved with painting and decorating both cycles and cars. Transferring this technique to canvas, Bengston made his first emblematic spray paintings in 1958; these eventually developed into his famous sergeants' stripes. Following his lead, Price adopted the spray technique for his ceramic sculpture.

Larry Bell (b. 1939) joined the Ferus Gallery in 1962. Bell came out of the late fifties Abstract Expressionist milieu at Chouinard along with Joe Goode, Edward Bereal and Ed Ruscha—all of whom were under the guidance of Richard Reuben, a radical teacher whose frequent visits to New York kept them in touch with the latest developments in painting. From Pollock-inspired student works, Bell turned to geometrically controlled paintings dealing with problems of isometric projection. Interested in their visual properties, Bell began setting pieces of glass and mirror into his canvases; he then worked directly in two-dimensional constructions and three-dimensional boxes. His early boxes, such as *Death Hollow* of 1963 (Figure 38) played off the transparency of the glass walls against the reflective surface of the mirror insets. Soon Bell was trying to combine the two effects into one surface, finally coming upon a commercial process for coating clear glass with vacuum-evaporated minerals. While in New York for a show at the Pace Gallery in 1965, Bell learned how to carry out the process himself; and he remained on the East Coast for the next two years. Bell's technique is a complex means of obtaining an objectively simple effect, and is regarded as an ultimate position among other Los Angeles artists. He maintains, however, that the equipment parallels the tools of any other artist and that his only concern is with the precision of his pieces, constituted by the elimination of all distractions from their surface.

Bell's concern, devoid of technical trappings, is shared by John McCracken (b. 1934), who has been working with simple fiberglass and wood objects since 1964. McCracken was studying painting at the California College of Arts and Crafts when he made a very smooth transition from Hard-Edge emblematic figures painted on canvas to Hard-Edge geometric shapes constructed in plywood. His first pieces, rectangular cubes with slotted faces, were directly inspired by the wood constructions of his teacher, Tony DeLap, who had been making abstract collages and assemblages during the fifties and who only adopted a geometric mode in 1963. McCracken moved to Los Angeles in 1965 when he was offered a show at the Nicholas Wilder Gallery. He began to add color directly into the resin used for fiberglassing, at first using only the primaries and gradually adding various metallic colors of sensuous hue. He tried a variety of configurations as well, including stacked blocks, pyramids, and post and lintel constructions. The most successful form, however, turned out to be a simple plank leaned casually against the wall, an idea which came to McCracken from the raw lumber stored in his studio (Figure 39a,b). Each plank is a product of preparatory drawings, scale models, and even masonite mockups that are used to bring size, shape, and color into precise harmony. McCracken's ideal of simplicity was shaped in part by the proto-Minimal canvases of Newman and Rothko, but he points out that he was equally influenced by the illusion of clean surfaces and contours of art magazine reproductions.

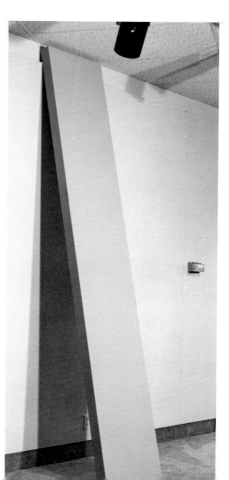

Figure 39. John McCracken. *Untitled.* 1966. Lacquer, fiberglass, plywood. (Collection, Robert Rowan. Photo: Frank J. Thomas.)

The versatility of materials made available to sculptors by the use of non-traditional materials accounts in large part for the demise of sharp distinctions between painting and sculpture—a phenomenon by no means peculiar to Bell and McCracken. Relieved of their commercial functions, fiberglass, plexiglass, liquid resins, acrylics, vinyls, and polyurethane have all become the working media of a number of California artists who were to expand on the Primary Structuralists' interest in non-traditional materials.

Another former painter, DeWain Valentine (b. 1936) works with poured resin as well as with fiberglass. Valentine first came in contact with fiberglass through his work in a boat shop; he also experimented with rough-surfaced fiberglass sculpture while teaching at the University of Colorado in 1964. Arriving in Los Angeles the following year, he began experimenting with smoothly lacquered surfaces; at the same time he started working with the newly-developed cast resins. Casting sleek discs and bulky geometric forms shaped in aluminum molds, Valentine further refined his surfaces over the next few years by spraying the color, along with metallic flecks, directly into the molds to fuse it with the fiberglass (Figure 40).

Craig Kauffman (b. 1932) uses a commercial process known as "vacuum forming" to cast plexiglass reliefs which he sprays with automobile lacquer. A very cerebral Abstract Expressionist painter during the fifties, Kauffman gradually simplified his images and bared his canvases in reaction to the congested compositions of the San Francisco painters. As his forms became more refined, he began looking for a way to enhance their clean appearance. In 1961, inspired by

Figure 40. DeWain Valentine. *Five Red Discs*. 1967. Fiberglass reinforced polyester resin, 63″ high. (Whitney Museum of American Art, New York.)

Figure 41. Craig Kauffman. *Untitled.* 1968. Vacuum formed plexiglass, 19″ x 55½″ x 10″. (Pasadena Art Museum, Pasadena, California.)

Duchamp's *Large Glass,* he tried painting on plexiglass, limiting himself to one elongated, organic shape directly related to his earlier paintings. Two years later he turned to the vacuum-forming process to have the form itself imprinted on the plexiglass before he painted it. In 1966, moving farther away from pictorial effects, he eliminated the figure-ground relationship in favor of a single undulating plexiglass shell. By 1968 while retaining a nominally sculptural lozenge shape, Kauffman returned to a more painterly attitude by using color as a source of light rather than mass (Figure 41), and serial forms to explore various color relationships.[33]

By 1967, the "primary structuralism" aesthetic had spread throughout the country, affecting not only many young sculptors just getting underway but also many older practitioners of other modes. At no time was this more apparent than when curator Maurice Tuchman organized the extraordinary "American Sculpture of the Sixties" show at the Los Angeles County Museum of Art.[34] Aside from the stylistic continuities of David Smith, Calder, and Noguchi, there was also clear evidence throughout the exhibition that the Surrealist-Constructivist dialectic of the forties had resurfaced as one of Pop Art and Primary Structures; subsumed in the dialectic were the connecting lines of Pop with Funk Art and Minimalism with the reductive tendencies of Los Angeles sculpture.

Around this time, however, a new generation of sculptors, under the general influence of Robert Morris, began to move beyond the discrete, finished forms of Minimal Art while avoiding the eccentricities of residual Abstract Expressionism and Pop Art. Some sculptors began to assert their art primarily as viable process, rather than the concrete fact of the object-commodity. Moreover, for the first time since the Hudson River School of American painting, art would become de-urbanized, as the sculptors moved into the rural and natural landscape; the object orientation of both Pop Art and Primary Structures would become one of systems and process as yet another phase of American sculpture got underway.

NOTES

1. Ad Reinhardt, "Twelve Rules for a New Academy," *Art News* 56, no. 3 (May 1957): 37–38, 56.

2. The term "Hard-Edge" was coined by critic Jules Langsner in 1959.

3. See Michael Fried, "Art and Objecthood," *Artforum* 5 (June 1967): 12–23. Also see Donald Judd, "Specific Objects," *Arts Yearbook* 8 (1965): 66.

4. Clement Greenberg, "Recentness of Sculpture," in *American Sculpture of the Sixties*, ed. Maurice Tuchman (Los Angeles: Los Angeles County Museum of Art, 1967): 25.

5. For further discussion of Kelly's sculpture see Barbara Rose, "The Sculpture of Ellsworth Kelly," *Artforum* 5, no. 10 (June 1967): 51–55.

6. Lucy Lippard, "New York Letter," *Art International* 9, no. 4 (May 1965): 57.

7. Barbara Rose, "New York Letter," *Art International* 7, no. 9 (December 5, 1963): 63.

8. In his anthology, *Minimal Art* (New York: Dutton, 1968), p. 387, Gregory Battcock credits Richard Wollheim with the application of the precise label "Minimal" to the new art. See Richard Wollheim, "Minimal Art," *Arts* 39, no. 4 (January 1965): 26–32. Donald Judd described Morris's work in a group show at Hartford's Wadsworth Atheneum as implying that "everything exists in the same way through existing in the most minimal way." See Donald Judd, "Black, White, and Grey," *Arts* 38, no. 6 (March 1964): 38.

9. Judd, "Black, White, and Grey," p. 37.

10. Robert Morris, "Notes on Sculpture," *Artforum* 4, no. 6 (February 1966): 42–44; Part II, *Artforum* 5, no. 2 (October 1966): 20–23; and Part III, *Artforum* 5, no. 10 (Summer 1967): 24–29.

11. David Bourdon, "Our Period Style," *Art and Artists* 1, no. 3 (June 1966): 54.

12. Robert Morris, "Anti Form," *Artforum* 6, no. 8 (April 1968): 33–35.

13. *Ibid.*

14. Quoted in Phyllis Tuckman, "An Interview with Carl Andre," *Artforum* 8, no. 10 (June 1970): 57.

15. Sam Hunter, *American Art of the Twentieth Century* (New York: Abrams 1972), p. 386.

16. *Ibid.*, p. 387.

17. Quoted in David Bourdon, "The Razed Sites of Carl Andre," *Artforum* 5, no. 2 (October 1966): 15.

18. Lucy R. Lippard, "New York Letter: Recent Sculpture as Escape," *Art International* 10, no. 2 (February 20, 1966): 50.

19. Donald Judd, "Specific Objects," *Contemporary Sculpture, Arts Yearbook*, no. 8 (1965): 79.

20. Morris, "Notes on Sculpture," Part II, *Artforum* 5, no. 2 (October 1966): 23.

21. Morris sent specifications to carpenters at the Art Institute of Chicago for their "68th American Exhibition" in 1966. See Jack Burnham, "Systems Esthetics," *Artforum* 7, no. 1 (September 1968): 32.

22. Quoted in Bruce Glaser with Lucy R. Lippard, ed., "Questions to Stella and Judd," *Art News* 65, no. 5 (September 1966): 60.

23. Dan Flavin, "in daylight or cool white," *Artforum* 4, no. 4 (December 1965): 20–24.

24. *Ibid.*, p. 23.

25. See the catalog of the exhibition "Systemic Painting," (New York: Solomon R. Guggenheim Museum, 1966).

26. Michael Benedikt, "New York: Notes on the Whitney Annual 1966," *Art International* 11, no. 2 (February 20, 1967): 56.

27. Samuel Wagstaff, Jr., "Talking with Tony Smith," in Gregory Battcock, ed., *Minimal Art*, p. 381.

28. Quoted in Elayne Varian in her Introduction to the catalog of the exhibition "'Schemata 7," (New York: Finch College Museum of Art, 1967).

29. For further discussion see Irving Sandler, "Ronald Bladen," *Artforum* 5, no. 2 (October 1966): 32.

30. Mel Bochner, "Primary Structures," *Arts* 40, no. 8 (June 1966): 32.

31. For this and a detailed account of the Park Place Group see David Bourdon, "E = MC² a Go-Go," *Art News* 64, no. 9 (January 1966): 22–25 ff.

32. Henry T. Hopkins, Curator of Exhibitions at the Los Angeles County Museum of Art, attributes the change in sensibility to the "Little Masters" exhibitions held at the Ferus Gallery at that time which included Albers, Schwitters, Morandi and Cornell. See Henry T. Hopkins's essay in "The West Coast Now" exhibition catalog (Portland, Oregon: Portland Art Museum, February 9–March 6, 1968).

33. A number of San Francisco artists also worked with plastics after the mid-sixties; but despite certain similarities in materials and techniques their work had little in common with that of the Los Angeles group. Among the more important in the San Francisco area were Jerrold Ballaine, Mel Henderson and Harold Paris.

34. See footnote 4.

EARTHWORKS AND PROCESS ART

VIII

The Primary Structuralists, or Minimalists, were essentially concerned with reconstituting the object as art to avoid illusion, allusion, and metaphor. For them the object emphasized the concrete physicality and spatial positioning of matter rather than matter as referential image. The basic nature of three-dimensional art was changed, according to Robert Morris, "from particular forms, to ways of ordering, to methods of production, and finally to perceptual relevance." [1] Morris noted that the fact that art did not have to end in a finished work allowed the detachment of art's energy from the production of an object to the reclamation of process thus refocusing art as an energy which was driving to change perception.[2] As explained further by Jack Burnham, "In the transition from an object-oriented to a systems-oriented culture, change emanates not from things, but from the way things are done." [3] This new approach to the problem of dimensionality takes the conditions of the visual field itself as the spatial basis for its material art. And, as Morris has also indicated, "It is a shift that is on the one hand closer to the phenomenal fact of seeing the visual field and on the other is allied to the heterogeneous spread of substances that make up that field. In another era, one might have said that the difference was between a figurative and landscape mode." [4]

Thus this shift to a more literal use of materials—and to a focus on process—was more a progression out of Minimal Art than a radical break in ideology. Many artists like Morris and the late Robert Smithson moved directly and easily from one movement to the other. The publication of Morris's "Anti-Form" had followed his exhibition in 1967 at the Leo Castelli Gallery which presented yet another alternative to "estheticizing form": compositions of grey felt tacked to the wall or piled in unstudied randomness on the floor (Figure 1). This first visual departure from the exacting austerity of his previous work confirmed Morris as a pioneer of the emerging Process aesthetic. The work remained nonetheless within the conceptual system he had established in his early object sculptures, channeled into the constructions, and pursued simultaneously in his Dance-Happenings, significantly alongside the archetypal "soft" sculptor, Claes Oldenburg. Similarly, Smithson was experimenting with serial sculpture of progressively increasing size such as *Plunge* (1966) (Figure 2) and *Alogon #2* (1966) when he made the shift to working with large outdoor sites.

Minimal artists had used basic literal, geometric forms rather than invented, illusionistic new ones; likewise, the Process sculptors used materials and environmental elements in their natural state. By departing from traditional formats which make art look like art, both Minimal and Process artists permitted the inherent properties of the materials or elements to come across more clearly. As the new format involved placing things in an environment, indoors or out, the work attained a more "real" presence for both sculptor and spectator.[5]

Much the same can be said for materials and fabrication (often industrial, as in the fabrication of Judd's galvanized iron boxes or Morris's I-beam pieces) that shrugged off the loaded content implicit in more malleable materials that *look like* "artists' materials" and accepted in their stead materials that had a kind of non-art reality. The hardness of the Minimalists' materials took a stand against "plasticity," whereas the Process artists' softness of materials, while expressing the same disdain for "art content," also worked against the *a priori*-sense of "art as form" by the use of materials that all but deny being formed. Both Minimal and Process artists employed a studied attitude of detachment—deadpan-ness in Judd's case especially —as if the distance between the artist and the material was essential to give the material autonomy, and therefore reality.

The move toward transcending the literal object of the Minimalists is now seen to have taken two major directions. Robert Smithson, Michael Heizer, Hans Haacke, Walter de Maria and Dennis Oppenheim, among others, began working outdoors with natural elements such as desert sand, dirt, salt, water, ice, rocks, and grass. Their results have been called "Earthworks," in that they worked with the existing natural landscape or with elements of the landscape, or site, which were brought back to the gallery and arranged there. The Process artists—at least most of them—worked indoors, using materials and elements that were without inherent object-value or object-durability such as string, cloth, rubber, lead, chalk, felt, graphite, glass, plastic, air, and light; they were essentially concerned with allowing the inherent properties of the materials to dictate possibilities of action and form.[6]

Figure 1. Robert Morris. *Untitled.* 1967–68. Felt, 1″ x 15′ x 6′.

Figure 2. Robert Smithson. *Plunge.* 1966. (Collection, Mr. & Mrs. John G. Powers.)

Process Art activity has engaged Robert Morris, Richard Serra, Carl Andre, Keith Sonnier, Eva Hesse, Bruce Nauman, and several others. Behind the ideas of some of them—and now as integral to the movement as the ideas of Duchamp—lies the early sixties work of the Düsseldorf artist, Joseph Beuys. Beuys was a major influence on Morris and Serra, particularly, though he was generally unknown in this country at the time. His work is distinctly political, constituting a vituperative attack on the capitalist system that he believes has fostered the art market and curtailed the freedom of all people—artists and art consumers alike. As did Duchamp, Beuys advocated freeing art from all restraints imposed by what art is supposed to be.

In this country, however, there developed a more subtle but perhaps more pervasive politic in Process Art of the sixties. Raw materials, presented not in a form for contemplation but for a shared moment of recognition between artist and audience, represent a coming to terms with the real "stuff" of life which lies beneath the slick and conventional veneer of twentieth-century urban society. Process Art can be seen as an implicit attack on modern values and the consumer ideology. People feel alienated by the impersonality of their lives, and discrete well-fabricated art could be seen as an extension of that artificial condition. Robert Morris wrote in 1969:[7]

241

An advanced, technological, urban environment is a totally manufactured one. Interaction with the environment tends more and more toward information processing in one form or another and away from interactions involving transformations of matter. The very means and visibility for material transformations become more remote and recondite. Centers for production are increasingly located outside the urban environment in what are euphemistically termed "industrial parks." In these grim, remote areas the objects of daily use are produced by increasingly obscure processes and the matter transformed is increasingly synthetic and unidentifiable. As a consequence our immediate surroundings tend to be read as "forms" that have been punched out of unidentifiable, indestructible plastic or unfamiliar metal alloys. It is interesting to note that in an urban environment construction sites become small theatrical arenas, the only places where raw substances and processes of its transformation are visible and the only places where random distributions are tolerated.

The concern with "raw substances" and "random distributions" is not a new one. The carve-direct and direct-metal sculptors had shared a similar interest in exposing the imprint of process and chance. But the salient characteristic of Process Art is the indeterminacy of formal boundaries. Morris's thread and mirror accumulation, which filled a room of the Leo Castelli Gallery in 1968, Serra's splashes of molten lead, Sonnier's wall flockings do not so much exist within space as they fill and define it. The ultimate indeterminate field, short of outer space, however, is the earth's surface. Artists dealing with natural processes found it artificial to display these phenomena within the walls of a gallery that defined, like a picture frame, the most non-delimited form as form. For that matter, even the studio of the artist became a delimiting and forming structure, like the geometric cage-like enclosures of Giacometti, Grippe, Lassaw and Lipton, or those of Ferber in the second half of the fifties, which contained the "indeterminate." "Happenings" had moved off the stage and into the environment (as Segal's compositions of figures gradually had shifted from "piece" to "tableau" to the placement of the figure in a real physical environment). So did several of the artists from the Minimalist milieu withdraw from the studio and gallery, and ultimately from urban imagery and industrial modes of sculpture production, to develop a new kind of landscape art executed in the landscape itself. Out of doors and especially on the surfaces of deserts, plains, and salt flats, the boundary conditions of the gallery and studio space were negated and the indeterminate field (of the kind sculptors had had before gallery arrangements became compositions *within* the framework of the gallery) was recovered. The form-defining environmental controls of the gallery— lighting, white walls, carpeted floors, silence, and stabilized climate—were also negated. In their stead the indeterminate behavior of nature was accepted.

Robert Smithson (1938–1973) was born in Passaic, New Jersey, and studied at the Art Students League. In 1966–67 he served as an artist-consultant to a group of engineers and architects who were developing an air terminal between Fort Worth and Dallas. Instead of art installed in and around the site, Smithson proposed the site itself as a sculptural experience: a progression of ground-hugging triangular concrete segments whose spiral configuration could be fully perceived only from the aircraft on takeoff and landing. Smithson envisioned a "total engagement with the building process," a dialectic between the "concatenation of aerial perceptions and the conception of the air terminal itself, firmly rooted in the earth." [8] Smithson noted at the time the geological processes, especially sedimentation of matter, that would become involved in his works. This he would later call "Pulverizations"—the idea that oxidation, hydration, carbonization, and solution (the major processes of rock and mineral disintegration) are processes that could be turned toward the making of art. Of the air terminal, he wrote:[9]

The entire project shall rest on an elevation of about 550 feet to 620 feet. The area is well drained and practically free of trees and natural obstructions. The sub-surface site of the project contains sediments from the Cretaceous Age. This underground site was penetrated by "auger borings" and "core borings." All the soil samples encountered in the borings were visually classified and tested. These samples ranged from clay to shale rock. The "boring" if seen as a discrete step in the development of the whole site has an esthetic value. It is an "invisible hole," and could be defined by Carl Andre's motto—"A thing is a hole in a thing it is not." The "boring," like other "earth works," is becoming more and more important to artists. Pavements, holes, trenches, mounds, heaps, paths, ditches, roads, terraces, etc., all have an esthetic potential.

In his 1968 article, "A Sedimentation of the Mind," Smithson wrote that heavy construction had a kind of devastating primordial grandeur, in many ways more powerful and interesting than the finished product, such as a road or a building.[10] He then became increasingly interested in excluding technological processes from the making of art in order that process of a more fundamental order might re-emerge. The break-up, or fragmentation of matter, he observed, makes one aware of the substrata of the Earth before it is overly refined by industry into sheet metal, aluminum, extruded I-beams, tubes, etc. The city makes one forget about earth. In his elegant manner, Smithson articulates the correspondence of mind and matter: "By refusing 'technological miracles,' the artist begins to know the corroded moments, the carboniferous states of thought, the shrinkage of mental mud, in the geological chaos—in the strata of esthetic consciousness. The fuses between mind and matter is a mine of information. . . . A sense of the Earth as a map undergoing disruption leads the artist to the realization that nothing is certain or formal. Language itself becomes mountains of symbolic debris." [11]

In his first earthwork in 1966, Smithson was concerned with converging the concept of the work with a chosen location, or site, which had to have an "oceanic de-differentiated" quality—vast total vision. His problem was to contain this "oceanic" site. As art is concerned with limits, Smithson saw the process of creating the work as a dialectic between concept and the mapping of a site; the finite object created is the limit. He called these works "Non-Sites," an interaction between the oceanic and the finite; he preferred to think of them as maps rather than as objects.

Non-Site #1 (1966) is the center of a hexagonal airfield in the Pine Barren Plains in South New Jersey. Six vanishing points lose themselves in a pre-existing earth mound; six runways radiate around a central axis, anchoring thirty-one subdivisions. The actual Non-Site is made up of 31 metal containers of painted blue aluminum, each containing sand from the site. In *Tar Pool and Gravel Pit* (1966) the spectator is made conscious of primal ooze. A molten substance is poured into a square sink that is surrounded by another square sink of coarse gravel; when the tar cools it flattens into a sticky level deposit. "This carbonaceous sediment brings to mind a tertiary world of petroleum, asphalts, ozokerite, and bitumeous agglomerations." [12] Here the work is not derived or evoked by a site, but creates a mental site of primordial time.

In constructing *Non-Site: Franklin, N.J.* in 1968, exhibited at the Dwan Gallery   243

Figure 3. Robert Smithson. *Non-site: Franklin, N.J.* 1968. Aerial map.

in the fall of that year, Smithson used a grid-system of parallel lines laid out as if on an inclined plane and overlaid on an aerial map of the Franklin area (Figure 3). The resulting five trapezoids were reproduced as five wood bins in which ore rocks from the site were placed (Figure 4). What is curious and characteristic of such Non-Sites is that they are fragments of the original landscape without the inherent sensation of the whole; there is only literal allusion to the original site. The Non-Site, as the absence of site reduced to constraint, negates the site rather than evokes it. As explained by Smithson, "The container is in a sense a fragment of itself, something that could be called a three-dimensional map. Without appeal to 'Gestalts' or 'anti-form' it actually exists as a fragment of a greater fragmentation. It is a three-dimensional *perspective* that has broken away from the whole, while containing the lack of its own containment. There are no mysteries in these vestiges, no traces of an end or a beginning." [13]

Figure 4. Robert Smithson. *Non-site: Franklin, N.J.* 1968. Painted wood bins filled with rocks, 16½″ x 82″ x 110″.

It is incongruous to see piles of rocks—rough fragments of a timeless expanse—contained within the immaculate metal bins which derive from Smithson's early Minimal pieces (and which keep his work within the large scope of sculpture that has always been a matter of contours containing an expansive force). But it is precisely this incongruity that makes the Non-Sites so provocative. Industrially fabricated, repetitive, slickly painted containers attempt to contain the uncontainable. Echoes of geologic eternity and entropic decay are heightened by these fragments, which have been wrenched from the earth and placed, work-of-art-like, in a 57th Street gallery.

In 1969 Smithson executed a series called *Mirror Displacements* (Figure 5), first in New York State and then in the Yucatan. Each displacement consisted of twelve square mirrors cantilevered from mounds of soil or sand or undergrowth (depending on the site), facing skyward. The sites were chosen for their ancient and deserted character, the mirror reflections displacing random fragments of both earth and sky. As described by Smithson: "The mirror displacement cannot be expressed in rational dimensions. The distances between the twelve mirrors are shadowed disconnections, where measure is dropped and incomputable. . . . The questions the mirrors ask always fall short of the answers." [14]

Michael Heizer, who was born in Berkeley, California, in 1944, attended the San Francisco Art Institute in 1963–64. As a teenager, he accompanied his father, the anthropologist Robert F. Heizer, on numerous archeological expeditions. After a period as a painter, he came to New York in 1966 and began to work with earth forms in 1967. Heizer, who has stated his refusal to create an object in a world already full of objects, called his earth projects the alternative to the absolute city system. "Artists have been misled into thinking that you have to create something in order to contribute to art. I want to create without creating a thing." [15] Heizer's *Circumflex*, commissioned by the New York taxi-cab magnate Robert Scull, is a 120-foot-long trench gouged out of the Nevada desert with pick axes, shovels, and wheelbarrows. *Compression Line* (Figure 6) records the effect of the earth pressing against the sides of two parallel lengths of plywood, causing them to converge into 245

Figure 8. Walter de Maria. *Half-Mile Long Drawing.* April 1968. Two chalk lines 12′ apart in Mojave Desert, California, ½ mile long.

Dennis Oppenheim, who was born in 1938 in Mason City, Washington, studied at the California College of Arts and Crafts and Stanford University. In 1967 he covered a New York City asphalt parking lot with salt; in 1968 he scattered V-shaped wood blocks in an avalanche that rolled down a Long Island Expressway escarpment. In both works, Oppenheim retaliates against technology by imposing materials where they are not welcome and out of context.

Haacke and Oppenheim bridge Earthworks and Minimal Art in a highly conceptual fashion. Oppenheim often draws analogies between person (both physical and mental presence) and landscape. In the spring of 1970 the Gibson Gallery showed various projects that involved both Oppenheim's bodily interaction with the land and the residual imprint of his presence. One such project was a 1969 photographic presentation of *Ground Mutations* (Figure 9). Wearing special shoes with four-inch diagonal grooves down the soles and heels, Oppenheim walked about New York and New Jersey, "connecting the patterns of thousands of individuals." In 1971–72 Oppenheim carried out *Polarities*—his most poetic and personal project to date. The artist chose two drawings: the first, one of the earliest drawings by his baby daughter, the second, presumably the last one by his father who had recently died. On a map Oppenheim enlarged both drawings to a scale of about 500 feet. He then plotted them with magnesium flares on the flat Long Island landscape. Aerial photographs were taken and displayed in the gallery along with the original drawings. Oppenheim's dialectic between autobiographical fact or action and cosmic theatre causes the viewer to identify with both extremes—the loneliness of personal artifact and the loneliness of infinite space into which that artifact has been mirrored.

248

KEARNY, N.J.

N.Y.C. (MIDTOWN)

JERSEY CITY, N.J.

KEARNY, N.J.

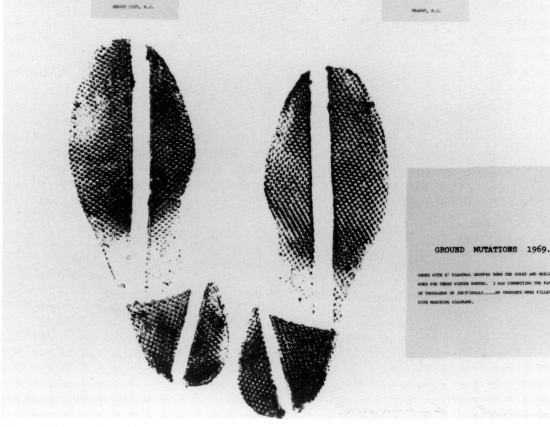

GROUND MUTATIONS 1969.

SHOES WITH ¼" DIAGONAL GROOVES DOWN THE SOLES AND HEELS WERE
WORN FOR THREE WINTER MONTHS. I WAS CONNECTING THE PATTERNS
OF THOUSANDS OF INDIVIDUALS.....MY THOUGHTS WERE FILLED
WITH MARCHING DIAGRAMS.

Figure 9. Dennis Oppenheim. *Ground Mutations.* 1969.

Figure 10. Robert Morris. *Observatory.* 1971. Earth, timber, granite, steel, water. 230′ across. (Photo: Peter Shuit.)

Similarly, the earthworks of Robert Morris involve an eclectic and synthetic composition of motives. During the summer of 1971 in Holland Morris executed an enormous work titled *Observatory* (Figure 10). Concentric, circular soil embankments surrounded by canals formed an imposing fortress-like structure which, by means of notches in the soil and sight lines, were oriented to the sun's equinox. Morris has written that "The *Observatory* is not a scientific instrument any more than it is an earthwork. . . . Enclosures and openings; the uses of earth, sky, and water; sight lines and walkways; changing levels—such things ally the work more to Neolithic and Oriental building complexes than to the sculptural qualities of earthworks." [18]

It is difficult therefore to categorize this work, as it is not left to be worked upon by the elements, nor is it an intervention in the landscape. A rather heroic, uncompromising gesture, the *Observatory* assumes the character of an anomalous, ritualistic configuration—mysteriously left whole, creating a psychological confrontation for the modern viewer who has been neither prepared nor initiated into its "use." [19]

Serra, Hesse, Sonnier, and Nauman are most strictly classifiable as Process artists. Richard Serra, who was born in 1939 in San Francisco, studied at the University of California, Berkeley, and Santa Barbara, and at Yale. He has been the most critically acclaimed of the young "Process" sculptors and the most admired by his fellow artists. In 1967 he exhibited several rubber works at the Noah Goldowsky Gallery. One piece consisted of nine sections of floppy rubber with each section comprised of twelve belt-like lengths fixed together and fastened to the wall by numerous bent nails. These thick harness-like assemblages looked improvisational and seemed to form random patterns, yet the position of each part was fixed and repeatable. A neon tube, acting as a linear counterpoint, underscored the work. In the multi-unit piece (Figure 11), a blue neon tube meandered through the rubber: it was both firm line and insubstantial luminosity, and it paralleled the duality of solid rubber and the impression of random softness.

Figure 11. Richard Serra. *Belts*. 1966–67. Vulcanized rubber and neon, 84″ x 288″ x 20″. (Collection, Count Panza.)

In 1968 Serra sensed the similar entropic qualities of rubber and lead. Involved with maximizing the possibilities of lead, accepting its limitations and specific qualities, he subjected it to a variety of processes: molting, slashing, diluting, rolling, folding, bending. In one of his earliest lead works, *Splash-piece*, exhibited at the Castelli warehouse exhibition in December 1968, and subsequently executed for a number of shows in Europe, molten lead was flung against the point at which the wall and floor met, lumping and obscuring the right angle of conjuncture.[20] For the spring 1969 Whitney exhibition "Anti-Illusion: Procedures and Materials" a different version of *Splash-piece* was created. In this instance, each imposition of lead against the wall was pried and scraped loose and laid down in parallel rows. The process was repeated eight to twelve times in a progression to the final splash that remained against the wall (Figure 12).

Figure 12. Richard Serra. *Casting*. 1969. Lead, 300″ x 180″.

Serra's work in 1969 brought a particular focus and tension to the gravitational problems of working with lead. In the Guggenheim Museum exhibition, "Nine Young Artists," installed in June of 1969, Serra showed nine works, described as "Props," which explored the capacity of two separate weights of lead within the tense, localized control of wall space. Each work posed a different gravitational problem: a large square of lead pinned a roll of lead slightly longer than itself against the wall; a three-foot-long tube of lead was projected from the wall about seven feet up, held in mutual balance by a sheet of lead projecting up from the floor; a one-hundred-inch square of lead was propped against the wall by a roll of lead that rose diagonally from the floor, *One Ton Prop* of 1969 (Figure 13). Neither the roll nor the sheets were affixed to each other in any of these works; the pieces demonstrated a mutually functioning role in the formal relationships of the parts. The contact of the two elements, the purely physical characteristics of his material—the force, weight, gravity—carry the expression. As an art of "overt materiality," [21] the emphasis is on action, event, and form; the result is aggrandized gesture and arrested motion,[22] an active aggressive sculpture, harnessing a potential for violence, controlling a space, defining a problem, and setting up a situation for the drama of the material. Serra has commented that he is interested in the logic of his material, as well as in the fallibility of physical process. In a short movie for the Whitney exhibition, he dropped bits of material before the lens. The only visible elements on the screen were his hand—along with his arm, the falling material, and his hand grasping for the falling bits, sometimes succeeding in catching them, only to release them again.

The contrast of Smithson's and Serra's work is the essential dialectic for most sculpture of the second half of the sixties. Smithson views Serra's art as "post-perfect pure art." Serra's work, he says, is not the result of formal judgment, but rather of a play of wit. It essentially illustrates the transformation of phenomena into physical entity. Of Smithson, Serra has said: "His ideas are brilliant, if he could only find his form." [23]

Figure 13. Richard Serra. *One Ton Prop.* 1969. Lead, 48″ x 55″ x 55″.

Figure 14. Richard Serra. *Shift*. 1970–72. (King City, Canada.) Six rectilinear concrete sections.

Serra has always been involved with what things "are," rather than with how things "look." In this sense he admires filmmaker Goddard for his simultaneity of process and his holding of an image. Since he is concerned with concretizing the process his forcible insistence on relationships deals with process as well as look. The power of his pieces is not so much in the beauty of their unitary images (though they are enduring as images) as in the act of harnessing energy and gravity at a precarious chosen moment. This amounts to an arrestation of time. He maximizes information about the material while remaining aware of the kind of information that is transmitted. He speaks of slow information and fast information, characterizing himself by the fast. Like most of the Process artists Serra insists on a subjective relationship between the work and the viewer.[24]

Serra's attitude is most forceful in *Shift*, executed from 1970–72 in King City, Canada (Figure 14). The site was staked out by two people walking the distance of a field. In commenting on this work he explains that "The boundaries of the work became the maximum distance two people could occupy and still keep each other in view. The horizon of the work was established by the possibility of maintaining this mutual viewpoint." [25] Six rectilinear cement slabs, five feet high by eight inches thick, were placed on the slopes of the site. Each slab, beginning flush with the ground, extended the distance it took for the land to drop five feet. The length and slope of each element was thereby determined by the contour of the land. Serra has written: "What I wanted was a dialectic between one's perception of the place in totality and one's relation to the field as walked. The result is a way of measuring oneself against the indeterminacy of the land. I'm not interested in looking at sculpture which is solely defined by its internal relationships." [26] The piece cannot be taken in at a glance, or even by an aerial photograph. It is a piece about walking around a field for forty-five minutes: "The work establishes a measure: one's relation to it and the land." [27]

253

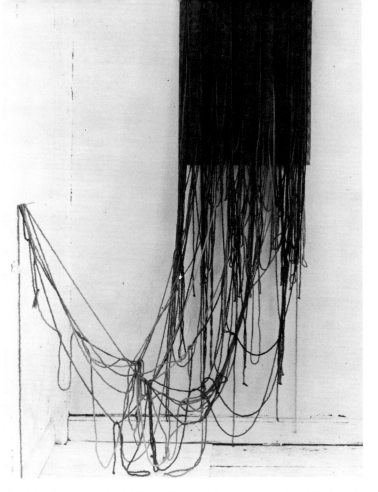

Figure 15. Eva Hesse. *Ennead*. 1966. Wood, plastic cord, acrylic, 36″ x 22″ x 1½″. (Collection, Mr. and Mrs. Victor Ganz.)

Eva Hesse gained critical acclaim in 1968, following her show at the Fischbach Gallery, and she was one of nine artists in the Castelli warehouse show of that same year. Hesse (1936–1970), who was born in Hamburg, Germany, came to New York with her parents in 1939. She studied at Cooper Union, New York, and then at Yale. Her work was well known and admired by other New York artists long before the public became aware of her accomplishments; a posthumous exhibition at the Guggenheim in 1972 consolidated her place among those at the forefront of the anti-formalist wing of Process artists. Her purposefully awkward compositions in plastic, Latex, and other "soft" materials are tenuously balanced between the ephemeral and the menacing. The informality and unpredictability of Hesse's work result in a strikingly personal statement, full of the presence and hand of the artist. In *Ennead* of 1966 (Figure 15), a vast number of plastic cords pulled through a board in a regular pattern, end up in an undefined tangle, that scrapes the floor. In a 1970 interview in *Artform* Hesse commented:[28]

I'm not conscious of materials as a beautiful essence . . . For me the great involvement is for a purpose—to arrive at an end—not that much of a thing in itself. . . . I am interested in finding out through working on the piece some of the potential and not the preconceived. . . . I want to allow myself to get involved in what is happening and what can happen and be completely free to let that go and change. . . . I do, however, have a very strong feeling about honesty—and in the process, I like to be, it sounds corny, true to whatever I use, and use it in the least pretentious and most direct way. . . . My attitude toward art is most open. It is totally unconservative—just freedom and willingness to work. I really walk on the edge.

Figure 16. Keith Sonnier. *Untitled.*
1968. Neon, cloth, 108″ x 60″. (Collection,
Herr Bönig, Germany. Photo: Peter Moore.)

Keith Sonnier was born in 1941 in Louisiana and graduated from the University of Louisiana in 1963. He became interested in the inherent properties of materials after viewing the work of Joseph Beuys while in Germany in 1964. Sonnier received an MFA from Rutgers in 1966. In 1968 he began to work with diaphanous materials and elements, such as mirrors, glass, plastic discs, and gauze—often in combination with neon lights. Sonnier's approach is painterly; he has always admired painters— Mondrian, Malevitch, Matisse, the early work of Poons, Stella, Peter Young—and he is concerned with pictorial space. He uses the gallery wall as a ground and has sometimes treated it as a pictorial plane. His materials generally function in low relief against the wall surface, and when materials are overlaid in his work, the space seems to recede rather than to carry forward, as in a relief. The linear extensions of his electrical cords and diaphanous materials trail into space as in his *Untitled* of 1968 (Figure 16).[29]

255

In an exhibition at the Leo Castelli Gallery in June 1969, Sonnier's piece displayed a tube of orange neon wrapped around the base of a white light bulb which then cast a white reflection on the wall, bleaching out the orange of the neon. The color-light was subtle; a black electric cord hung randomly down and across the piece, contradicting the fragile beauty of the light. Although the contrast of the controlled neon and cord looked arbitrary, its arbitrariness was intentional, as if the cord was a manifestation of process. Sonnier will deny the importance of process. He maintains instead that he is concerned with the final image, though he remains free to incorporate any element that the process reveals into the final work.

The Californian Bruce Nauman was perhaps the most enigmatic of the Process artists. Admired by his fellow artists, he was also the most harshly attacked by critics. His pieces often displayed an unfinished look: the fiberglass works of 1965 resembled molds for sculptures yet to be cast more than finished works. The "throw-away," limped look was intensified in the later rubber on cloth backing pieces that he produced late in 1965.

Nauman was born in 1941 in Fort Wayne, Indiana. In 1965, he attended the University of California, Davis, studying under William T. Wiley and Robert Arneson with fellow students Frank Owen and Stephen Kaltenbach. While his earlier pieces were concerned with form as such, those after 1966 involved efforts at a more direct communication of thought process between Nauman and the spectator; the title was the catalyst for the spectator's perception and understanding of the work. Around 1967 the titles of his works became integral to their meanings as their particular quality lay between the poetic evocation of titles and the visual form. In a *Foot of Lead Pressed Between My Palms* (1969), a square of lead several inches thick rests on a wooden support which is raised slightly off the floor. The viewer must arbitrate between the title and the piece, thus participating in the process of the work, just as Nauman himself participates in using his own body as the measurement of some of his works.[30] *From Hand to Mouth* of 1967 (Figure 17) is a sculptural fragment cast from his hand to his chin and mouth: his *Device for Left Armpit* (1967) is a mold of his armpit. Nauman's imagery is a spin-off from San Francisco Funk Art.

Nauman considers himself the American equivalent of Marcel Duchamp. He functions somewhat outside definition; his works outrage, especially his use of elaborate titles and puns which reflect his Duchampian legacy in their quotations of Duchamp's work. Duchamp had made a neon spirograph of an alphabetical letter; likewise Nauman, using blue and peach neon, spelled out *The True Artist Helps the World by Revealing Mystic Truths*. He has also executed a transparent rose-colored mylar banner which reads *The True Artist Is an Amazing Luminous Fountain* (1967). A photograph titled *15″ x 138″* reads *A Composite Photo of My Name as Though It Were Written on the Surface of the Moon* (1967).

Art critic Knute Stiles, reviewing a 1966 exhibition of Nauman's works in San Francisco, observed that "all the pieces are so ambiguous as to be infinitely suggestive."[31] And it is precisely this element that some of Nauman's fellow sculptors—especially Serra and Sonnier, appreciate and that his critics detest. His work is not overtly available to a single interpretation. Max Kozloff, reviewing the December 1968 Castelli "Nine in a Warehouse" exhibition, wrote of Nauman that he "repels both attentive looking and conceptual openness in a Dada gesture that is too frivolous for me."[32] Serra sees Nauman's separation of image and word (object and title) as surrealistic paradox, which he recognizes as the essential content of Nauman's work. It is the nonchalance of Nauman's attitude that is most compelling—the kind of cool indifference to art that has always been admired in Duchamp.

256

In 1967, Nauman discussed an outdoor piece that he had in mind:[33]

I thought that outdoor sculpture was usually big and durable but that seemed very dumb, because it's already nice outside with trees and fields, and I didn't want to put something there and change it all. I thought maybe I'd make something which fell apart after a while—which would return to nature. Like dirt or paper, that would disintegrate. Then I made this piece which is a plaque which you put on a tree. After a few years the tree would grow over it, and finally cover it up, and it would be gone . . . Then I made plastic copies and I thought maybe I could send them to people I knew all over the world. It reads "A rose has no teeth." I got it from Wittgenstein. He's talking about language and he says to think about the difference between "A rose has no teeth" and "A baby has no teeth." With the first one, you don't know what it means, because they have as much to do with nature as anything I could think of.

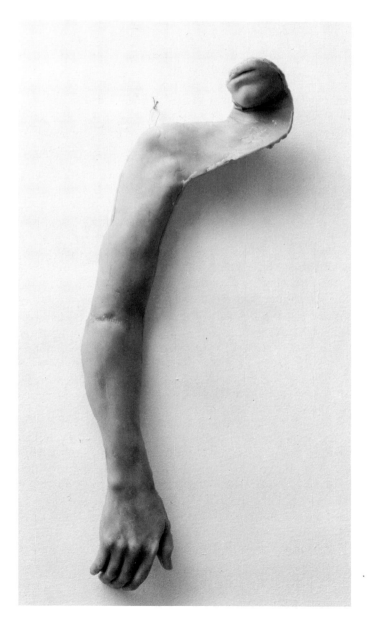

Figure 17. Bruce Nauman. *From Hand to Mouth*. 1967. Wax over cloth, 30″ x 10″ x 4″. (Collection, Joseph Helman, New York.)

Figure 18. Robert Smithson. *Spiral Jetty.* 1970. (Great Salt Lake, Utah.) 1500′ long.

The Process artists have reinvested recent art with a kind of immediate vitalism, just as the Earthworks artists have reinstated an oceanic romanticism about the form of nature and the "vitalistic" processes of geological motion, time, and space. The inertness of Morris's felt pieces or of Serra's lead configurations, their absolute silence or their deadness and limpness, evoke feelings of immense duration, which is itself a sense of immense space. In his film on the construction of his *Spiral Jetty* (Figure 18), in the Great Salt Lake, Smithson, as narrator, wanders back through the space of time to when the lake was thought to have an underground outlet, or inlet, from the Pacific Ocean. He locates the site of the outlet, imagines the whirlpool, the spiraling eddy; and with a monstrous bulldozer, filmed at times as if it were a primordial dinosaur uprooting the earth with its brute energy, constructs a "positive" stone spiral that mirrors in solidity the "negative" eddy of the displaced water. The spiral in place, Smithson had the bulldozer pass over it with a ripping blade. In the film the phallus-shaped blade lowers and penetrates the surface of the eddy and rips furrows in its body like a plow furrowing the body of the earth at seeding time.

Smithson takes us back through much of the history of American sculpture in the process of creating this work. One recognizes the geometry of the work as formed by the energy of process: the whirlpool in the artist's mind becoming the spiral jetty, which registers the process as physical fact. In constructing it, a form is imposed on the idea; in texturing it with the ripping blade, the artist's "hand" is imprinted in the form (as, for example, Lipton had textured the surface of his sculpture with molten metal, or as David Smith had textured his *Cubii* with a grinding wheel). Gone from tradition, however, is the anthropomorphic imagery and the discrete object-quality of sculpture that was originated and sustained for centuries by the primacy of the human and animal as the subject matter of sculpture.

The evolution from a vertical and delimiting anthropomorphism to a kind of horizontal indeterminacy of Earthworks and Process Art may be one manifestation of a significant change in modern life and attitudes. Jack Burnham has written that the progress of art is indicative of the direction and end-purpose of a civilization. He quotes Sigfried Giedion, who pointed out that prehistoric art, frontal and relief-like, paralleled the period of man's total integration with the natural world, that free-standing, anthropomorphic sculpture evolved along with man's homeocentric rise above the animal world. Burnham goes on to propose very tentatively that technological art signals that an irreversible technology is replacing organic life with very sophisticated forms of synthetic life.[34] Burnham's assumption must be challenged, however, on the evidential ground that technological art has *never* proven to have been more than incidentally in the vanguard of art; nor, for that matter, has technology ever been more than incidentally in the vanguard of science. On the other hand, Earthworks and Process Art have brought about pervasive changes in art methodology, art criticism, and the sociology of art—even in the general lifestyle of artists. Faced then with Earthworks and Process Art, which reject not only anthropomorphism but a sophisticated technology as well, one might interpret such developments as teleological auguries of an end to humanism and a return to yet a new naturalism, heralding a new time, cyclical or a-logical perhaps, rather than "progressive." Or rather, one could view them as manifestations of a romantic yearning for what *seems* irrevocably past. For in the on-going process of art, as in the process of life, nothing is ever left behind; nothing is ever final.

The history of sculpture is all of a piece in the evolving present; there is neither a past nor a future except in the alchemical formula of the *now*. To predict that synthetic life will replace organic life, or that technological art will replace organic art is only to preach from a new pulpit the futuristic prophecies of the Constructivists, whose moralistic predictions proved to be as pathetically lacking in wisdom as doomsday predictions based on man's immorality. Just as Classicism was (and not just incidentally) a moralistic rejection of the sensuousness of Romanticism, Constructivism was motivated to a large extent by moral conflict with any art that registered below the head or behind the present. In the classic partitioning of human sensibility, consciousness and morality (the Constructivist state of mind) are present- and future-oriented—the dreams of the Constructivist are invariably wide-awake daydreams, unfolding solely in the mind and in the eye that looks straight ahead. On the other hand, the unconscious, which is associated with fleshiness, viscera, intuitions, night dreams, and dark passions, harbors the residue of an evolutionary past that surfaces, symptom-like, as immorality. This duality, which a reductionist Darwinianism, a reductionist Freudianism—and a reductionist art criticism—have bestowed upon us is, in the final analysis, just the Heaven-Hell dichotomy of Western theology all over again. By whatever simplistic form it is given: Upper World/Under World, ego/id, conscious/unconscious, synthetic/organic, mind/body, morality/immorality, Classicism/Romanticism, Constructivism/Surrealism—it's all the same thing: the opposition of complements that generates awareness and spurs humanity toward a homeostasis that in turn it rejects as boring. If sculpture plays a part in shaping human destiny it is surely not, as Burnham says, shaping it as "a post-human species," as if the terrestrial ego will one day—like the coming of Christ—capitulate completely to a deified super-ego and, following "some unseen plan," enter into an eternal phase of synthetic life in which neither animalism, humanism, nor naturalism would figure. Surely that's not the kind of hereafter that the Creator had in mind. The machinomorphic idealism of the thirties may have reemerged in the sixties as the technomorphic, but just as Surrealism checked the theo-technology of Constructivism in the forties, Earthworks and Process Art in the sixties checked the belief that a new technological art would propel us into a synthetic future. In fact, no period of human sensibility has experienced a closer integration of the human with the form, substance, and creatures of the earth than the 1970's thus far.

259

NOTES

1. Robert Morris, "Notes on Sculpture, Part 4: Beyond Objects," *Artforum* 7, no. 8 (April 1969): 54.

2. *Ibid.*

3. Jack Burnham, "Systems Esthetics," *Artforum* 7, no. 1 (September 1968): 31.

4. Morris, "Notes on Sculpture," p. 51.

5. Gregoire Müller, "Robert Morris Presents Anti-Form," *Arts* 43, no. 4 (February 1969): 30.

6. Marcia Tucker in *Anti-Illusion: Procedures/Materials* (New York: Whitney Museum of American Art, 1969), p. 39.

7. Morris, "Notes on Sculpture," p. 54.

8. Robert Smithson, "Aerial Art," *Studio International* 177, no. 910 (April 1969): 180. (Smithson had invited Andre, LeWitt and Morris to participate in this project.)

9. Robert Smithson, "Toward the Development of an Air-Terminal Site," *Artforum* 5, no. 10 (June 1967): 38.

10. Robert Smithson, "A Sedimentation of the Mind," *Artforum* 7, no. 1 (September 1968): 50.

11. *Ibid.*, p. 50.

12. *Ibid.*, p. 45.

13. *Ibid.*, p. 50. For more on Smithson's "Non-Sites" see Lawrence Alloway, "Robert Smithson's Development," *Artforum* 11, no. 3 (November 1972): 53–60.

14. Robert Smithson, "Incidents of Mirror Travel in the Yucatan," *Artforum* 8, no. 1 (September 1969): 30.

15. David Shirey, "Impossible Art—What It Is," *Art in America* 57, no. 3 (May–June 1969): 34.

16. See Smithson, "A Sedimentation of the Mind," p. 50.

17. See the introduction to *Earthworks* (Ithaca, New York: Andrew Dickson White Museum, Cornell University, 1969).

18. Robert Morris, "Observatory," *Avalanche*, no. 3 (Fall 1971): 35.

19. Several of the younger artists working today are similarly interested in constructing ritualistic structures which imply "use" by their very wholeness and careful execution and yet deny "function" as we know it. In 1972 Alice Aycock constructed on a field in Pennsylvania a large wooden maze. The local youth have taken great pains to make their way to this isolated structure, using it as a meeting and festival place. They have no idea why or when it was built. The following year Aycock constructed a "house" which consisted solely of a sodded roof with stone gables lying on the ground; the gable was only three feet from the ground; the eaves rested on ground beams. Object-function was denied; one had to crawl on the ground to enter and experience the space—an attic space at ground level. Function and action approach ritual as the experience of attic occurs on the "ground" floor (not completely unlike the experience of the sky reflected in a mirror that lies on the ground).

20. It has been observed by critics that the method and appearance of the *Splash-piece* is akin to Abstract Expressionism, but Serra denies that there is any connection. *Splash-piece* also seems reminiscent of Joseph Beuys's margarine piece in which the right angle of floor and wall is covered, but in a more carefully finished manner.

21. Barbara Rose, "Problems of Criticism, VI," *Artforum* 7, no. 9 (May 1969): 48.

22. See the catalog *Nine Young Artists* (New York: The Solomon R. Guggenheim Museum, 1969)

23. Interview with Richard Serra conducted on my behalf by Judith Wechsler, 1971.

24. See note 22.

25. Richard Serra, "Shift," *Arts* 47, no. 6 (April 1973): 50.

26. *Ibid.*

27. *Ibid.*, p. 52.

28. Cindy Nemser, "An Interview with Eva Hesse," *Artforum* 8, no. 9 (May 1970): 60.

29. Max Kozloff, "Nine in a Warehouse," *Artforum* 7, no. 6 (February 1969): 41.

30. This description and interpretation is essentially as given me by Judith Wechsler.

31. Knute Stiles, "San Francisco," *Artforum* 5, no. 4 (December 1966): 65–66.

32. Kozloff, "Nine in a Warehouse," p. 42.

33. Joe Raffaele and Elizabeth Baker, "The Way-Out West; Interviews with Four San Francisco Artists," *Art News* 66, no. 4 (Summer 1967): 41.

34. Jack Burnham, *Beyond Modern Sculpture* (New York: Braziller, 1967), p. 371.

In formulating this chapter I benefitted not only from the research assistance of Judith Wechsler but also from many discussions with Meg Shore during the time we jointly organized the "Interventions in Landscape" show at M.I.T. in the spring of 1974.

BIBLIOGRAPHY

BOOKS

AMAYA, MARIO. *Pop Art and After.* New York: Viking Press, 1965. Selected bibliography.

ARNASON, H. H. *Alexander Calder.* Princeton, N.J.: Van Nostrand, 1966.

ARNASON, H. H. *Calder.* London: Thames and Hudson, 1971.

ARNASON, H. H. *History of Modern Art: Painting, Sculpture, Architecture.* New York: Abrams, 1968. Bibliography.

ASHTON, DORE. *Modern American Sculpture.* New York: Abrams, 1968.

ASHTON, DORE. *The Unknown Shore: A View of Contemporary Art.* Boston, Mass.: Little, Brown, 1962.

BARO, GENE. *Claes Oldenburg: Drawings and Prints.* New York: Chelsea House, 1969. Includes catalogue raisonné of drawings from 1958–1967; bibliography.

BARR, ALFRED H., JR., ed. *Masters of Modern Art.* New York: Simon & Schuster, 1954.

BATTCOCK, GREGORY, ed. *Minimal Art: A Critical Anthology.* New York: Dutton, 1968.

BAUR, JOHN I. H. *Revolution and Tradition in Modern American Art.* The Library of Congress Series on American Civilization. Cambridge, Mass.: Harvard University Press, 1951.

BRUMMÉ, C. LUDWIG. *Contemporary American Sculpture.* Foreword by William Zorach. New York: Crown, 1948. Bibliography.

BURNHAM, JACK. *Beyond Modern Sculpture: The Effects of Science and Technology on the Sculpture of This Century.* New York: Braziller, 1968.

CALDER, ALEXANDER. *Calder.* New York: Pantheon, 1966.

COPLANS, JOHN. *Ellsworth Kelly.* New York: Abrams, 1972.

COPLANS, JOHN, ed. *Roy Lichtenstein.* New York: Praeger, 1972.

CRAVEN, WAYNE. *Sculpture in America.* New York: Crowell, 1968.

ELSEN, ALBERT E. *The Partial Figure in Modern Sculpture.* Baltimore, Md.: Baltimore Museum of Art, 1969.

ELSEN, ALBERT. *Seymour Lipton.* New York: Abrams, 1970.

FINCH, CHRISTOPHER. *Pop Art: Object and Image.* New York: Dutton, 1968.

FORGE, ANDREW. *Robert Rauschenberg.* New York: Abrams, 1969.

FRANK, W.; MUMFORD, L.; NORMAN, D.; ROSENFELD, P.; RUGG, H., eds. *America and Alfred Stieglitz.* Garden City, N.Y.: Doubleday, 1934.

GABO, NAUM. *Gabo: Constructions, Sculpture, Paintings, Drawings, Engravings.* Introductions by Herbert Read and Leslie Martin. Cambridge, Mass.: Harvard University Press, 1957.

GIEDION-WELCKER, CAROLA. *Contemporary Sculpture: An Evolution in Volume and Space.* New York: Wittenborn, 1955. Biographical and bibliographical notes on Calder, Ferber, Hare, Lassaw, Lippold, Lipton, Smith.

GLIMCHER, ARNOLD B. *Louise Nevelson.* New York: Praeger, 1972.

GOLDWATER, ROBERT. *What Is Modern Sculpture?* New York: Museum of Modern Art, 1969.

GOOSEN, E. C. "Herbert Ferber." In *Three American Sculptors.* New York: Grove, 1959.

GOOSEN, E. C.; GOLDWATER, R.; SANDLER, I. *Three American Sculptors: Ferber, Hare, Lassaw.* New York: Grove, 1959.

GRAY, CLEVE, ed. *David Smith by David Smith.* New York: Holt, Rinehart and Winston, 1968.

GREENBERG, CLEMENT. *Art and Culture: Critical Essays.* Boston: Beacon, 1961.

GUGGENHEIM, PEGGY, ed. *Art of This Century.* New York: Arno, 1942.

HANSEN, AL. *A Primer of Happenings and Time/Space Art.* New York: Something Else, 1965.

HUNTER, SAM. "American Art Since 1945." In *New Art Around the World: Painting and Sculpture.* New York: Abrams, 1966, pp. 9–58.

Janis, Harriet, and Blesh, Rudi. *Collage.* Philadelphia: Chilton, 1967.

Jean, Marcel. *The History of Surrealist Painting.* New York: Grove, 1967.

Kaprow, Allan. *Assemblage, Environments and Happenings.* New York: Abrams, 1966.

Kirby, Michael. *Happenings, An Illustrated Anthology.* New York: Dutton, 1966.

Kozloff, Max. *Jasper Johns.* New York: Abrams, 1967.

Kozloff, Max. *Renderings: Critical Essays on a Century of Modern Art.* New York: Simon & Schuster, 1969.

Kramer, Hilton. *The Age of the Avant-Garde: An Art Chronicle of 1956–1971.* New York: Farrar, Straus & Giroux, 1973.

Krauss, Rosalind. *Terminal Iron Works: The Sculpture of David Smith.* Cambridge, Mass.: M.I.T., 1971.

Kuh, Katharine. *The Artist's Voice, Talks with Seventeen Artists.* New York: Harper & Row, 1962.

Kultermann, Udo. *The New Sculpture, Environments and Assemblages.* New York: Praeger, 1968. Selected bibliography.

Lassaw, Ibram. "On Inventing Our Own Art." In *American Abstract Artists: Three Annual Yearbooks.* New York: Arno, 1969, pp. 23–24. Reprint of 1939 edition.

Lippard, Lucy R. *Changing: Essays in Art Criticism.* New York: Dutton, 1971.

Lippard, Lucy R., ed. *Pop Art.* New York: Praeger, 1966. Articles by Lawrence Alloway, Nancy Marmer, Nicolas Calas.

Mellow, James R., ed. *The Art World,* Arts Yearbook, no. 7. New York: Art Digest, 1964. Articles by Clement Greenberg, Hilton Kramer, Don Judd, Michael Fried, Vivian Raynor, Sidney Tillim.

Noguchi, Isamu. *A Sculptor's World.* London: Thames and Hudson, 1967.

Oldenburg, Claes. *Claes Oldenburg: Proposals for Monuments and Buildings, 1965–1969.* Chicago: Big Table, 1969.

Oldenburg, Claes. *Store Days.* New York: Something Else, 1967.

Popper, Frank. *Kinetic Art.* Greenwich, Conn. and London: New York Graphic Society/ Studio-Vista, Ltd., 1968. Bibliography.

Rickey, George. *Constructivism: Origins and Evolution.* New York: Braziller, 1967. Comprehensive bibliography.

Ritchie, Andrew C. *Abstract Painting and Sculpture in America.* New York: Museum of Modern Art, 1951. Bibliography on American art.

Ritchie, Andrew. *Sculpture of the Twentieth Century.* New York: Museum of Modern Art, 1952.

Rose, Barbara. *American Art Since 1900: A Critical History.* New York: Praeger, 1967. Selected bibliography.

Rose, Barbara. *Claes Oldenburg.* New York: Museum of Modern Art, 1969. Monograph published on the occasion of Oldenburg's retrospective; extensive bibliography.

Rose, Barbara. *Readings in American Art Since 1900: A Documentary Survey.* New York: Praeger, 1968. Bibliography.

Rosenberg, Harold. *The Anxious Object: Art Today and Its Audience.* 2nd ed. New York: Horizon, 1966.

Rosenberg, Harold. *Artworks and Packages.* New York: Horizon, 1969.

Rosenberg, Harold. *Tradition of the New.* New York: Horizon, 1959.

Roszak, Theodore. *In Pursuit of an Image.* Chicago: Art Institute of Chicago, Time to Time Publications, 1955.

Rubin, William S. *Dada and Surrealist Art.* New York: Abrams, 1968.

Rublowsky, John. *Pop Art.* New York: Basic Books, 1965.

Russell, John, and Gablik, Suzi. *Pop Art Redefined.* London: Thames and Hudson, 1969.

Sandler, Irving. "Ibram Lassaw." In *Three American Sculptors.* New York: Grove, 1959.

Sandler, Irving. *The Triumph of American Painting: A History of Abstract Expressionism.* New York: Praeger, 1970. Bibliography.

Seitz, William C., ed. *Contemporary Sculpture,* Arts Yearbook, no. 8. New York: Art Digest, 1965. Articles by Sidney Geist, Robert Goldwater, Don Judd.

Seuphor, Michel. *The Sculpture of This Century.* New York: Braziller, 1960.

Seymour, Charles. *Tradition and Experiment in Modern Sculpture.* Washington, D.C.: American University, 1949.

Smithson, Robert. "The Spiral Jetty." In *Arts of the Environment.* Gyorgy Kepes, ed. New York: Braziller, 1972, pp. 222–32.

Steinberg, Leo. *Jasper Johns.* New York: Wittenborn, 1963.

Tomkins, Calvin. *The Bride and The Bachelors.* New York: Viking, 1965.

Tuchman, Maurice. *The New York School: Abstract Expressionism in the 40's and 50's.* London: Thames and Hudson, 1969. Comprehensive bibliography.

Waldman, Diane. *Ellsworth Kelly: Drawings, Collages and Prints.* Greenwich, Conn.: New York Graphic Society, 1971. Catalogue raisonné of graphics; bibliography.

Wittenborn, Schultz. *American Abstract Artists.* New York: 1946.

EXHIBITION CATALOGUES

Albright-Knox Art Gallery, Buffalo. *Kinetic and Optic Art Today.* Essay by Gordon Smith. Buffalo, 1965.

Andrew Dickson White Museum of Art, Cornell University. *Earth.* Essays by Willoughby Sharp and William C. Lipke. Ithaca, 1969.

Art Institute of Chicago, Chicago. *Abstract and Surrealist Art: 58th American Annual.* Chicago, 1947.

Brooklyn Museum, Brooklyn. *Louise Nevelson: Prints and Drawings, 1953–1966.* Essay by Una E. Johnson; research by Jo Miller; bibliography. New York, 1967.

City Art Museum of St. Louis, St. Louis. *7 for 67: Works by Contemporary Sculptors.* St. Louis, 1967.

Contemporary Arts Museum, Houston. *Irons in the Fire.* Introduction by Sam Hunter. Houston, 1957.

Corcoran Gallery of Art, Washington, D.C. *Robert Morris.* Catalogue essay by Annette Michelson; selected bibliography. Washington, D.C., 1969.

Corcoran Gallery of Art, Washington, D.C. *Scale as Content: Ronald Bladen, Barnett Newman, Tony Smith.* Pamphlet by Eleanor Green. Washington, D.C., 1967.

David Porter Gallery, Washington, D.C. *A Painting Prophecy—1950.* Catalogue with statements of artists in the show, with a forward by David Porter; Statement by Louise Bourgeois. Washington, D.C., 1945.

Dwan Gallery, Los Angeles. *Boxes.* Exhibition catalogue. Los Angeles, 1964.

Exposition Internationale du Surréalisme, Paris. *Le Surréalisme en 1947.* Paris, 1947.

Finch College Museum of Art, New York. *Art in Process: The Visual Development of a Structure.* Exhibition and catalogue foreword by Elayne H. Varian. New York, 1966.

Fischbach Gallery, New York. *Eccentric Abstraction.* Exhibition and catalogue essay by Lucy R. Lippard. New York, 1966.

Fogg Art Museum, Cambridge, Mass. *David Smith: A Retrospective Exhibition.* Introduction by Jane Harrison Cone; bibliography. Cambridge, Mass., 1966.

Galerie Louis Carré, Paris. *Calder.* Essay by Jean-Paul Sartre. Paris, 1946.

Gemeentemuseum, The Hague. *Carl André.* Exhibition and catalogue by Enno Develing. The Hague, 1969.

Gemeentemuseum, The Hague. *Sol Lewitt.* Exhibition and catalogue organized by Enno Develing. The Hague, 1970.

Gemeentemuseum, The Hague. *Minimal Art.* Introduction by Enno Develing; text by Lucy R. Lippard; artists' statements; selected biographies and bibliographies. The Hague, 1968.

Solomon R. Guggenheim Museum, New York. *Alexander Calder: A Retrospective Exhibition.* Introduction by Thomas Messer; bibliography. New York, 1964.

Solomon R. Guggenheim Museum, New York. *Carl André.* Exhibition and catalogue essay by Diane Waldman; comprehensive bibliography. New York, 1970.

Solomon R. Guggenheim Museum, New York. *John Chamberlain.* Essay by Diane Waldman. New York, 1971.

Solomon R. Guggenheim Museum, New York. *Joseph Cornell.* Essay by Diane Waldman. New York, 1967.

Solomon R. Guggenheim Museum, New York. *Guggenheim International Exhibition, 1967. (Sculpture from Twenty Nations.)* Text by Edward F. Fry. New York, 1967.

Solomon R. Guggenheim Museum, New York. *Guggenheim International Exhibition, 1971.* Exhibition and catalogue essays by Diane Waldman and Edward F. Fry. Artists' and general bibliographies. New York.

Solomon R. Guggenheim Museum, New York. *David Smith.* Introduction by Edward F. Fry; brief bibliography. New York, 1969.

Howard Wise Gallery, New York. *On the Move.* Essay by Douglas MacAgy. New York, 1964.

Indiana University Art Museum, Bloomington. *Noguchi and Rickey and Smith.* Text by Daniel Mato. Bloomington, Indiana, 1970.

263

Institute of Contemporary Art, Boston. *George Rickey: Kinetic Sculptures.* Exhibition catalogue. Boston, 1964.

The Jewish Museum, New York. *Jasper Johns.* Essays by Alan Solomon and John Cage; bibliography. New York, 1964.

The Jewish Museum, New York. *Primary Structures: Younger American and British Sculptors.* Exhibition and introduction by Kynaston McShine; bibliographies. New York, 1966.

The Jewish Museum, New York. *Recent American Sculpture.* Introduction by Hans van Weeren Griek; critical essays; bibliographies. New York, 1964.

M. Knoedler & Co., New York. *Tony Smith: Recent Sculpture.* Interviews with the artist by Lucy R. Lippard; chronology. New York, 1971.

Kunsthalle, Berne. *When Attitudes Become Form: Works, Concepts, Processes, Situations, Information.* Exhibition organized by Harald Szeemann; essays by Scott Burton, Gregoire Muller, Tommaso Trini; biographies and bibliographies. Bern, 1969.

Los Angeles County Museum of Art, Los Angeles. *American Sculpture of the Sixties.* Exhibition and introduction by Maurice Tuchman; essays by Lawrence Alloway, Wayne Andersen, Dore Ashton, John Coplans, Clement Greenberg, Max Kozloff, Lucy R. Lippard, James Monte, Barbara Rose, Irving Sandler; bibliographies. Los Angeles, 1967.

Los Angeles County Museum of Art, Los Angeles. *H. C. Westermann.* Essay by Max Kozloff. Los Angeles, 1968.

Los Angeles County Museum of Art, Los Angeles. *A Report on the Art and Technology Program of the Los Angeles County Museum of Art: 1967–1971.* Exhibition and catalogue by Maurice Tuchman. Los Angeles, 1971.

Marlborough-Gerson Gallery, New York. *Seymour Lipton: Recent Works.* Exhibition catalogue. New York, 1971.

Martha Jackson Gallery, New York. *New Forms–New Media I.* Essays by Lawrence Alloway and Allan Kaprow. New York, 1960.

The Metropolitan Museum of Art, New York. *New York Painting and Sculpture: 1940–1970.* Exhibition and catalogue essay by Henry Geldzahler; articles by Harold Rosenberg, Robert Rosenblum, Clement Greenberg, William S. Rubin, Michael Fried. Artists' biographies and bibliographies. New York, 1969.

Moderna Museet, Stockholm. *Amerikanst pop-konst.* Introduction by Alan K. Solomon. Stockholm, 1964.

Moderna Museet, Stockholm. *Edward Kienholz: 11 + 11 Tableaux.* Exhibition and catalogue by K. G. Pontus Hulten. Stockholm, 1970.

Museu de Arte Moderna, São Paulo. *V Bienal de arte. Catalogue: Guston, Smith, Francis, Frankenthaler, Goldberg, Kadish, Kohn, Leslie, Marca-Relli, Metcalf, Mitchell, Rauschenberg.* Text by Sam Hunter. Minneapolis Institute of Arts, Minneapolis, 1959.

Museu de Arte Moderna, São Paulo. *VII Bienal de arte. The United States of America: 1. Adolph Gottlieb, 2. Ten Sculptors.* Exhibition and catalogue by Martin Friedman; brief biographies and selected bibliography. Walker Art Center, Minneapolis, 1963.

Museum of Contemporary Art, Chicago. *Art by Telephone.* Exhibition organized by Jan van der Marck; recorded telephone instructions from the artists. Chicago, 1969.

Museum of Contemporary Art, La Jolla. *José de Rivera.* Retrospective Exhibition 1930–1971. La Jolla, 1972.

Museum of Modern Art, New York. *Abstract Painting and Sculpture in America.* Edited by A. C. Ritchie. New York, 1951.

Museum of Modern Art, New York. *Alexander Calder.* Essay by James Johnson Sweeney; bibliography. New York, 1951.

Museum of Modern Art, New York. *Americans 1963.* Exhibition and catalogue foreword by Dorothy C. Miller; artists' statements. New York, 1963.

Museum of Modern Art, New York. *American Painting and Sculpture, 1862–1932.* Text by H. Cahill. New York, 1932.

Museum of Modern Art, New York. *The Art of Assemblage.* Text by William C. Seitz. New York, 1961.

Museum of Modern Art, New York. *The Art of the Real: U.S.A. 1948–1968.* Exhibition and catalogue essay by E. C. Goossen. Artists' and general bibliographies. New York, 1968.

Museum of Modern Art, New York. *Fifteen Americans.* Edited by D. C. Miller; Statements by the artists. New York, 1952.

Museum of Modern Art, New York. *Fourteen Americans.* Edited by D. C. Miller; Statements by the artists. New York, 1946.

Museum of Modern Art, New York. *Nakian.* Essay by Frank O'Hara. New York, 1966.

Museum of Modern Art, New York. *New Images of Man.* Introduction by Peter Selz. New York, 1959.

Museum of Modern Art, New York. *Recent American Sculpture.* Text by James Thrall Soby. New York, 1959.

Museum of Modern Art, New York. *The Responsive Eye.* Exhibition and catalogue essay by William C. Seitz. New York, 1965.

Museum of Modern Art, New York. *Sixteen Americans.* Exhibition and catalogue foreword by Dorothy C. Miller; artists' statements. New York, 1959.

Museum of Modern Art, New York. *Spaces.* Exhibition and catalogue essay by Jennifer Licht. New York, 1969.

Museum of Modern Art, New York. *Twelve Americans.* Edited by D. C. Miller; Statements by the artists. New York, 1956.

National Gallery of Canada, Ottawa. *Fluorescent Light, etc. from Dan Flavin.* Exhibition and catalogue by Brydon Smith; essays by Mel Bochner and Don Judd; comprehensive bibliography. Ottawa, 1969.

New Jersey State Museum, Trenton. *Burgoyne Diller: 1906–1965.* Exhibition catalogue. Trenton, 1966.

New Jersey State Museum, Trenton. *Sculptures by George Rickey and James Seawright.* Foreword by Zoltan Buki; essay by Rickey. Trenton, 1969.

New York University, Loeb Student Center, New York. *Concrete Expressionism.* Exhibition and catalogue essay by Irving Sandler. New York, 1965.

Otto Gerson Gallery, New York. *James Rosati–Recent Sculpture.* Introduction by Dore Ashton. New York, 1962.

Pace Gallery, New York. *Chryssa.* Exhibition catalogue. (New York, March–April, 1966).

Pace Gallery; Hayden Gallery, Massachusetts Institute of Technology. *Trova: Selected Works. 1953–1966.* Text by Lawrence Alloway; bibliography. New York, and Cambridge, Massachusetts, 1967.

Pasadena Art Museum, Pasadena. *Don Judd.* Exhibition, catalogue essay, and interview with the artist by John Coplans; bibliography. Pasadena, 1971.

Pasadena Art Museum, Pasadena. *New American Sculpture.* Text by Walter Hopps. Pasadena.

Pasadena Art Museum, Pasadena. *Serial Imagery.* Exhibition and catalogue essay by John Coplans. Pasadena, 1968.

Perls Galleries, New York. *Calder–Bronze Sculptures of 1944.* New York, 1969.

Rhode Island School of Design, Providence. *Contemporary Boxes and Wall Sculpture.* Text by Daniel Robbins. Providence.

Sculpture Center, New York. *American Sculpture 1928–1953: The Tumultuous Quarter-Century.* Introduction by Sahl Swarz. New York, 1953.

Stedelijk Museum, Amsterdam. *Claes Oldenburg.* Foreword by E. de Wilde, introduction by Alicia Legg. Amsterdam, 1970.

Stedelijk Museum, Amsterdam. *Op Losse Schroeven situaties en cryptostructuren (Square Pegs in Round Holes).* Exhibition organized by Wim Berren; introduction by E. de Wilde; essays by Berren, Piero Gilardi, Harald Szeemann. Amsterdam, 1968.

Stedelijk van Abbemuseum, Eindhoven. *Don Judd.* Exhibition and catalogue by Jan Leering. Second catalogue by Manfred de la Motte, published by Kunstverein, Hanover, Germany, 1970.

Tate Gallery, London. *Robert Morris.* Exhibition and catalogue by Michael Compton and David Sylvester. London, 1971.

Tate Gallery, London. *Warhol.* Text by Richard Morphet. London, 1971.

Terry Ditenfass Gallery, New York. *William King.* Introductory essay by Hilton Kramer. New York, 1970.

University of California Art Museum, Berkeley. *Directions in Kinetic Sculpture.* Essays by Peter Selz and George Rickey; artists' statements. Berkeley, 1966.

University of Illinois, Urbana. *Contemporary American Painting and Sculpture.* Catalogues of the biennial exhibitions. Urbana, 1948 and later.

University of Pennsylvania, Institute of Contemporary Art, Philadelphia. *7 Sculptors.* Exhibition by Samuel Green; critical texts; artists' biographies. Philadelphia, 1965.

XXVII Venice Biennale, American Pavilion. *2 Pittori: De Kooning, Shahn. 3 Scultori: Lachaise, Lassaw, Smith.* Exhibition organized by Museum of Modern Art, New York; text and artists' statements in Italian and English. Venice, 1954.

XXIX Venice Biennale. *Lipton, Rothko, Smith, Tobey*. Catalogue by Museum of Modern Art, New York; texts by Sam Hunter and Frank O'Hara. Venice, 1958.

Walker Art Center, Minneapolis. *Eight Sculptors: The Ambiguous Image*. Essays by Martin Friedman and Jan van der Marck. Minneapolis, 1966.

Walker Art Center. Minneapolis, Dayton's Auditorium, *14 Sculptors: The Industrial Edge*. Essays by Barbara Rose, Christopher Finch, Martin Friedman; bibliographies. Minneapolis, 1969.

Walker Art Center, Minneapolis. *Light, Motion, Space*. Essay by Willoughby Sharp. Minneapolis, 1967.

Walker Art Center, Minneapolis. *Richard Stankiewicz and Robert Indiana*. Essay by Jan van der Marck. Minneapolis, 1963.

Walker Art Center, Minneapolis. *The Sculpture of Herbert Ferber*. Accompanying monograph by Wayne Andersen; bibliography. Minneapolis, 1962.

Walker Art Center, Minneapolis. *Ten American Sculptors*. Minneapolis, 1964.

Walker Art Center, Minneapolis. *Theodore Roszak*. Text by H. H. Arnason. Minneapolis, 1957.

Washington Gallery of Modern Art, Washington, D.C. *Edward Kienholz: Work From the 1960's*. Exhibition and catalogue essay by Walter Hopps. Washington, D.C., 1968.

Washington Gallery of Modern Art, Washington, D.C. *Phillip Pavia*. Introduction by Gerald Nordland. Washington, D.C., 1966.

Whitechapel Art Gallery, London. *Robert Rauschenberg: Paintings, Drawings and Combines 1949–1964*. Preface by Bryan Robertson; essays by Henry Geldzahler, John Cage, Max Kozloff. London, 1964.

Whitney Museum of American Art, New York. *Annual Exhibition 1964 Contemporary American Sculpture*. New York, 1964.

Whitney Museum of American Art, New York. *Annual Exhibition 1966 Sculpture and Prints*. New York, 1966.

Whitney Museum of American Art, New York. *Anti-Illusion: Procedures/Materials*. Exhibition and catalogue essays by Marcia Tucker and James Monte; bibliography. New York, 1969.

Whitney Museum of American Art, New York. *Contemporary American Sculpture: Selection 1*. Text by John I.H. Baur. New York.

Whitney Museum of American Art, New York. *Don Judd*. Exhibition and catalogue by William C. Agee. New York, 1968.

Whitney Museum of American Art, New York. *Isamu Noguchi*. Exhibition and catalogue by John Gordon. New York, 1966.

Whitney Museum of American Art, New York. *Light: Object and Image*. Exhibition and catalogue essay by Robert Doty. New York, 1968.

Whitney Museum of American Art, New York. *Louise Nevelson*. Exhibition and catalogue by John Gordon; bibliography. New York, 1967.

Whitney Museum of American Art, New York. *The New Decade: 35 American Painters and Sculptors*. Text by John I.H. Baur. New York, 1955.

Whitney Museum of American Art, New York. *Pioneers of Modern Art in America*. Text by L. Goodrich. New York, 1946.

Whitney Museum of American Art, New York. *Robert Morris*. Exhibition and catalogue essay by Marcia Tucker; selected bibliography. New York, 1970.

Whitney Museum of American Art, New York. *Theodore Roszak*. Essay by H.H. Arnason. New York, 1956.

Whitney Museum of American Art, New York. *Young America*. New York, 1965.

World's Fair, American Express Pavilion, New York. *Art '65: Lesser Known and Unknown Painters: Young American Sculpture—East to West*. Catalogue text by Brian O'Doherty and Wayne Andersen. New York, 1965.

World's Fair, Seattle. *Art Since 1950*. Text by Sam Hunter. Seattle, 1962.

ARTICLES AND MAJOR REVIEWS

"A Symposium on Pop Art," *Arts* 37 (April 1963): 36–45. Moderated by Peter Selz with Dore Ashton, Henry Geldzahler, Hilton Kramer, Stanley Kunitz and Leo Steinberg.

ADRIAN, DENNIS. "Walter De Maria: Word and Thing," *Artforum* 5 (January 1967): 28–29.

ALDRICH, LARRY. "New Talent U.S.A.," *Art in America* 54 (July–August 1966): 22–69.

ALLOWAY, LAWRENCE. "Roy Lichtenstein," *Studio International* 175 (January 1968): 25–31.

"American Sculpture," *Artforum* 5 (Summer 1967). Special issue with articles by Philip Leider, Michael Fried, Robert Morris, Barbara Rose, Robert Smithson, Max Kozloff,

Sidney Tillim, James Monte, Wayne Andersen, Fidel A. Danieli, Jane Harrison Cone, Sol Lewitt, Robert Pincus-Witten, Charles Frazier.

ANDERSEN, WAYNE. "American Sculpture: The Situation in the Fifties," *Artforum* 5 (Summer 1967): 60–67.

ANDERSEN, WAYNE. "Calder at the Guggenheim," *Artforum* 3 (March 1965): 37–42.

ANDERSEN, WAYNE. "Fusion in Modern Sculpture." Unpublished College Art Association paper given at the Walker Art Center, Minneapolis. (January, 1961)

ANDERSEN, WAYNE. "Interview With Herbert Ferber." Files of Wayne Andersen. (September 1961.)

ANDERSEN, WAYNE. "La Scultura Americana." *L'Arte Moderna* 8 (1969): 241–80.

ANDERSEN, WAYNE. "Note on Three-Dimensional Quality," *Connection* 4 (Fall 1966): 36–38.

ANTIN, DAVID. "Art and Information, 1: Grey Paint, Robert Morris," *Art News* 65 (April 1965): 22–24; 56–58.

APPLE, BILLY. "Live Stills," *Arts* 5 (February 1967): 46–47.

ARNASON, H. H. "Nakian." *Art International* 7 (April 1963): 36–43.

ASHTON, DORE. "James Rosati–World of Inner Rhythms," *The Studio* 167 (May 1964): 196–99.

ASHTON, DORE. "José de Rivera," *Arts and Architecture* 72 (July 1955): 10 ff.

ASHTON, DORE. "La sculpture américaine," *XX Siècle* 15 (November 1960): 85–91.

ASHTON, DORE. "Roszak: Draftsman," *The Art Digest* 27 (February 15, 1953): 16.

ASHTON, DORE. "Sculpture of José de Rivera," *Arts* 30 (April 1956): 38–41.

ASHTON, DORE. "Unconventional Techniques in Sculpture: New York Commentary," *Studio International* 169 (January 1965): 22–25.

BAKER, ELIZABETH C. "Critic's Choice: Serra," *Art News* 69 (February 1970): 26–27.

BARO, GENE. "American Sculpture: A New Scene," *Studio International* 175 (January 1968): 9–19.

BARO, GENE. "Tony Smith: Toward Speculation in Pure Form," *Art International* 11 (Summer 1967): 27–30.

BERKSON, W. "Sculpture of Larry Rivers," *Arts* 40 (November 1965): 49–52.

BEWLEY, MARIUS. "An Introduction to Louise Bourgeois," *Tiger's Eye* 12 (March 1949): 89–92.

BLOK, C. "Minimal Art at The Hague," *Art International* 12 (May 1968): 18–24.

BOCHNER, MEL. "Primary Structures," *Arts Magazine* 40 (June 1966): 32–35.

BOCHNER, MEL. "Serial Art Systems: Solipsism," *Arts Magazine* 41 (Summer 1967): 39–43.

BOCHNER, MEL. "The Serial Attitude," *Artforum* 6 (December 1967): 28–33.

BOURDON, DAVID. "E = mc² a go-go," *Art News* 64 (January 1966): 22–25; 57–59; illus. 22–25.

BOURDON, DAVID. "Our Period Style," *Art and Artists* 1 (June 1966): 54–57.

BOURDON, DAVID. "Walter De Maria: The Singular Experience," *Art International* 12 (December 1968): 39–43; 72.

BOURGEOIS, LOUISE. Statement in *Design Quarterly*, no. 30 (1954): 18.

BURNHAM, JACK. "Problems of Criticism, IX: Art and Technology," *Artforum* 9 (January 1971): 40–45.

BURTON, SCOTT. "New York: Robert Smithson's 'Non-sites'," *Art Scene* (April 1969): 22–23.

BURTON, SCOTT. "Old Master at the New Frontier," *Art News* 65 (December 1966): 52–55; 68–70.

"California Sculpture Today," *Artforum* (special issue) (August 1963).

CAMFIELD, WILLIAM A. "The Machinist Style of Francis Picabia," *Art Bulletin* 48 (September–December 1966): 309–22.

CAMPBELL, LAWRENCE. "Diller: The Ruling Passion," *Art News* 6 (October 1968): 36–37.

CAMPBELL, LAWRENCE. "Lassaw Makes a Sculpture: Clouds of Magellan," *Art News* 53 (March 1954): 24–27; 66–67.

CAMPBELL, LAWRENCE. "Lippold Makes a Construction," *Art News* 55 (October 1956): 30–32 ff.

CAMPBELL, LAWRENCE. "Marisol's Magic Mixtures," *Art News* 63 (March 1964): 38–41.

CANADAY, JOHN. "Good-by Forever," *The New York Times* II (May 19, 1963): 11.

CONTESI, ALEXANDRE. "Cornell," *Artforum* 4 (April 1966): 27–31.

COPLANS, JOHN. "Abstract Expressionist Ceramics," *Artforum* 5 (November 1966): 34–41.

COPLANS, JOHN. "Assemblage: The Savage Eye of Edward Kienholz," *Studio International* 170 (September 1965): 112–15.

COPLANS, JOHN. "Circle of Styles on the West Coast," *Art In America* 52 (June 1964): 24–41; illus. 24–41.

COPLANS, JOHN. "The Earlier Work of Ellsworth Kelly," *Artforum* 7 (Summer 1969): 48–55.

COPLANS, JOHN. "Formal Art," *Artforum* 2 (Summer 1964): 42–43; illus. 43.

COPLANS, JOHN. "The New Abstraction on the West Coast U.S.A.," *Studio International* 169 (May 1965): 192–99; illus. 192–99.

COPLANS, JOHN. "The New Paintings of Common Objects," *Artforum* 1 (November 1962): 26–29.

COPLANS, JOHN. "Notes on the Nature of Joseph Cornell," *Artforum* 1 (February 1963): 27–29.

COPLANS, JOHN. "Robert Smithson, the 'Amarillo Ramp'," *Artforum* 12 (April 1974): 36–45.

COPLANS, JOHN. "Sculpture in California," *Artforum* 2 (August 1963): 3–6.

COPLANS, JOHN. "Talking with Roy Lichtenstein," *Artforum* 5 (May 1967): 34–39.

COPLANS, JOHN. "Voulkos: Redemption Through Ceramics," *Art News* 64 (Summer 1965): 38–39.

"Dada and Surrealism," *Bulletin of the Museum of Modern Art* 4 (November–December 1936): 30. Essays by Georges Hugnet.

DANIELI, FIDEL A. "The Art of Bruce Nauman," *Artforum* 6 (December 1966): 65–66.

DANIELI, FIDEL A. "Robert Hudson," *Artforum* 6 (November 1967): 32–35.

ELSEN, ALBERT. "Lipton's Sculpture as Portrait of the Artist," *College Art Journal* 24 (Winter 1964–1965): 113–18.

ELSEN, ALBERT E. "The Sculptural World of Seymour Lipton," *Art International* 9 (February 1965): 12–16.

ELSEN, ALBERT. "Seymour Lipton: Odyssey of the Unquiet Metaphor," *Art International* 5 (February 1, 1961): 39–44.

FLAVIN, DAN. " '. . . In Daylight or Cool White,' An Autobiographical Sketch," *Artforum* 4 (December 1965): 20–24.

FLAVIN, DAN. ". . . on an American Artist's Education," *Artforum* 6 (March 1968): 28–32.

FRIED, MICHAEL. "Art and Objecthood," *Artforum* 5 (June 1967): 12–23.

FULLER, MARY. "San Francisco Sculptors," *Art In America* 52 (June 1964): 52–59; illus. 52–59.

GEIST, SIDNEY. "A Memoir of Zadkine," *Artforum* 8 (June 1970): 65–69.

GEIST, SIDNEY. "Color It Sculpture," *Contemporary Sculpture, Arts Yearbook*, no. 8 (New York: Art Digest): 91–98.

GEIST, SIDNEY. "Face Front," *It Is*, no. 3 (1959): 32–33.

GEIST, SIDNEY. "Month in Review," *Arts* 32 (December 1957): 46.

GEIST, SIDNEY. "New Sculptor: Mark di Suvero," *Arts Magazine* 35 (December 1960): 40–43.

GEIST, SIDNEY. "Prelude: The 1930's," *Art* 30 (September 1956): 49–55.

GELDZAHLER, HENRY. "An Interview with George Segal," *Artforum* 3 (November 1964): 26–29.

GLASER, BRUCE, moderator. "Lichtenstein, Oldenburg, Warhol: A Discussion," *Artforum* 4 (February 1966): 20–24.

GLASER, BRUCE and LIPPARD, LUCY R., eds. "Questions to Stella and Judd," *Art News* 65 (September 1966): 55–61. (See bibl. 6.)

GOLDIN, AMY. "Beyond Style," *Art and Artists* 3 (September 1968): 32–35.

GOLDWATER, ROBERT. "David Hare," *Art in America* 44 (Winter 1956–57): 18–20.

GOLDWATER, ROBERT. "Everyone Knew What Everyone Else Meant," *It Is*, no. 4 (Autumn 1959): 35.

GOLDWATER, ROBERT. "Problems of Criticism, I: Varieties of Critical Experience," *Artforum* 6 (September 1967): 40–41.

GOLDWATER, ROBERT. "Reflections on the New York School," *Quadrum* 7–8 (1960): 17–36.

GOLDWATER, ROBERT. "Reuben Nakian," *Quadrum*, no. 11 (1961): 95–102.

GOOSEN, E. C. "The End of the Object," *Art International* 3 (1959): 40–42; illus. 40–42.

GREENBERG, CLEMENT. "America Takes the Lead: 1945–1965," *Art in America* 53 (August 1965): 108–29.

GREENBERG, CLEMENT. " 'American-Type' Painting," *Partisan Review* 22 (Spring 1955): 180.

GREENBERG, CLEMENT. "Avant-Garde Attitudes: New Art in the Sixties," *Studio International* 179 (April 1970): 142–45.

GREENBERG, CLEMENT. "David Smith," *Art in America* 44 (Winter 1956): 30 ff.

GREENBERG, CLEMENT. "The New Sculpture," *Partisan Review* 16 (June 1949): 637–42.

GREENBERG, CLEMENT. "The Present Prospects of American Painting and Sculpture," *Horizon*, nos. 93–94 (October 1947): 20–30.

GREENBERG, CLEMENT. "Recentness of Sculpture," *Art International* 11 (April 1967): 9–21.

GRIPPE, PETER. "The City of Peter Grippe." *Connection* 4 (Fall 1966): 24–27. Introduction by Wayne Andersen.

GRUEN, JOHN. "The Artist Speaks: Isamu Noguchi," *Art in America* 56 (March–April 1968): 28–31.

Hess, Thomas B. "The Disrespectful Handmaiden," *Art News* 63 (January 1965): 38–39; 57.

Hess, Thomas B. "Isamu Noguchi," *Art News* 55 (September 1946): 34–38 ff.

Hess, Thomas B. "U.S. Painting: Some Recent Directions," *Art News Annual* 25 (1956): 76–98; 174–80; 199.

Hess, Thomas B. "U.S. Sculpture: Some Recent Directions," *Portfolio* (including *Art News Annual*), no. 1 (1959): 112–27; 146; 148; 150–52.

Hickey, Dave. "Earthscapes, Landworks and Oz," *Art in America* 59 (September–October 1971): 40–49.

Hooton, Bruce. "Interview with Philip Pavia" (January 19, 1965) *Archives of American Art*.

Hopkins, Henry T. "Kenneth Price," *Artforum* 2 (August 1963): 41.

Hopps, Walter. "An Interview with Jasper Johns," *Artforum* 3 (March 1965): 32–36.

Hopps, Walter. "Boxes," *Art International* 8 (March 1964): 38–42.

Hudson, Andrew. "Scale as Content," *Artforum* 6 (December 1967): 46–47.

Hutchinson, Peter. "Earth in Upheaval: Earthworks and Landscapes," *Arts Magazine* 43 (September 1968): 44–50.

Hutchinson, Peter. "Earth in Upheaval: Earthworks and Landscapes," *Arts Magazine* 43 (November 1968): 19.

Johnson, Ellen H. "The Sculpture of George Segal," *Art International* 8 (March 1964): 46–49.

Judd, Don. "Black, White and Gray," *Arts Magazine* 38 (March 1964): 36–38.

Judd, Don. "Chamberlain: Another View," *Art International* 7 (January 1964): 38–39.

Judd, Don. "Complaints, Part 1," *Studio International* 177 (April 1969): 182–88.

Judd, Don. "Exhibition at Chalette Gallery," *Arts Magazine* 37 (January 1963): 52.

Judd, Don. "Specific Objects," *Contemporary Sculpture, Arts Yearbook*, no. 8 (1965): 74–82.

Kaprow, Allan. "Experimental Art," *Art News* 65 (March 1966): 60–63; 77–82.

Kaprow, Allan. "The Happenings are Dead–Long Live the Happenings," *Artforum* 4 (March 1966): 36–39.

Kaprow, Allan. "The Legacy of Jackson Pollock," *Art News* 57 (October 1958): 24 ff.

Kaprow, Allan. "Segal's Vital Mummies," *Art News* 62 (February 1964): 30–33; 65.

Karp, Ivan C. "Anti-Sensibility Painting," *Artforum* 11 (September 1963): 26–27.

Kobler, John. "Experiments in Sound–John Cage: 'Everything We Do is Music'," *Saturday Evening Post* 241 (October 19, 1968): 46 ff.

Kozloff, Max. "American Sculpture in Transition," *Arts* 38 (May–June, 1964): 19–24.

Kozloff, Max. "Art and the New York Avant-Garde," *Partisan Review* 31 (Fall 1964): 535–44; 549–54; illus. 545–48.

Kozloff, Max. "Further Adventures of American Sculpture," *Arts Magazine* 39 (February 1965): 24–31.

Kozloff, Max. "Mark di Suvero," *Artforum* 5 (Summer 1967): 41–46.

Kozloff, Max. "New York Letter," *Art International* 6 (September 1962): 35.

Kozloff, Max. "9 in a Warehouse," *Artforum* 7 (February 1969): 38–42.

Kozloff, Max. "'Pop' Culture, Metaphysical Disgust and the New Vulgarians," *Art International* 6 (March 1962): 34–36.

Kramer, Hilton. "An Apology to Trajan," *Arts* 33 (June 1959): 26–33.

Kramer, Hilton. "The Emperor's New Bikini," *Art in America* 57 (January–February 1969): 48–55.

Kramer, Hilton. "Episodes from the Sixties," *Art in America* 58 (January–February 1970): 56–61.

Kramer, Hilton. "The New American Painting." *Partisan Review* 20 (July–August 1953): 421–27.

Kramer, Hilton. "'Realists' and Others," *Arts Magazine* 38 (January 1964): 18–23.

Kramer, Hilton. "The Sculpture of James Rosati," *Arts Magazine* 33 (March 1959): 26–31.

Kramer, Hilton. "The Sculpture of Louise Nevelson," *Arts Magazine* 32 (June 1958): 26–29.

Krasne, Belle. "A Theodore Roszak Profile," *Art Digest* 27 (October 15, 1952): 9 ff.

Krasne, Belle. "Three Who Carry the Acetylene Torch of Modernism," *Art Digest* 25 (April 15, 1951): 15.

Krauss, Rosalind. "Allusion and Illusion in Donald Judd," *Artforum* 4 (May 1966): 24–26.

Krauss, Rosalind. "The Essential David Smith, Part 1," *Artforum* 7 (February 1969): 43–49.

Krauss, Rosalind. "The Essential David Smith, Part 2," *Artforum* 7 (April 1969): 34–41.

Krauss, Rosalind. "Problems of Criticism, X: Pictorial Space and the Question of Documentary," *Artforum* 10 (November 1971): 68–71.

Kunitz, Stanley. "Sitting for Rosati the Sculptor." *Art News* 58 (March 1959): 36–39 ff.

Leger, Fernand. Statement in *Derrière Le Miroir*, no. 31 (July 1950).

LEIDER, PHILIP. "Kinetic Sculpture at Berkeley," *Artforum* 4 (May 1966): 40–44.

LIPPARD, LUCY R. "Eva Hesse: The Circle," *Art in America* 59 (May–June 1971): 68–73.

LIPPARD, LUCY R. "Homage to the Square," *Art in America* 55 (July–August 1967): 50–57.

LIPPARD, LUCY R. "New York Letter," *Art International* 9 (March 1965): 46; 48; illus. 48.

LIPPARD, LUCY R. "New York Letter: Recent Sculpture as Escape," *Art International* 10 (February 1966): 48–58.

LIPPARD, LUCY R. "New York Letter: Rejective Art," *Art International* 9 (September 1965): 57–61.

LIPPARD, LUCY R. "Rejective Art," *Art International* 10 (October 20, 1966): 33–36; illus. 37.

LIPPARD, LUCY R. "Sol Lewitt: Non-Visual Structures," *Artforum* 5 (April 1967): 42–46.

LIPPARD, LUCY R. "The Third Stream: Constructed Paintings and Painted Structures," *Art Voices* 4 (Spring 1965): 44–49.

LIPPARD, LUCY R. "Tony Smith: 'The Ineluctable Modality of the Visible'," *Art International* 11 (Summer 1967): 24–26.

LIPPOLD, RICHARD. "On Hanging, Seeing and Maintaining *Variation Number Seven: Full Moon*," typed manuscript in the files of Wayne Andersen.

LIPTON, SEYMOUR. "Some Notes on My Work," *Magazine of Art* 40 (November 1947): 264–65.

LUCAS, JOHN. "In the Wake of a Brazen Hussy," *Arts* 38 (October 1963): 18–22.

MATTOX, CHARLES. Sculpture by Charles Mattox, untitled, *Artforum* 4 (February 1966).

MEADMORE, CLEMENT. "New York: Scene I: Sculpture," *Art and Australia* 3 (September 1965): 124–29; illus. 124–29.

MEADMORE, CLEMENT. "Thoughts on Earthworks, Random Distribution, Softness, Horizontality and Gravity," *Arts Magazine* 43 (February 1969): 26–28.

MELLOW, JAMES R. "New York Letter," *Art International* 13 (February 1969): 50.

MEYER, CHARLES E. "Seymour Lipton and His Place in Twentieth Century Sculpture," *The Register of the Museum of Art*, University of Kansas 11 (April 1962): 36–43.

MICHELSON, ANNETTE. "Noguchi: Notes on a Theatre of the Real," *Art International* 8 (December 1964): 21–25.

MONTE, JAMES. "Polychrome Sculpture," *Artforum* 3 (November 1964): 40–43; illus. 40–43.

MORRIS, ROBERT. "Anti-Form," *Artforum* 6 (April 1968): 33–35.

MORRIS, ROBERT. "Notes on Sculpture, Part 1," *Artforum* 4 (February 1966): 42–44.

MORRIS, ROBERT. "Notes on Sculpture, Part 2," *Artforum* 5 (October 1966): 20–23.

MORRIS, ROBERT. "Notes on Sculpture, Part 3: Notes and Nonsequiturs," *Artforum* 5 (Summer 1967): 24–29.

MORRIS, ROBERT. "Notes on Sculpture, Part 4: Beyond Objects," *Artforum* 7 (April 1969): 50–54.

MORRIS, ROBERT. "Some Notes on the Phenomenology of Making: The Search for the Motivated," *Artforum* 8 (April 1970): 62–66.

MORRIS, ROBERT. Untitled essay, *Artforum* 4 (February 1966): 42–44.

MOTHERWELL, ROBERT. "The Painter and His Audience," *Perspectives U.S.A.*, no. 9 (1954): 107–12.

MOTHERWELL, ROBERT. "The Rise and Continuity of Abstract Art," *Arts and Architecture* 68 (September 1951): 20–21.

MULLER, GREGOIRE and SMITHSON, ROBERT. ". . . The Earth, Subject to Cataclysms, Is a Cruel Master," *Arts Magazine* 46 (November 1971): 36–41.

MUNRO, ELEANOR. "Explorations in Form: A View of Some Recent American Sculpture," *Perspectives U.S.A.*, no. 16 (Summer 1956): 160–72.

NAUMAN, BRUCE. An interview with the artist, *Avalanche* I, no. 2 (Winter 1971): 22–31.

NAVARETTA, C. A. "Agostini Makes a Sculpture," *Art News* 61 (May 1962): 27–30.

NEMSER, CINDY. "An Interview with Eva Hesse," *Artforum* 8 (May 1970): 59–63.

NEMSER, CINDY. "Sculpture and the New Realism," *Arts Magazine* 44 (April 1966): 39–41.

NODELMAN, SHELDON. "Sixties Art: Some Philosophical Perspectives," *Perspecta 11: The Yale Architectural Journal* (1967): 72–89.

NOGUCHI, ISAMU. "A Reminiscence of Four Decades," *Architectural Forum* 136 (January–February 1972): 59.

NORDLAND, GERALD J. "A Succession of Visitors," *Artforum* 2 (Summer 1964): 64–68.

OLDENBURG, CLAES. "*Extracts from the Studio Notes (1962–64)*," *Artforum* 4 (January 1966): 32–33.

PEARLSTEIN, PHILIP. "The Private Myth," *Art News* 60 (September 1961): 42–45.

PIENE, NAN R. "Light Art," *Art in America* 55 (May–June 1967): 24–47.

PIERCE, JAMES S. "Design and Expression in Minimal Art," *Art International* 12 (May 1968): 25–27.

Pincus-Witten, Robert. "Eva Hesse: Post-Minimalism into Sublime," *Artforum* 10 (November 1971): 32–44.

Pincus-Witten, Robert. "Slow Information: Richard Serra," *Artforum* 8 (September 1969): 34–39.

Porter, Fairfield. "Stankiewicz Makes a Sculpture," *Art News* 54 (September 1955): 36–39.

Rauschenberg, Robert. "The World Is a Painting," *Vogue* 146 (October 15, 1965): 101 ff.

Reinhardt, Ad. "Twelve Rules for a New Academy," *Art News* 56 (May 1957): 37–38.

Reise, Barbara. "Sol Lewitt Drawings, 1968–1969," *Studio International* 178 (December 1969): 222–25.

Reise, Barbara. " 'Untitled 1969': A Footnote on Art and Minimalstylehood," *Studio International* 177 (April 1969): 166–72.

Ritchie, Andrew C. "Seymour Lipton," *Art in America* 44 (Winter 1956): 14–17.

Robbins, Daniel. "Sculpture by Louise Bourgeois," *Art International* 8 (October 20, 1964): 29–31.

Robins, Corinne. "Object, Structure or Sculpture: Where are We?" *Arts Magazine* 40 (September–October 1966): 33–37.

Rose, Barbara. "ABC Art," *Art in America* 53 (October–November 1965): 57–69.

Rose, Barbara. "Blowup—The Problem of Scale in Sculpture," *Art in America* 56 (July–August 1968): 80–91.

Rose, Barbara. "Claes Oldenburg's Soft Machines," *Artforum* 5 (June 1967): 30–35.

Rose, Barbara. "Dada Then and Now," *Art International* 7 (January 1963): 23–28.

Rose, Barbara. "Ellsworth Kelly as Sculptor," *Artforum* 5 (Summer 1967): 51.

Rose, Barbara. "Looking at American Sculpture," *Artforum* 3 (February 1965): 29–36.

Rose, Barbara. "Nakian at the Modern," *Artforum* 5 (October 1966): 18–19.

Rose, Barbara. "New York Letter: Recent American Sculpture," *Art International* 8 (December 1964): 47–48; illus. 47.

Rose, Barbara. "On Chamberlain's Interview," *Artforum* 10 (February 1972): 44–45.

Rose, Barbara. "The Sculpture of Ellsworth Kelly," *Artforum* 5 (June 1967): 51–55.

Rose, Barbara and Sandler, Irving. "Sensibility of the Sixties," *Art in America* 55 (January–February 1967): 44–57.

Rosenberg, Harold. "The American Action Painters," *Art News* 51 (December 1952): 22–23.

Rosenblum, Robert. "Louise Nevelson," *Arts Yearbook III* (1959): 137–38.

Rosenblum, Robert. "The New Decade" [at the Whitney Museum and the Museum of Modern Art], *Arts Digest* 29 (May 15, 1955): 20–23.

Rosenblum, Robert. "Pop and Non-Pop: An Essay in Distinction," *Canadian Art* 23 (January 1966): 50–54.

Rosenstein, Harris. "Climbing Mt. Oldenburg," *Art News* 64 (February 1966): 21 ff.

Rosenstein, Harris. "Di Suvero: The Pressures of Reality," *Art News* 65 (February 1967): 36–39.

Roszak, Theodore. "Problems of Modern Sculpture," *7 Arts*, no. 3 (1955): 58–68.

Rubin, William S. "Ellsworth Kelly: The Big Form," *Art News* 62 (November 1963): 32–35.

Rubin, William S. "Some Reflections Prompted By the Recent Work of Louise Bourgeois," *Art International* 13 (April 1969): 17–20.

Sandler, Irving. "The Club," *Artforum* 4 (September 1965): 27–31.

Sartre, Jean-Paul. "Existentialist or Mobilist," *Art News* 46 (December 1947): 22; 55; 56.

Sawin, Martica. "Ibram Lassaw," *Arts Magazine* 30 (December 1955): 22–26.

Sawin, Martica. "Richard Stankiewicz," *Arts Yearbook III* (1959): 157–59.

Seckler, Dorothy Gees. "The Artist Speaks: Louise Nevelson," *Art in America* 55 (January–February 1967): 32–43.

Secunda, Arthur. "Two Motion Sculptors: Tinguely and Rickey," *Artforum* 1 (June 1962): 16–18.

Segal, Jeanne. "The Artist and the New Media," Interview with Roy Lichtenstein, 1968, on WBAI. Taped.

Seitz, William C. "Assemblage: Problems and Issues," *Art International* 6 (February 1962): 26–34.

Seitz, William C. "Spirit, Time and Abstract Expressionism," *Magazine of Art* 46 (February 1953): 80–87.

Selz, Peter. "A Symposium on Pop Art," *Arts Magazine* 37 (April 1963): 36–45. Symposium held at the Museum of Modern Art, New York, December, 1963.

Serra, Richard. "Play It Again Sam," *Arts Magazine* 44 (February 1970): 24–27.

Simon, Sidney. "George Sugarman," *Art International* 11 (May 1967): 22–26.

Smith, David. "Gonzalez: First Master of the Torch," *Art News* 54 (February 1956): 35 ff.

Smith, David. "Notes on My Work," *Arts Magazine* 34 (February 1960): 44.

SMITH, DAVID. "Second Thoughts on Sculpture." *College Art Journal* 13 (Spring 1954): 203–07.

SMITH, DAVID. "Thoughts on Sculpture." *College Art Journal* 13 (Winter 1954): 97–100.

SMITHSON, ROBERT. "A Sedimentation of the Mind: Earth Proposals," *Artforum* 7 (September 1968): 44–50.

SMITHSON, ROBERT. "Aerial Art–Proposals for the Dallas-Fort Worth Regional Airport," *Studio International* 177 (April 1969): 180–81.

SMITHSON, ROBERT. "Discussions with Heizer, Oppenheim, Smithson," *Avalanche* (Fall 1970): 48–71.

SMITHSON, ROBERT. "Entropy and the New Monuments," *Artforum* 4 (June 1966): 26–31.

SMITHSON, ROBERT. "Frederick Law Olmsted and the Dialectical Landscape," *Artforum* 11 (February 1973): 62–68.

SMITHSON, ROBERT. "Incidents of Mirror-Travel in the Yucatan," *Artforum* 8 (September 1969): 28–33.

SMITHSON, ROBERT. "Smithson's Non-Site Sights," Interview by Anthony Robbins. *Art News* 67 (February 1969): 50–53.

SMITHSON, ROBERT. "Quasi-infinities and the Waning of Space," *Arts Magazine* 41 (November 1966): 28–31.

SOLOMON, ALAN. "The New American Art," *Art International* 8 (February 1964): 50–55.

SPEAR, ATHENA T. "Sculptured Light," *Art International* 11 (December 1967): 29–49.

STONE, WARREN R. "The Contemporary Movement in American Sculpture," *Art*, no. 15 (June 9, 1955): 6–7.

SWENSON, G. R. "An Interview with Roy Lichtenstein," *Art News* 62 (November 1963): 24 ff.

SWENSON, G. R. "The New American 'Sign Painters'," *Art News* 61 (September 1962): 44–47; 60–62.

TILLIM, SIDNEY. "Earthworks and the New Picturesque," *Artforum* 7 (December 1968): 42–45.

TILLIM, SIDNEY. "Scale and the Future of Modernism," *Artforum* 6 (October 1967): 14–18.

TILLIM, SIDNEY. "The Underground Pre-Raphaelitism of Edward Kienholz," *Artforum* 4 (April 1965): 38–40.

TUCHMAN, MAURICE. "A Decade of Edward Kienholz," *Artforum* 4 (April 1965): 41–45.

TUCHMAN, MAURICE. "Art and Technology," *Art in America* 58 (March–April 1970): 78–79.

TUCHMAN, PHYLLIS. "An Interview with Carl Andre," *Artforum* 8 (June 1970): 55–61.

TUCHMAN, PHYLLIS. "An Interview with Herbert Ferber," *Artforum* 9 (April 1971): 52–57.

TUCHMAN, PHYLLIS. "An Interview with John Chamberlain," *Artforum* 10 (February 1972): 38–43.

TUCHMAN, PHYLLIS. "George Segal," *Art International* 12 (September 1968): 51–53.

TUCKER, MARCIA. "PheNAUMANology," *Artforum* 9 (December 1970): 38–44.

TWORKOV, JACK. "Four Excerpts from a Journal," *It Is*, no. 4 (Autumn 1959): 12–13.

VAN DER MARCK, JAN. "Ernest Trova–Idols for the Computer Age," *Art in America* 54 (November–December 1966): 64–67.

VVV. Nos. 1–4. New York, 1924–44. Edited by David S. Hare. Editorial advisers: A. Breton, M. Duchamp, M. Ernst.

WALDMAN, DIANE. "Chryssa," *Art International* 12 (April 1968): 42–44.

WALDMAN, DIANE. "Holding the Floor," *Art News* 69 (October 1970): 60–62; 75–79.

"Waldorf Panel 2," *It Is* (Autumn 1965): 77–80; 109–13; illus. 17–56; 65–72; 81–108; 117–31.

WASSERMAN, EMILY. "Process: Whitney Museum," *Artforum* 8 (September 1969): 56–58.

WECHSLER, JUDITH. "Why Scale?" *Art News* 66, no. 4 (Summer 1967): 32–35; 66–67.

"What Abstract Art Means to Me," *Bulletin of the Museum of Modern Art* 18, no. 3 (Spring 1951). Statements by A. Calder, S. Davis, W. de Kooning, F. Glarner, G. L. K. Morris, R. Motherwell.

WOLLHEIM, RICHARD. "Minimal Art," *Arts Magazine* 39 (January 1965): 26–32.

INDEX

275

276